Easy Use and Interpretation of SPSS for Windows: Answering Research Questions With Statistics

Easy Use and Interpretation of SPSS for Windows: Answering Research Questions With Statistics

George A. Morgan and Orlando V. Griego

School of Education
Colorado State University

LEA
LAWRENCE ERLBAUM ASSOCIATES, PUBLISHERS
1998   MAHWAH, NEW JERSEY   LONDON

Figure 16.7 on page 205 is adapted from: Data Analysis for Research Designs, by Keppel and Zedeck, copyright © 1989 by W.H. Freeman and Company. Used with permission.

Lawrence Erlbaum Associates, Inc., Publishers
10 Industrial Avenue
Mahwah, New Jersey 07430

Library of Congress Cataloging-in-Publication Data

Morgan, George A. (George Arthur) 1936-
    Easy use and interpretation of SPSS for Windows : answering
research questions with statistics / George A. Morgan and Orlando
V. Griego.
        p.   cm.
    Includes bibliographical references and index.
    ISBN 0-8058-2959-8 (alk. paper)
    1. SPSS for Windows. 2. Social sciences--Statistical methods--
Computer programs.   I. Griego, Orlando V. II. Title.
    HA32.M65 1997
    519.5'078'55369--dc21
                                                            98-11193
                                                               CIP

Books published by Lawrence Erlbaum Associates are printed
on acid-free paper, and their bindings are chosen
for strength and durability.

Printed in the United States of America

10 9 8 7 6 5 4

To Felix E. Goodson,

who made statistics understandable to students

TABLE OF CONTENTS

Appendices

PREFACE

This book is designed to help students and professionals learn how to analyze research data using SPSS 7.5 for Windows. However, the statistics problems in this book have been solved with earlier versions of SPSS. Both the procedures and outputs were quite similar, and we expect future Windows versions to be very similar.

SPSS 7.5 for Windows is quite easy to use, especially in contrast to earlier mainframe and DOS versions, but the outputs provide a wide variety of options and statistics which can be difficult to interpret. This book demonstrates how to produce a wide variety of statistics, several of which are quite complex and are rarely included in basic statistics courses even though they are common in the literature. Our goal has been to describe the use and interpretation of these statistics as much as possible in nontechnical, jargon-free language. Also, we have provided a bibliography of some of the books we have found useful. You will find it helpful to read about each statistic before doing the lab assignments in this book.

Helping you learn how to choose the appropriate statistics, interpret the outputs, and develop skills in writing about the meaning of the results are the main goals of this book. Thus, we have combined material on a) how the appropriate choice of a statistic is based on the design of the research, b) how to use SPSS to answer a number of research questions about one realistic data set, and c) how to interpret SPSS outputs. This will help you develop skills that cover the whole range of the design, data entry, analysis, and interpretation process. The high school and beyond data (HSB), used in this book are similar to what you might have for a thesis, dissertation, or faculty research project. Therefore, we think it can serve as a model for your analysis.

Our approach in this book is to present the concept of how to use and interpret SPSS in the context of actually proceeding as if these were the data from your research project. Thus, before starting the SPSS assignments, we have three introductory chapters. The first chapter describes research problems, variables, and questions/hypotheses, and it identifies a number of specific research questions related to the HSB data. Appendix A provides some guidelines for phrasing or formatting research questions. In chapter 2 and Appendix D, we describe the HSB data set in more detail. In chapter 2, we also provide an overview of SPSS 7.5 and of the many statistics and other manipulations possible with this sophisticated package. Of course, the goal is to use SPSS as a tool to help answer the research questions that were posed. Chapter 3 discusses scales of measurement and how they are related to the appropriate use of statistics. This chapter also includes a brief review of descriptive statistics.

Our approach to design and statistics in chapters 1, 3, and 7 is somewhat nontraditional because we have found that students have a great deal of difficulty with some aspects of statistics but not others. Most can "crunch" the numbers quite easily and accurately with a calculator or with a computer. However, many have trouble knowing what statistics to use and how to interpret the results. They do not seem to have a "big picture" or see how research design influences data analysis. Part of the problem is inconsistent terminology. We are reminded of Bruce Thompson's frequently repeated, intentionally facetious remark at his many national workshops: "We use these different terms to confuse the graduate students." For these reasons we have tried to present a semantically consistent and coherent big picture of what we call research approaches (experimental, etc.) and how they lead to three basic kinds of research questions (difference, associational, and descriptive) which, in turn, lead to three kinds or groups of statistics with the same names. We realize that these and other attempts to develop and utilize a consistent framework are both nontraditional and somewhat of an oversimplification. However, we think the framework and consistency pay off in terms of student understanding and ability to actually use statistics to answer their research questions. Professors who are not persuaded that this framework is useful can skip chapters 1, 3, and 7 and still have a book that helps them and their students use SPSS.

Assignments A - G (chapters 4 - 11) are organized in very much the way you might proceed to analyze the data if this were your project. For example, we begin by examining and checking the data for errors. Then, we calculate a variety of descriptive statistics, check certain statistical assumptions, make some data transformations, and check the reliability of several measures. Much of what is done in the first seven assignments is preliminary analyses to get ready to answer the research questions that you might state in a report. Chapter 7 describes research designs, data entry formats, and how to select an appropriate inferential statistic. Chapters 8 - 16 (assignments D - N) are designed to answer the research questions posed in chapter 1 as well as a number of additional questions that should give you a good idea of the variety of statistics that can be computed with SPSS.

Hopefully, seeing how the research questions and design lead naturally to the choice of statistics will become apparent after using this book. In addition, it is our hope that interpreting what you get back from the computer will become more clear after doing these assignments, studying the outputs, and answering the interpretation questions.

With the permission of our colleague Jeffrey Gliner, this book borrows sections from Gliner and Morgan (in press), *Research Design and Analysis in Applied Settings*. We also would like to acknowledge the assistance of the students who have used earlier versions of this manual and provided helpful suggestions for improvement. Bob Fetsch provided a good draft of Appendix E, Answers to the Interpretation Questions. We could not have completed the task or made it look so good without our word processor, Linda White, and several capable work study students. Bill Sears, LaVon Blaesi, Jenny Kou, and Mei-Huei Tsay assisted with earlier classes and the development of materials for the DOS and earlier Windows versions of the assignments. Our colleagues, Karen Barrett, Jeff Gliner, and Jim zumBrunnen, and three reviewers provided editorial advice and suggestions about the selection and interpretation of statistics and options. Bart Beaudin, Don Quick, and Mei-Huei Tsay provided helpful feedback from an adult education point of view. We also want to acknowledge the financial assistance of two instructional improvement grants from the College of Applied Human Sciences at Colorado State University. Finally, the patience and help of our wives, Hildy and Lise, enabled us to complete the task.

G. M. and O. G.
Fort Collins, Colorado

CHAPTER 1

Research Problems, Approaches, and Questions

Research Problems

The research process begins with a problem. *What is a research problem?* Kerlinger (1986) formally describes a problem as "...an interrogative sentence or statement that asks: *What relation exists between two or more variables?*" (p. 16). Note that almost all research studies have more than two variables. Kerlinger suggests that prior to the problem statement "...the scientist will usually experience an obstacle to understanding, a vague unrest about observed and unobserved phenomena, a curiosity as to *why something is as it is*" (p. 11). Appendix A provides templates to help you phrase your research problem, and provides examples from the high school and beyond (HSB) data set.

Variables

A *variable* has one defining quality. *It must be able to vary or have different values.* For example, *gender* is a variable because it has two values, female or male. *Age* is a variable that has a large number of values. *Type of treatment/intervention* (or *type of curriculum*) is a variable if there is more than one treatment or a treatment and a control group. *Number of days to learn something or to recover from an ailment*, common measures of the effect of a treatment, are also variables. Similarly, *amount of mathematics knowledge* is a variable because it can vary from none to a lot. If a concept has one value in a particular study it is not a variable, e.g., ethnic group is not a variable if all participants are Caucasian.

Definition of a variable. We can define the term "variable" as a characteristic of the participants or situation of a given study that has different values in that study. In quantitative research, variables are defined operationally and are commonly divided into independent variables (active or attribute), dependent variables, and extraneous variables. Each of these topics will be dealt with in the following sections.

Operational definitions of variables. An operational definition describes or defines a variable in terms of the operations or techniques used to elicit or measure it. When quantitative researchers describe the variables in their study, they specify what they mean by demonstrating how they measured the variable. Demographic variables like age, gender, or ethnic group are usually measured simply by asking the participant to choose the appropriate category from a list. Types of treatment (or curriculum) are usually described/defined much more extensively so the reader can understand what the researcher meant by, for example, a cognitively enriching curriculum or sheltered work. Likewise, abstract concepts like mathematics knowledge, self-concept, or mathematics anxiety need to be defined operationally by spelling out in some detail how they were measured in a particular study. To do this, the investigator may provide sample questions, append the actual instrument, or provide a reference where more information can be found.

Independent Variables

Active independent variables. This first type of variable is often called a manipulated independent variable. A frequent goal of research is to investigate the effect of a particular intervention. An example might be the effect of a new kind of therapy compared to the traditional treatment. A second example might be the effect of a new teaching method, such as cooperative learning, on student performance. In the two examples provided above, the variable of interest was something that was *given to* the participants. Therefore, an *active independent variable* is a variable, such as a workshop, new curriculum, or other intervention, one level of which *can be given to a group of participants*, usually within a specified period of time *during the study*.

In traditional experimental research, independent variables are those that the *investigator can manipulate*; they presumably cause a change in some resulting behavior, attitude, or physiological measure of interest. An independent variable is considered to be manipulated or active when the investigator has the option to give one value to one group (experimental condition), and another value to another group (control condition).

However, there are many circumstances, especially in applied research, when we have an active independent variable but this variable *is not directly manipulated by the investigator*. Consider the situation where the investigator is interested in a new type of treatment. In order to carry out the study, it turns out that rehabilitation center *A* will be using that treatment. Rehabilitation center *B* will be using the traditional treatment. The investigator will compare the two centers to determine if one treatment works better than the other. Notice that the independent variable is active but has *not* been manipulated *by the investigator*.

Thus, active independent variables are *given* to the participants in the study but are not necessarily manipulated by the experimenter. They may be given by a clinic, school, or someone, other than the investigator. From the participants' point of view the situation was manipulated.

Attribute independent variables. Unlike some authors of research methods books, we do not restrict the term "independent variable" to those variables that are manipulated or active. We define an independent variable more broadly to include any predictors, antecedents, or *presumed* causes or influences under investigation in the study. Attributes of the participants as well as active independent variables fit within this definition. For the social sciences, education, and disciplines dealing with special needs populations, attribute independent variables are especially important. Type of disability or level of disability is often the major focus of a study. Disability certainly qualifies as a variable since it can take on different values even though they are not "given" in the study. For example, cerebral palsy is different from Down syndrome which is different from spina bifida, yet all are disabilities. Also, there are different levels of the same disability. People already have defining characteristics or *attributes* which place them into one of two or more categories. The different disabilities are already present when we begin our study. Thus, we are also interested in studying a class of variables that cannot be given during the study, even by other persons, schools, or clinics.

A variable which cannot be given, yet is a major focus of the study, is called an attribute independent variable (Kerlinger, 1986). In other words, the values of the independent variable are attributes of the persons or the environment that are not manipulated during the study. For example, *gender*, *age*, *ethnic group*, or *disability* are attributes of a person.

Other labels for the independent variable. SPSS uses a variety of terms such as **factor** (chapters 5, 15, 16, 17 and 18), **covariate** (chapter 13), and **grouping variable** (chapters 14, 15). In other cases (chapters 5, 9) SPSS does not make a distinction between the independent and dependent variable, just labeling them variables. Another common label for an attribute independent variable is a measured variable. However, we prefer attribute so it is not easily confused with the dependent variable, which is also measured. Sometimes variables such as gender or ethnic group are called moderator or mediating variables because they serve these functions; however, SPSS does not use these terms so we will not either in this book.

Type of independent variable and inferences about cause and effect. When we analyze data from a research study, the statistical analysis does not differentiate whether the independent variable is an active independent variable or an attribute independent variable. However, even though SPSS and most statistics books use the label independent variable for both active and attribute variables, there is a crucial difference in interpretation. A significant change or difference following manipulation of the active independent variable may reasonably lead the investigator to infer that the independent variable *caused* the change in the dependent variable.

However, a significant change or difference between or among values of an attribute independent variable should *not* lead one to the interpretation that the attribute independent variable caused the dependent variable to change. A major goal of scientific research is to be able to identify a causal relationship between two variables. For those in applied disciplines, the need to demonstrate that a given intervention or treatment causes change in behavior or performance is extremely important. Only the approaches that have an active independent variable (the randomized experimental and to a lesser extent the quasi-experimental) can be successful in providing data that allow one to infer that the independent variable caused the dependent variable.

Although studies with attribute independent variables are limited in what can be said about causation, they can lead to solid conclusions about the differences between groups and about associations between variables. Furthermore, they are the *only* available approach if the focus of your research is on attribute independent variables. The descriptive approach, as we define it, does not attempt to identify relationships. It focuses on describing variables.

As implied above, this distinction between active and attribute independent variables is important because terms such as *main effect* and *effect size* used by SPSS and most statistics books might lead one to believe that if you find a significant difference the independent variable *caused* the difference. These terms are misleading when the independent variable is an attribute.

Values of the independent variable. In defining a variable, we said that it must have more than one value. When describing the different categories of an independent variable, SPSS uses the word *values*. This does *not* necessarily imply that the values are ordered.[1] Suppose that an investigator is performing a study to investigate the effect of a treatment. One group of participants is assigned to the treatment group. A second group does not receive the treatment. The study could be conceptualized as having one independent variable (*treatment type*), with two values or levels (treatment and no treatment). The independent variable in this example would be classified as an active independent variable. Instead, suppose the investigator was interested primarily in comparing two different treatments but decided to include a third no-treatment group as a control group in the study. The study still would be conceptualized as having one active independent variable (treatment type), but with three values (the two treatment conditions and the control condition). This variable could be diagrammed as follows:

Variable Label	Values	Value Labels
	1	= Treatment 1
Treatment type	2	= Treatment 2
	3	= No treatment (control)

As an additional example, consider gender, which is an attribute independent variable with two values, male and female. It could be diagrammed as follows:

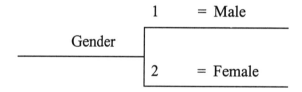

Note that in SPSS each variable is given a label; the values, which are numbers, may also have labels. It is especially important to know the value labels when the variable is nominal; i.e., when the values of the variable are just names and, thus, are not ordered.

Dependent Variables

The dependent variable is the presumed outcome or criterion. It is assumed to measure or assess the effect of the independent variable. Dependent variables are often test scores, ratings on questionnaires, readings from instruments (electrocardiogram, galvanic skin response, etc.), or measures of physical performance. When we discuss measurement in chapter 3, we are usually referring to the dependent variable. SPSS also uses a number of other terms for the dependent variable. The most common is **dependent list**, used in cases where you can do the same statistic several times, for a list of dependent variables. In discriminant analysis (chapter 13), the dependent variable is called the **grouping variable**. The term **test variable** is used in several of the chapters on *t* tests and analysis of variance.

---

[1] The terms categories, levels, groups, or samples are sometimes used interchangeably with the term values, especially in statistics books. Likewise the term factor is often used instead of independent variable.

Extraneous Variables

These are variables that are *not* of interest in a particular study but could influence the dependent variable. Environmental factors (e.g., temperature or distractions), time of day, and characteristics of the experimenter, teacher, or therapist are some possible extraneous variables that need to be controlled. SPSS does not use the term extraneous variable. However, sometimes such variables are controlled using statistics. For example, one can use analysis of covariance and enter the variable to be controlled as the covariate (see chapter 16, problems 3 and 4).

Research Approaches

Basic Research Approaches

Table 1.1 shows the five basic research approaches and the criteria that distinguish them. We use the term basic to indicate that there is one independent variable or factor (i.e., a single factor design). In the basic descriptive approach there is only one type of variable, which we call the dependent variable.

The randomized experimental approach. In order for a research approach to be called randomized experimental, two criteria must be met. The first criterion is that the researcher must *randomly assign participants to groups* or conditions. We have used the word condition in addition to group because under certain circumstances a group can undergo both the control and experimental conditions. As you can see from Table 1.1, this criterion is what differentiates randomized (or true) experiments from quasi-experiments, but it is the most difficult to achieve. Much applied research involves groups that are already "intact" (in existence) such as classrooms or rehabilitation settings, and it is not possible to change those assignments. Thus, such research is *not* considered to be experimental.

The second criterion that must be satisfied for the research approach to be considered experimental is that the *independent variable* must be *active* as defined previously. In addition, the researcher usually is able *to control the independent variable*. In other words, the researcher can decide exactly what the treatment will be and when and to whom it will be given. She or he will be able to randomly assign one level of the independent variable to the experimental condition and the other level of the independent variable to the control condition. These aspects of experiments are also shown in Table 1.1.

Quasi-experimental approach. The quasi-experimental research approach is similar to the randomized experimental approach but fails to satisfy the condition of random assignment of subjects to groups. Note in Table 1.1 that quasi-experimental designs have an *active independent variable* with a *few values* and also *involve a comparison* between, for example, an experimental and a control condition. However, there is a word of caution about the active independent variable. In the experimental approach, the researcher usually has control over the independent variable in that one level can be randomly assigned to the experimental condition, and one level can be randomly assigned to the control condition. The *strength* of the quasi-experimental design is based, in part, on how much control the investigator actually has in manipulating the independent variable and deciding which group will receive which treatment. The strength of the design influences how confident we can be about whether the independent variable was *the cause* of any change in the dependent variable.

Table 1.1. *A Comparison of Five Basic Quantitative Research Approaches*

Criteria	Randomized Experimental	Quasi-Experimental	Comparative	Associational	Descriptive
Random assignment of subjects to groups by investigator	Yes	No	No	No (only one group)	No groups
Independent variable is active	Yes	Yes	No (attribute)	No (attribute)	No Independent variable
Independent variable is controlled *by the investigator*[1]	Usually	Sometimes	No	No	No
Independent variable has only a few levels/values[2]	Yes	Yes	Yes	No[2] (many)	No Independent variable
Relationships between variables (comparison of groups or association of variables)	Yes (comparison)	Yes (comparison)	Yes (comparison)	Yes (association)	No

[1] Although this is a desired quality of experimental and quasi-experimental designs, it is not sufficient for distinguishing between the experimental and quasi-experimental approaches.

[2] This distinction is made for heuristic/educational purposes and is only "usually" true. In the associational approach, the independent variable is *assumed to be continuous*; i.e., it *has many values/levels*. We consider the approach to be associational if the independent variable has five or more *ordered* categories. Except for this difference and the statistics typically used with them, the comparative and associational approaches are the same.

Basic comparative approach. The comparative research approach differs from the experimental and quasi-experimental approaches because the investigator *cannot randomly assign participants to groups* and because there is *not an active independent variable*. Table 1.1 shows that, like experiments and quasi-experiments, comparative designs usually have a few levels or categories for the independent variable and make comparisons between groups. Studies that use the comparative approach examine the presumed effect of an *attribute independent variable*.

An example of the comparative approach is a study that compared two groups of children on a series of motor performance tests. The investigators attempted to determine whether the differences between the two groups were due to perceptual or motor processing problems. One group of children, who had motor handicaps, was compared to a second group of children who did not have motor problems. Notice that the independent variable in this study was an attribute independent variable with two levels, motor handicapped and not handicapped. Thus, it is not possible for the investigator to randomly assign participants to groups, or "give" the independent variable; the independent variable was not active. The independent variable had only two values or categories so a statistical comparison between the groups would be performed. It is, of course, possible for comparisons to be made between three or more groups.[2]

Basic associational approach. Now, we would like to consider an approach to research where the independent variable is usually continuous or has several ordered categories, usually five or more. Suppose that the investigator is interested in the relationship between giftedness and self-perceived confidence in children. Assume that the dependent variable is a self-confidence scale for children. The independent variable is giftedness. If giftedness had been divided into high, average, and low groups (a few values or levels), we would have called the research approach comparative because the logical thing to do would be to compare the groups. However, in the typical associational approach, the independent variable is continuous or has at least five ordered levels or values.[3] All participants would be in a single group with two continuous variables--giftedness and self-concept. A correlation coefficient could be performed to determine the strength of the relationship between the two variables.

As implied above, it is somewhat arbitrary whether a study is considered to be comparative or associational. For example, a continuous variable such as age can always be divided into a small number of levels such as young and old. However, we make this distinction for two reasons. First, we think it is usually unwise to divide a variable with many ordered levels into a few because information is lost. For example, if the cut point for "old age" was 65, persons 66 and 96 would be lumped together as would persons 21 and 64. Second, different types of statistics are usually used with the two approaches (see Fig. 1.1). We think this distinction and the similar one made in the section on research questions will help you decide on an appropriate statistic, which we have found is one of the hardest parts of the research process for students.

Basic descriptive approach. This approach is different from the other four in that only one variable is considered at a time so that no relationships are made. Table 1.1 shows that this lack of comparisons or associations is what distinguishes this approach from the other four. Of course, the descriptive approach does not meet any of the other criteria such as random assignment of participants to groups.

Most research studies include some descriptive questions (at least to describe the sample), but do not stop there. It is rare these days for published quantitative research to be purely descriptive; we almost always study several variables and their relationships. However, political polls and consumer surveys are sometimes only interested in describing how voters *as a whole* react to issues or what products a group of consumers will buy. Exploratory studies of a new topic may just describe what people say or feel about that topic.

Most research books use a considerably broader definition for descriptive research. Some use the phrase "descriptive research" to include all research that is not randomized experimental or

---

[2] It is also possible to compare relatively large numbers of groups (e.g., 5 or 10) if one has enough participants that the group sizes are adequate, but this is atypical.

[3] It is possible, as we will see in chapters 7 and 8, to use the associational approach and statistics when one has fewer than five ordered values of the variables and even with unordered nominal variables, but this is not typical.

quasi-experimental. Others do not seem to have a clear definition, using descriptive almost as a synonym for exploratory or sometimes "correlational" research. We think it is clearer and less confusing to students to restrict the term descriptive research to questions and studies that use only *descriptive statistics*, such as averages, percentages, histograms, and frequency distributions, and do not test null hypotheses with inferential statistics.

Complex Research Approaches

It is important to note that most studies are more complex than implied by the above examples. In fact, almost all studies have more than one hypothesis or research question and may utilize more than one of the above approaches. It is common to find a study with one active independent variable (e.g., type of treatment) and one or more attribute independent variables (e.g., gender). This type of study combines the randomized experimental approach (if the participants were randomly assigned to groups) and the comparative approach. Most "survey" studies include both the associational and comparative approaches. As mentioned above, most studies also have some descriptive questions so it is common for published studies to use three or even more of the approaches.

Research Questions/Hypotheses

Next, we divide research questions into three broad types: *difference, associational,* and *descriptive*. For the difference type of question, we compare groups or values of the independent variable on their scores on the dependent variable. This type of question typically is used with the randomized experimental, quasi-experimental, and comparative approaches. For an associational question, we associate or relate the independent and dependent variables. Descriptive questions are not answered with inferential statistics; they merely describe or summarize data.

Basic Difference Versus Associational Research Questions or Hypotheses

Hypotheses are defined as *predictive statements about the relationship between variables*. Fig. 1.1 shows that both difference and associational questions/hypotheses have as a *general purpose* the exploration of relationships between variables: This similarity is in agreement with the statement by statisticians that all parametric inferential statistics are relational, and it is consistent with the notion that the distinction between the comparative and associational approach is somewhat arbitrary.[4] However, we believe that the distinction is educationally useful. Note that difference and associational questions differ in specific purpose and the kinds of statistics they use to answer the question.

---

[4] We use the term associational for this type of research question, approach, and statistics rather than relational or correlational to distinguish them from the *general purpose* of both difference and associational questions/hypotheses described above. Also we wanted to distinguish between correlation, as a specific statistical technique, and the broader types of approach, questions, and group of statistics.

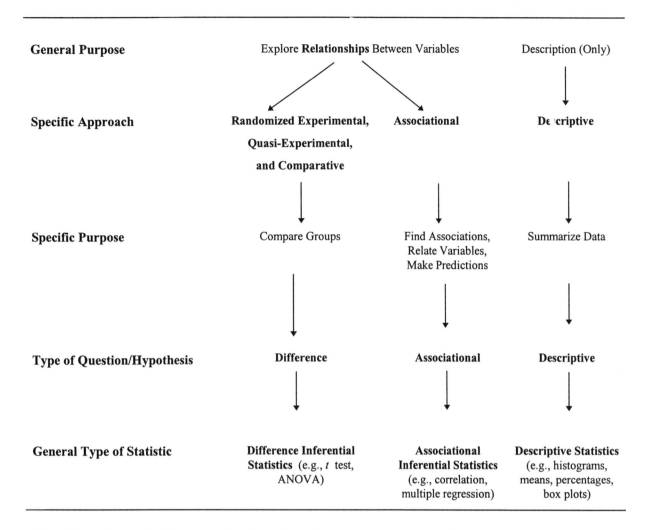

Fig. 1.1. Schematic diagram showing how the purpose, approach and type of research question correspond to the general type of statistic used in a study.

Table 1.2 provides the general format and one example of a basic *difference hypothesis* and of a basic *associational hypothesis*. Research questions are similar to hypotheses, but they are stated in question format. We think it is advisable to use the question format when one does not have a clear directional prediction and for the descriptive approach. More details and examples are given in Appendix A.

Table 1.2. *Examples of Basic Difference and Associational Hypotheses*

---

1.   *Difference (group comparison) Hypothesis*

- For this type of hypothesis, the levels or values of the independent variable (e.g., gender) are used to divide the participants into groups (male and female) which are then compared to see if they differ in respect to the average scores on the dependent variable (e.g., empathy).
- An example of a directional research hypothesis is: Women will score higher than men on empathy scores. In other words, the average empathy scores of the women will be significantly higher than the average empathy scores for men.

2.   *Associational (relational) Hypothesis*

- For this type of hypothesis, the scores on the independent variable (e.g., self-esteem) are associated with or related to the dependent variable (e.g., empathy). *It is often arbitrary which variable is considered the independent variable* but most researchers have an idea about what they think is the predictor (independent) and what is the outcome (dependent) variable.
- An example of a directional research hypothesis is: There will be a positive association (relation) between self-esteem scores and empathy scores. In other words, those persons who are high on self-esteem will tend to have high empathy, those with low self-esteem will tend also to have low empathy, and those in the middle on the independent variable will tend to be in the middle on the dependent variable.

Six Types of Research Questions

Table 1.3 expands our overview of research questions to include both basic and complex questions of each of the three types: *descriptive, difference,* and *associational.* The table also includes references to the tables in chapters 3 and 7, designed to help you select an appropriate statistic and examples of the types of statistics that we include under each of the six types of questions. Appendix A and the last section in this chapter provide examples of research questions for each of the six types. We use the terms basic and complex because the more common names, univariate and multivariate, are not used consistently in the literature.

Note that some complex descriptive statistics (e.g., a cross-tabulation table) could be tested for significance with inferential statistics; if they were so tested they would no longer be considered descriptive. We think that most qualitative/constructivist researchers ask complex descriptive questions because they consider more than one variable/concept at a time but do not use inferential/hypothesis testing statistics. Furthermore, complex descriptive statistics are used to check reliability (e.g., Cronbach's alpha) and to reduce the number of variables (e.g., factor analysis).

Table 1.3. *Summary of Types of Research Questions*

Type of Research Questions (Number of Variables)	Statistics (Example)
1) **Basic Descriptive Questions** – 1 variable	See Table 3.2 (mean, standard deviation, frequency distribution)
2) **Complex Descriptive Questions** – 2 or more variables, but no use of inferential statistics	(box plots, cross-tabulation tables, factor analysis, measures of reliability)
3) **Basic Difference Questions** – 1 independent and 1 dependent variable. Independent variable usually has a few values (ordered or not).	Table 7.1 (*t* test, one-way ANOVA)
4) **Complex Difference Question** – 3 or more variables. Usually 2 or a few independent variables and 1 or more dependent variables considered together.	Table 7.3 (factorial ANOVA, MANOVA)
5) **Basic Associational Questions** – 1 independent variable and 1 dependent variable. Usually at least 5 ordered values for both variables. Often they are continuous.	Table 7.2 (correlation tested for significance)
6) **Complex Associational Questions** – 2 or more independent variables and 1 or more dependent variables. Usually 5+ ordered values for all variables but some or all can be dichotomous variables.	Table 7.4 (multiple regression)

Difference versus associational inferential statistics. We think it is educationally useful, although not common in statistics books, to divide inferential statistics into two types corresponding to difference and associational hypotheses/questions. Difference inferential statistics are used for the experimental, quasi-experimental, and comparative approaches, which test for *differences between groups* (e.g., using analysis of variance). Associational inferential statistics test for *associations or relationships between variables* and use correlation or multiple regression analysis.[5] We will utilize this contrast between difference and associational inferential statistics in chapter 7 and later in this book.

---

[5] We realize that all parametric inferential statistics are relational so this dichotomy of using one type of data analysis procedure to test for differences (when there are a few values or levels of the independent variables) and another type of data analysis procedure to test for associations (when there are continuous independent variables) is somewhat artificial. Both continuous and categorical independent variables can be used in a general linear model

A Sample Research Problem - The High School and Beyond (HSB) Study

Imagine that you are interested in the general problem of what factors influence mathematics achievement at the end of high school. You might have some hunches or hypotheses about such factors based on your experiences and your reading of the research and popular literature. Some factors that might influence mathematics achievement are commonly called demographics; e.g., gender, ethnic group, and mother's and father's education. A probable influence would be the mathematics courses that the student has taken. We might speculate that grades in math and in other subjects could have an impact on math achievement.[6] However, other "third" variables, such as students' IQ or parent encouragement and assistance, could be the actual causes of high math achievement. Such extraneous variables could influence what courses one took, the grades one received, and might be correlates of the demographic variables. We might wonder how spatial performance scores such as pattern/mosaic score and visualization score might enter into a more complete understanding of the problem and whether these skills seem to be influenced by the same factors as math achievement. Finally, students' attitudes about mathematics might be factors affecting these math achievement scores.

Before we state the research problem and questions in more formal ways, we need to step back and discuss the types of variables and the approaches that might be used to study the above problem. Think about what are the *independent/antecedent* (presumed causes) *variables* and what are the *dependent/outcomes variable(s)* in the above problem. Hopefully, it is obvious that math achievement is the primary dependent variable.

Given the above research problem, which focuses on achievement tests at the end of the senior year, the number of math courses taken is best considered to be an antecedent or independent variable in this study. What about father's and mother's education and gender? How would you classify ethnic group in terms of the type of variable? What about grades? Like IQ and parent encouragement they would be independent variables, but, as with any study, we were not able to measure all the variables that might be of interest. Visualization and mosaic pattern scores could probably be either independent or dependent variables depending upon the specific research question. Finally, the math attitude questions and the resulting composite or scale scores derived from them also could be either independent or dependent variables, but probably independent/antecedent variables in this study. Note that student's class or grade level is not a variable in this study because all the participants are high school seniors (i.e., it does not vary; it is the population of interest).

As we have discussed, independent variables can be *active* (given to the participant or manipulated by the investigator) or *attributes* of the participants or their environments. Are there

---

(regression) approach to data analysis. However, the practical implications are that most researchers adhere to the above dichotomy in data analysis.

[6] We have decided to use the short version of mathematics (i.e., math) throughout the book to save space, because it is used in common language, and because it is the name of several variables (e.g., *mathach, mathgr*) in the sample study.

any *active* independent variables in this study? No! There is no intervention, new curriculum, or something similar. All the independent variables, then, are attribute variables because they are attributes or characteristics of these high school students. Given that all the independent variables are attributes, the research approach *cannot be experimental or quasi-experimental*. The proposed study is basically an individual differences one that will use the *comparative, associational*, and *descriptive approaches*. This means that we will *not* be able to draw definite conclusions about cause and effect (i.e., we will find out what is related to math achievement, but we will not know for sure what *causes* math achievement).

Research Questions for the Modified HSB Study[7]

We will generate a large number of research questions from the modified HSB data set for Assignments A - L and N. Assignment M uses a different data set that you will enter. In this section, we will list one research question to be answered in each of the assignments to give you an idea of the range of types of questions that one might have in a typical research project like a thesis or dissertation. In addition to the *difference* and *associational questions* that are commonly seen in a research report, we have asked *descriptive questions* and questions about assumptions in the early assignments. Templates for writing the research problem and research questions/ hypotheses are given in Appendix A; it should help you write questions for your own research. The questions below correspond to the lab assignments in Chapters 4-18.

1) Often, we start with basic *descriptive questions* about the demographics of the sample. Thus, we could answer, with the results of Assignment A, the following basic descriptive question: "What is the average educational level of the fathers of the students in this sample?"

2) Additional basic *descriptive questions* about the sample will be answered in Assignment B. For example, "What percentages of the students are male and female?"

3) In Assignment C, we produce a number of new/transformed variables such as three summated scales assessing math attitudes. In this assignment we will examine whether the dependent and continuous independent variables (those that might be used to answer associational questions) are distributed normally, an *assumption* of many statistics. The question is, "Are the frequency distributions of the three math attitude scales markedly different from the normal curve distribution?"

4) We will produce cross-tabulation tables in Assignment D and ask "Is the association between gender and math grades statistically significant?" This is a basic associational question.

---

[7] The High School and Beyond (HSB) study was conducted by the National Opinion Research Center (1980). The example, discussed here and throughout the book, is based on 13 variables obtained from a random sample of 75 out of 28,240 high school seniors. These variables include achievement scores, grades, and demographics. The raw data for the 13 variables were obtained from an appendix in Hinkle, Wiersma, and Jurs (1994). Note that additional variables (ethnicity and math attitudes) with realistic but fictitious data have been added to the HSB data set in order to provide examples of common additional types of analysis (e.g., summated scales and Cronbach's alpha).

5) In Assignment E, we will answer additional basic *associational* research questions (using Pearson product-moment correlation coefficients) such as, "Is there a positive association/relationship between grades in high school and a math achievement?"

This assignment also will produce a correlation matrix of all the associations among seven key variables including math achievement. Similar matrixes will provide the basis for the answers to the issues raised in Assignments F, G, and H.

6) Assignments F and G are not really intended to provide answers to the research problem posed at the beginning of this section. Assignment F will deal with the issue of whether our conceptualization that there are three aspects of attitudes about mathematics (pleasure, motivation, and competence) is consistent with the ways the students answered the 13 attitude items. The research question might be phrased, "Using the SPSS factor analysis program, will the 13 math attitude items/questions cluster into the same three sets of questions that we proposed conceptually?" This is a complex descriptive question.

7) Whether there is internal consistency reliability of the summated scale scores (determined conceptually or from factor analysis) is another important *assumption* to test before proceeding with the formal research questions. This issue could be phrased, "Are the three scale scores computed from the math attitude questions internally consistent?" There are also other important measures of reliability that will be computed in Assignment G.

8) Assignment H will ask and answer a key research question which is a *complex associational question*: "Is there a combination of math attitudes (motivation, competence, and pleasure), grades, father's and mother's education, and gender that predicts math achievement better than any one of them alone, and, if so, what is the best combination?" Assignment I will answer similar questions.

9) Several basic *difference questions* will be asked in Assignment J. For example, "Do males and females differ on math achievement and grades in high school?"

10) *Basic difference questions* in which the independent variable has three or more values will be asked in Assignment K. For example, "Are there differences among Euro-American, African-American, Hispanic-American, and Asian-American students on math achievement?"

11) *Complex difference questions* will be asked in Assignment L. One *set* of three questions is as follows: (1) "Is there a difference between students who have fathers with no college, some college, and a BS or more with respect to the student's math achievement?" (2) "Is there a difference between students who had an A or B math grade average and those with less than a B average on a math achievement test at the end of high school?" and (3) "Is there an interaction between father's education and math grades with respect to math achievement?"

12) Assignment M will deal with repeated measures and mixed ANOVA questions using a different data set that you will enter into the computer.

13) Finally, Assignment N will answer *complex difference questions* similar to those in Assignments J and K when more than one dependent variable is considered simultaneously.

Another way to group these research questions that we have found useful is as follows:

a) Descriptive statistics about the *demographics of the sample.*
b) *Tests of assumptions* such as that the key variables are distributed normally and the instruments are assessed reliably.
c) Tests of the specific *research questions* posed by the researcher, based on the research problem. These can be *descriptive, associational,* and/or *difference* questions.
d) In addition, we often test other *supplementary questions*, which may be side issues or may arise after we have written the proposal or even after the data have been collected and analyzed.

This introduction to the research problem and questions raised by the HSB data set should help make the assignments meaningful, and it should provide a guide and examples for your own research.

CHAPTER 2

Overview of the High School and Beyond (HSB) Data Set and SPSS 7.5

The Modified Hsbdata File

The file name of the data set used with this manual is hsbdata; it stands for high school and beyond data. It is based on a national sample of data from more than 28,000 high school students. The current data set is a sample of 75 students drawn randomly from the larger population. The data that we have from this sample includes school outcomes such as grades and the number of mathematics courses of different types that the students took in high school. Also there are several kinds of standardized test data and demographic data such as gender and mother's and father's education. To provide an example of questionnaire type data, we have included 13 questions about math attitudes. These data were developed for this manual and, thus, are not really the math attitudes of the 75 students in this sample. The questions, however, are based on ones used by the authors to study mastery motivation. Also we made up ethnic group data which, although somewhat realistic overall, do not represent the actual ethnic groups of the 75 students in this sample. This enables us to do some additional analyses.

We have provided you with a disk which contains the data for each of the 75 participants on 28 variables. The hsbdata file, shown in Table 2.1, has already been entered and labeled to enable you to get started on analyses quickly. In Assignments A and M, you will enter some additional data to practice entering it yourself. Also you will, in several assignments, label variables and their values so that your printouts will include the new variable names and the value labels.

The Raw HSB Data and Data Editor

Notice the short variable names at the top of the hsbdata file. (Actually we have transferred the HSB file from the SPSS data editor to Excel and reduced it so that it would fit on two pages, but in SPSS it will look very similar to Table 2.1.) Be aware that the subjects/participants are listed down the page from ID 1 to ID 75 at the bottom of the second page, and the variables are listed across the top. You will always enter data this way. If a variable is measured more than once, such as a pretest and posttest, it will be entered as two variables perhaps called Pre and Post. This method of entering data follows that suggested in chapter 7. Note that most of the values are single digits but that *visual, mosaic,* and *mathach* include some decimals and even minus numbers. Notice also that some cells like variable Q09 for participant ID 1 are blank because a datum is missing. Perhaps participant 1 did not answer question 9 and participant 2 did not answer question 4, etc. Blank is the "system missing" value that can be used for any missing data in an SPSS data file. However, other values also can be used for missing data. Notice that for father's and mother's education level we have used -1 for the missing values, and for ethnic group we have defined 9 as missing. For your purposes, however, we suggest that you leave missing data blank, but you may run across "user defined" missing data codes like -1 or 9 in other researchers' data.

Table 2.1. *Hsbdata Data Set in the SPSS Data Editor*

ID	VISUAL	MOSAIC	GRADES	MATHGR	ALG1	ALG2	GEO	TRIG	CALC	MATHACH	FAED	MAED	GEND	Q01	Q02	Q03	Q04	Q05	Q06	Q07	Q08	Q09	Q10	Q11	Q12	Q13	ETHNIC
1	8.75	31.0	4	0		0	0	0	0	9.00	10	10	2	10	4	3		4	2	2	3	.	1		3	3	2
2	4.75	56.0	5	0		0	0	0	0	10.33	2	2	2	3	40	3	.	1	2	3	3	3	1	1	4	2	3
3	4.75	25.0	6	0	1	0	0	0	0	7.67	2	2	1	1	1	1	4	4	4	1	3	4		4	4	1
4	1.00	22.0	3	0	1	0	0	0	0	5.00	3	3	1	1	2	1	4	3	4	1	3	4	3	4	4	3
5	2.25	17.5	3	0	1	0	0	0	0	-1.67	-1	3	2	1	4	3	4	4	4	3	4	1	4	2	2
6	1.00	23.5	5	0	1	0	0	0	0	1.00	3	2	2	1	1	3	2	4	4	1	4	1	1	3	2
7	2.50	28.5	6	0	1	0	0	0	0	12.00	9	6	1	.	1	3	4	3	3	2	3	3	3	3
8	3.50	29.5	4	0	1	0	0	0	0	8.00	5	6	2	1	1	3	2	4	2	1	2	2	2	3	3	2
9	3.50	28.0	7	0	1	0	0	0	0	13.00	3	3	2	3	1	.	1	4	2	1	3	3	2	3	4	2
10	3.75	27.5	5	0	1	0	0	0	0	3.67	8	2	1	4	3	1	3	4	2	1	4	4	4	4
11	11.00	27.0	6	0	1	0	0	0	0	21.00	3	4	1	4	4	4	2	3	2	1	4	2	1	3	3
12	4.75	26.5	8	0	1	0	0	0	0	23.67	8	9	2	3	4	4	2	4	3	1	4	3	3
13	1.00	13.0	5	0	1	0	0	0	0	4.00	2	3	2	3	4	3	2	2	4	2	4	4	2
14	1.00	18.0	2	0	1	0	0	0	0	9.00	6	3	1	3	4	4	3	3	1	4	3	3	3
15	4.75	25.0	3	0	1	0	0	0	0	5.33	2	3	2	4	4	3	2	3	3	2	4	1	3	1
16	13.50	33.0	7	0	1	0	0	0	0	19.67	-1	-1	1	4	4	3	3	3	2	1	4	4	3
17	-.25	33.0	5	0	1	0	0	0	0	7.67	3	7	2	4	4	3	3	3	4	2	3	2	4	4	3
18	6.00	27.0	6	0	1	0	0	0	0	14.33	9	7	2	4	3	3	3	3	4	1	4	4	3
19	9.75	26.0	6	0	1	0	0	0	0	14.33	3	3	2	4	3	3	2	4	4	3	3	4	2	3
20	8.75	25.0	8	0	1	0	0	0	0	19.67	8	3	2	4	4	2	4	3	2	3	3	3	4
21	-.25	41.0	5	0	1	0	0	0	0	17.00	5	5	2	2	4	4	2	4	4	2	3	4	4	4
22	7.25	27.0	5	0	1	0	0	0	0	7.67	2	1	2	4	4	3	2	3	3	2	4	1	3	3
23	4.75	22.0	5	1	1	1	0	0	0	19.67	9	7	1	3	4	3	2	3	4	3	4	4	4	3
24	1.00	53.0	4	0	1	0	0	0	0	6.67	2	2	2	4	4	3	2	4	2	2	2	2	3	3
25	9.75	27.0	7	0	1	0	0	0	0	14.33	6	6	2	3	4	4	2	4	3	3	3	3	3
26	7.25	31.0	5	0	1	0	0	0	0	10.67	5	5	2	3	4	3	2	3	3	3	3	2	3
27	2.25	29.0	6	0	1	0	0	0	0	14.33	3	6	2	4	4	4	2	3	4	3	3	4	3
28	2.25	26.0	5	0	1	0	0	0	0	14.33	3	2	2	3	4	3	2	3	3	1	4	2	3	4
29	1.00	22.0	6	1	1	1	0	0	0	14.33	5	3	2	2	3	3	3	4	4	3	3	2	3	3
30	13.50	31.0	3	1	1	1	0	0	0	9.00	2	3	2	2	3	4	2	2	2	4	3	2	3
31	9.75	27.0	6	1	1	1	0	0	0	17.00	2	3	1	2	4	2	3	4	3	4	3	1	3	3
32	9.50	34.0	6	1	1	1	0	0	0	23.67	9	5	1	3	4	4	2	4	4	2	4	4	4
33	9.75	24.5	4	1	1	1	0	0	0	18.33	5	7	2	4	4	3	3	4	3	3	4	3	3
34	6.00	23.0	7	1	1	1	0	0	0	15.67	8	8	2	3	4	3	2	2	2	3	3	3	4
35	2.25	32.5	8	0	1	0	0	0	0	17.00	4	6	2	3	3	3	3	3	2	4	4	2	3
36	9.75	29.5	6	0	1	0	0	0	0	15.67	8	6	1	3	3	3	3	2	3	3	3	4	2
37	-.25	33.0	7	1	1	1	0	0	0	7.67	3	3	2	3	4	4	3	4	4	4	4	3	3
38	3.75	24.0	7	1	1	1	0	0	0	22.67	2	2	2	4	4	4	3	2	4	4	4	4
39	6.00	11.0	7	0	1	0	0	0	0	14.33	4	4	2	4	4	2	3	2	3	4	4	2	4
40	6.50	23.0	5	1	1	1	0	0	0	21.00	2	2	2	2	4	2	3	3	3	3	3	3	2
41	1.00	26.0	6	1	1	1	0	0	0	6.33	3	2	2	4	2	3	2	3	3	2	3	3	1
42	6.00	22.5	6	0	1	0	0	0	0	3.67	10	6	1	3	4	4	4	3	4	3	4	2	2
43	3.50	20.5	6	1	1	1	0	0	1	10.33	10	10	2	4	3	3	3	3	3	3	2	3	3	3
44	3.50	28.0	8	1	1	1	0	0	1	23.67	8	8	2	3	4	3	2	1	4	3	4	1	4	3

Table 2.1. Hsbdata Data Set in the SPSS Data Editor (continued)

ID	VISUAL	MOSAIC	GRADES	MATHGR	ALG1	ALG2	GEO	TRIG	CALC	MATHACH	FAED	MAED	GEND	Q01	Q02	Q03	Q04	Q05	Q06	Q07	Q08	Q09	Q10	Q11	Q12	Q13	ETHNIC
45	1.00	16.0	7	1	1	1	0	0	0	4.00	2	3	2	4	4	3	3		2	2	3	3	1	1	3	2	2
46	-.25	30.0	6	0	1	1	0	0	0	17.00	4	6	2	3	4	3	1		2	4		3	1	1	3	3	1
47	-.25	23.5	6	0	1	0	1	0	0	6.33	10	9	2	2	4	2	4		3		3	3	1	2	2	2	1
48	-.25	20.5	5	0	1	0	0	0	0	3.67	2	2	2	3	4	3	3	2	2	1	3	3	1	1	3	3	1
49	4.75	22.5	5	0	1	0	0	0	0	9.00	3	5	2	4	3	4	3		2	4	2	4	1	1	2	3	4
50	5.00	24.0	6	0	1	0	0	0	0	20.33	8	7	2	3	4	3	3		3	3	2	4	2	1	3	3	9
51	4.75	37.0	6	0	1	0	0	0	0	13.00	2	2	2	4	4	4	2		3	4		3	1	3	3	3	3
52	4.75	31.0	5	1	1	1	0	0	0	12.00	6	2	2	3	3	4	3		2	3	3	4	2	3	2	2	3
53	5.00	56.0	6	0	1	0	0	0	0	17.00	6	2	1	3	3	3	1		2	2	2	3		3	2	3	4
54	11.00	35.5	8	1	1	1	1	0	0	23.67	5	7	1	3	4	3	2		2	3	2	3	2	3	3	3	9
55	11.00	28.0	8	1	1	1	1	0	0	21.00	2	2	2	3	3	3	1		2	3	1	3		2	3	3	3
56	7.25	36.0	7	0	1	1	0	0	0	2.33	10	9	2	3	4	3	3		2	4	3	4		1	3	2	1
57	3.50	35.0	3	1	1	0	1	0	0	22.33	10	5	2	4	4	3	3		1	2	3	2	4	1	1	3	3
58	7.25	44.0	8	0	1	0	1	0	0	5.00	2	2	2	4	4	2	2		2	2	3	3		3	3	3	2
59	-3.50	-4.0	7	0	1	0	0	0	0	5.00	2	3	2	2	3	3	2		3	3	3	3	2	3	3	3	3
60	6.00	24.5	5	0	1	0	0	0	0	10.33	2	3	2	3	4	3	2	2	3	3	1	3		3	3	2	2
61	9.75	25.0	8	0	1	0	0	0	0	5.00	3	3	1	4	4	3	4		2	4	4	4	4	4	4	4	4
62	2.25	51.5	3	0	1	0	1	0	0	1.00	10	3	1	3	4	2	1		3	4	2	3		3	3	3	3
63	1.00	25.0	4	0	1	0	0	0	0	13.00	2	3	1	4	3	4	2		3	4	2	4		4	3	4	9
64	-3.50	30.5	4	0	1	0	0	0	0	9.33	3	3	2	4	4	2	2		3	4	3	3		3	3	3	3
65	4.75	29.0	4	0	1	0	0	0	0	10.33	2	3	2	3	3	3	2		3	3	4	4		4	4	3	1
66	-.25	20.0	7	1	1	0	1	0	0	23.67	9	3	1	4	4	4	2		3	3	2	3	1	3	3	3	1
67	4.75	22.0	7	1	1	0	0	1	1	25.67	5	5	1	4	4	3	2		3	3	1	4	1	3	3	3	9
68	6.00	7.5	3	0	1	0	0	0	0	5.00	5	5	1	3	4	2	1		3	3	1	3		2	3	2	1
69	7.25	32.0	8	1	1	0	1	0	0	23.67	9	8	1	4	4	4	3		2	3	1	4		4	4	4	1
70	1.00	23.0	5	0	1	0	0	0	0	14.67	3	3	1	4	4	3	3		3	4	1	2	2	4	4	4	1
71	11.00	24.5	4	0	1	0	0	0	0	18.67	7	3	1	3	4	1	2	3	4	4	1	2		3	3	1	1
72	8.50	23.0	7	0	1	1	0	0	0	11.67	5	4	1	4	4	4	2	2	4	4	3	3	2	2	3	3	1
73	8.50	30.5	4	0	1	0	0	0	0	14.33	3	6	1	2	2	2	2	2	3	3	2	3	3	2	2	3	1
74	14.75	13.5	5	0	1	0	1	0	0	11.67	3	3	1	3	3	2	3	2	2	3	3	3	3	2	3	2	1
75	14.75	30.0	7	1	1	1	1	0	1	14.33	6	3	1	3	3	3	3		3	3	1	4	2	3	3	3	1

The HSB Variables

The following 28 variables (with the range of their values in parentheses) are found in the hsbdata file. Note that a complete codebook and how to generate it in SPSS are found in Appendix D.

1.   Identification number (1 to 75)
2.   Visualization score (-4 to 16)
3.   Mosaic, pattern test score (-4 to 56)
4.   Grades in h.s. (1 to 8)
5.   Math grades (0=low, 1=high)
6.   Algebra 1 in h.s. (1=taken, 0=not taken)
7.   Algebra 2 in h.s. (1=taken, 0=not taken)
8.   Geometry in h.s. (1=taken, 0=not taken)
9.   Trigonometry in h.s. (1=taken, 0=not taken)
10.   Calculus in h.s. (1=taken, 0=not taken)
11.   Math achievement score (-8.33 to 25)
12.   Father's education (2 to 10)
13.   Mother's education (2 to 10)
14.   Gender (1=male, 2=female)

Math Attitude Questions 1 - 13 (rated from 1=very atypical to 4=very typical) and Ethnicity

15.   Q01:   I practice math skills until I can do them well. (math motivation)
16.   Q02:   I feel happy after solving a hard problem. (math pleasure)
17.   Q03:   I solve math problems quickly. (math competence)
18.   Q04:   I give up easily instead of persisting if a math problem is difficult. (low motivation)
19.   Q05:   I am a little slow catching on to new topics in math. (low competence).
20.   Q06:   I do not get much pleasure out of math problems. (low pleasure)
21.   Q07:   I prefer to figure out how to solve problems without asking for help. (motivation)
22.   Q08:   I do not keep at it very long when a math problem is challenging. (low motivation)
23.   Q09:   I am very competent at math. (competence)
24.   Q10:   I smile only a little (or not at all) when I solve a math problem. (low pleasure).
25.   Q11:   I have some difficulties doing math as well as other kids my age. (low competence)
26.   Q12:   I try to complete my math problems even if it takes a long time to finish. (motivation)
27.   Q13:   I explore all possible solutions of a complex problem before going on to another one. (motivation)

28.   Ethnicity (1=Euro-American, 2=African-American, 3=Hispanic-American, 4=Asian-American)

Statistical Package for the Social Sciences (SPSS 7.5)

Overview of the Program

SPSS is a sophisticated and complex package of statistical programs for the social sciences including education. It is widely used and available in many formats. This manual is based on SPSS 7.5 which has been developed for microcomputers with Windows 95 or NT. There are similar versions of SPSS for the Macintosh and Windows 3.1, but they have somewhat different windows and less sophisticated outputs. There is also a student version of SPSS 7.5 which includes almost all the statistics used in this manual (except for some or all in Assignments G, I, M, and N.

SPSS has a large number of options both for analyzing data and for printing the outputs. This manual only illustrates and discusses some of the more common options. However, we include a wide variety of useful statistics, some of which are quite complex and not covered in basic statistics books or in the *SPSS Base 7.5 for Windows Users Guide* and the *SPSS Base 7.5 Applications Guide*, which are important references for serious users. Also important for advanced users are the *SPSS 7.5 Advanced Statistics* and *SPSS 7.5 Professional Statistics* manuals.

The SPSS tutorial and Help screens are other valuable sources of information about what SPSS can do and how to use it. It is best to study the tutorial in relatively small segments because it is packed with information and options.

Menu Overview

Fig. 2.1 shows the SPSS pull-down menus. As you can see, there are a wide variety of subcommands under the 10 basic menus. We have marked the commands most often used in this manual with an X to the right of the menu. Also we have put the names of specific menus and commands in bold in this section and throughout the book. You will, as in all Windows applications, use the **file** menu frequently to **open, save,** and **print** files, and you may use the **edit** and **view** menus in the usual way.

The **data** menu can be used in a variety of ways but in this manual we have used it to **define** and label **variables** and to **select cases** from a sample to analyze separately from the rest of the sample. Using the **transform** commands, we have created, in Assignment C, several new or revised variables with the **compute, count,** and **recode** commands.

The **statistics** pull-down menu is the one used in this manual for all the descriptive and inferential statistics that you will learn. We will discuss the statistics submenus more below when we describe Fig. 2.1.

The **graphs** menu can be used for making a variety of graphs or charts such as **box plots, scatter** plots, and **histograms,** and we will do so in several assignments (e.g., B, C, and E). When we

Fig. 2.1. SPSS pull-down menus with frequently used submenus marked with an X.

discuss the high school and beyond data set in the next section, we will indicate how to use the **file info** submenu, under **utilities,** to create a codebook. The **Windows** menu includes a line indicating the current file in the SPSS data editor. The **tutorial** for **SPSS,** which you should browse before getting too deeply involved into the assignments, is under the **help** menu.

Statistics Submenus

Fig. 2.2 shows the several submenus under the statistics menu. Beside each submenu are X's for the programs that are used in this manual. We suggest that you tab this key figure or make a copy so that you can refer to it easily when selecting a statistic.

Summarize. This menu provides a variety of descriptive statistics, produced in Assignments A-D, such as frequency distributions, means, and standard deviations. Many of these descriptive statistics are found not only under the **frequencies** submenu but also under the **descriptives** and **explore** submenus. The latter is used to develop box plots which we will do in Assignment B. The **crosstabs** submenu is used to cross-tabulate two categorical variables, making a cross-tabulation table and providing some basic nonparametric measures of association. The **case summaries** submenu could be used to print out or list the scores of several participants on a new or computed variable so that one could check to make sure that the computations produced the desired new variable.

Compare Means. This menu is used in Assignment J to compare the means of two groups with the **independent samples *t* test** or two related samples with a **paired samples *t* test**. It is also used in Assignment K to compare three or more independent samples or groups with a **one-way ANOVA.**

General Linear Model. This very sophisticated program is used for a variety of types of analysis of variance. We will use it in Assignment L for **general factorial** ANOVAs as well as ANCOVA, in Assignment M for **repeated measures** (and mixed) ANOVAs, and in Assignment N for **multivariate** analyses of variance (MANOVAs).

Correlate. We will use the **bivariate** submenu to do Pearson, Spearman, and Kendall's Tau correlations in Assignment E. Although we will not use the partial correlation program in this manual you may want to be aware of its existence.

Regression. In Assignment H, we will use the **linear** subprogram to compute linear multiple regression statistics. Several other complex regressions are included on this menu. We will use **logistic** regression in Assignment I.

We will not use the **loglinear** menus in this manual. It is a complex statistic similar to chi-square, but with more than two variables.

Classify. In Assignment I, we will use **discriminant** analysis.

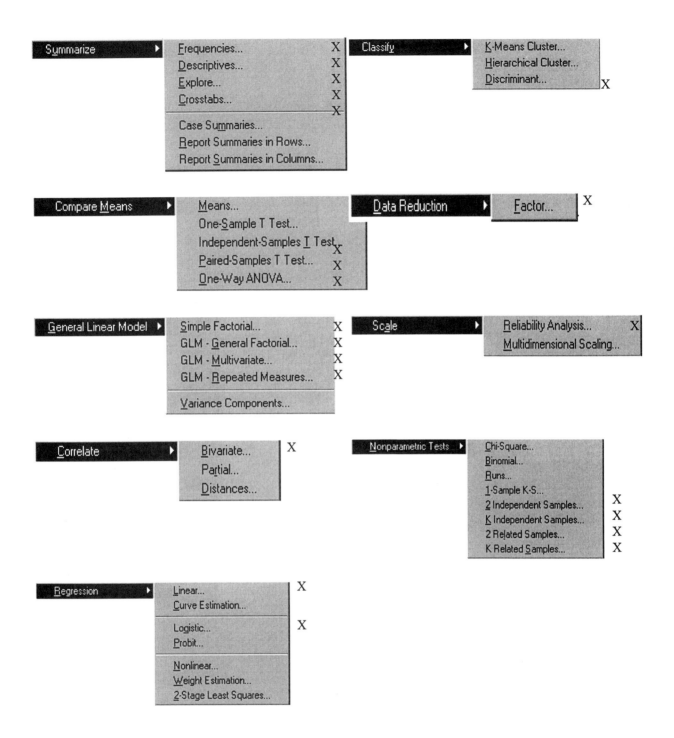

Fig. 2.2. Statistics submenus with statistics used in this manual indicated with an X.

Data Reduction. The **factor** subprogram will be used in Assignment F to do factor analysis for the purpose of reducing a sizable number of variables to a smaller number of composite factors or variables.

Scale. The reliability analyses subprogram includes **Cronbach's alpha** which we will do in Assignment G. Note that several measures of reliability such as **test-retest** and **alternate forms reliability** are done using a correlation coefficient and the Correlate menu described above. **Kappa** is done from the crosstabs submenu.

Nonparametric Tests. Chi-square is available both under crosstabs, where we will use it, and here for goodness of fit. This menu will be used to produce the nonparametric equivalents of t tests and ANOVAs. The **two independent samples** submenu will be used to produce the Mann-Whitney U which is the nonparametric equivalent for the independent samples t test. The **K independent samples** menu will be used to produce the Kruskal-Wallis nonparametric statistic which is similar to a one-way ANOVA. The **two related samples** program will be used to generate the Wilcoxon test which is similar to a paired t test. And finally the **K related samples** Friedman test is a nonparametric equivalent of the repeated measures ANOVA. These will be used in Assignments J-M along with the equivalent parametric analysis.

We hope that this overview of the HSB data file and SPSS has given you enough background for the assignments that follow. After a brief introduction to measurement and descriptive statistics, you should be ready to start Assignment A. Good computing.

CHAPTER 3
Measurement and Descriptive Statistics

According to S. S. Stevens (1951), "In its broadest sense measurement is the assignment of numerals to objects or events according to rules" (p.1). As we have seen in chapter 1, the process of research begins with a problem that is made up of a question about the relationship between two, or usually more, variables. Measurement is introduced when these variables are operationally defined by certain rules which determine how the participants' responses will be translated into numerals. These numbers can represent nonordered categories in which the numerals do not indicate a greater or lesser degree of the characteristic of the variable. Stevens went on to describe four scales or levels of measurement that he labeled: nominal, ordinal, interval, and ratio. Stevens and most writers since then have argued that the level or scale of measurement used to collect data is one of the most important determinants of the types of statistics that can be done appropriately with that data. As implied by the phrase "levels of measurement," these types of measurements vary from the most basic (nominal) to the highest level (ratio). However, since none of the statistics that are commonly used in social sciences or education require the use of ratio scales we will not discuss them to any extent.

Nominal Scales/Variables

These are the most basic or primitive forms of scales in which the numerals assigned to each category stand for the name of the category, but have no implied order or value. Males may be assigned the numeral 1 and females may be coded as 2. This does not imply that females are higher than males or that two males equal a female or any of the other typical mathematical uses of the numerals. The same reasoning applies to many other true nominal categories such as ethnic groups, type of disability, section number in a class schedule, or marital status (e.g., never married, married, divorced, or widowed). In each of these cases the categories are distinct and nonoverlapping, but not ordered, thus each category in the variable marital status is different from each other but there is no necessary order to the categories. Thus, the four categories could be numbered 1 for never married, 2 for married, 3 for divorced, and 4 for widowed or the reverse, or any combination of assigning a number to each category. What this obviously implies is that you must *not* treat the numbers used for identifying the categories in a nominal scale as if they were numbers that could be used in a formula, added together, subtracted from one another, or used to compute an average. Average marital status makes no sense. However, if one asks a computer to do average marital status, it will blindly do so and give you meaningless information. The important thing about nominal scales is to have clearly defined, nonoverlapping or mutually exclusive categories which can be coded reliably by observers or by self-report.

Qualitative or naturalistic researchers rely heavily, if not exclusively, on nominal scales and on the process of developing appropriate codes or categories for behaviors, words, etc. Although using qualitative/nominal scales does dramatically reduce the types of statistics that can be used with your data, it does not altogether eliminate the use of statistics to summarize your data and make inferences. Therefore, even when the data are nominal or qualitative categories, one's research may benefit from the use of appropriate statistics. We will return shortly to discuss the types of statistics, both descriptive and inferential, that are appropriate for nominal data.

Dichotomous Variables

It is often hard to tell whether a dichotomous variable, one with two values or categories (e.g., Yes or No, Pass or Fail), is nominal or ordered and researchers disagree. We argue that, although some such dichotomous variables are clearly nominal (e.g., gender) and others are clearly ordered (e.g., math grades--high and low), all dichotomous variables form a special case. Statistics such as the mean or variance would be meaningless for a three or more category nominal variable (e.g., ethnic group or marital status, as described above). However, such statistics do have meaning when there are only two categories. For example, in the HSB data the average gender is 1.55 (with males = 1 and females = 2). This means that 55% of the participants were females. Furthermore, we will see in Chapter 12, multiple regression, that dichotomous variables, called dummy variables, can be used as independent variables along with other variables that are interval scale. Thus, it is not necessary to decide whether a dichotomous variable is nominal, and it can be treated as if it were interval scale.

Table 3.1. *Descriptions of Scales of Measurement With Dichotomous Variables Added*

Scale	Description
Nominal	= 3 or more unordered or nominal categories
Dichotomous	= 2 categories either nominal or ordered (special case)
Ordinal	= 3 or more ordered categories, but *clearly unequal intervals* between categories or *ranks*
Interval	= 3 or more ordered categories, and *approximately equal intervals* between categories
Ratio	= 3 or more ordered categories, with equal intervals between categories and a true zero

Ordinal Scales/Variables (i.e., Unequal Interval Scales)

In ordinal scales there are not only mutually exclusive categories as in nominal scales, but the categories are ordered from low to high in much the same way that one would *rank* the order in which horses finished a race (i.e., first, second, third, ...last). Thus, in an ordinal scale one knows which participant is highest or most preferred on a dimension but the intervals between the various ranks are not equal. For example, the second place horse may finish far behind the winner but only a fraction of a second in front of the third place finisher. Thus, in this case there are unequal intervals between first, second, and third place with a very small interval between second and third and a much larger one between first and second.

Interval and Ratio Scales/Variables (i.e., Equal Interval Scales)

Interval scales have not only mutually exclusive categories that are ordered from low to high, but also the categories are equally spaced (i.e., have equal intervals between them). Most physical measurements (length, weight, money, etc.) are ratio scales because they not only have equal intervals between the values/categories, but also have a true zero, which means in the above examples, no length, no weight, or no money. Few psychological scales have this property of a true zero and thus even if they are very well constructed equal interval scales, it is not possible to say that one has no intelligence or no extroversion or no attitude of a certain type. While there are differences between interval and ratio scales, the differences are not important for us because we can do all of the types of statistics that we have available with interval data. As long as the scale has equal intervals, it is not necessary to have a true zero.

Distinguishing Between Ordinal and Interval Scales

It is usually fairly easy to tell whether three categories are ordered or not, so students and researchers can distinguish between nominal and ordinal data, except perhaps when there are only two categories, and then it does not matter. The distinction between nominal and ordinal makes a lot of difference in what statistics are appropriate. However, it is considerably harder to distinguish between ordinal and interval data. While almost all *physical* measurements provide either ratio or interval data, the situation is less clear with regard to psychological measurements.

When we come to the measurement of psychological characteristics such as attitudes, often we cannot be certain about whether the intervals between the ordered categories are equal, as required for an interval level scale. Suppose we have a five-point scale on which we are to rate our attitude about a certain statement from strongly agree as 5 to strongly disagree as 1. The issue is whether the intervals between a rating of 1 and 2, 2 and 3, 3 and 4, and 4 and 5 are all equal or not. One could argue that because the numbers are equally spaced on the page, and because they are equally spaced in terms of their numerical values, the subjects will view them as equal intervals. However, especially if the in-between points are identified (e.g., strongly agree, agree, neutral, disagree, and strongly disagree), it could be argued that the difference between strongly agree and agree is not the same as between agree and neutral; this contention would be hard to disprove. Some questionnaire or survey items have response categories that are not exactly equal intervals. For example, let's take the case where the subjects are asked to identify their age as one of five categories: 21 to 30, 31 to 40, 41 to 50, 51 to 60, and 61 and above. It should be clear that the last category is larger in terms of number of years covered than the other four categories. Thus, the age intervals are not exactly equal. However, we would consider this scale and the ones above to be at least *approximately interval*.

On the other hand, an example of an ordered scale that is clearly not interval would be one that asked how frequently subjects do something. The answers go something like this: every day, once a week, once a month, once a year, once every 5 years. You can see that the categories become wider and wider and, therefore, are not equal intervals. There is clearly much more difference between 1 year and 5 years than there is between 1 day and 1 week. Most of the above information is summarized in the top of Table 3.2.

Table 3.2. *Selection of Appropriate Descriptive Statistics for One Dependent Variable*

	Level/Scale of Measurement of Variable		
	Nominal	**Ordinal**	**Interval or Ratio**
Characteristics of the Variable	- Qualitative data - Not ordered - True categories: only names, labels	- Quantitative data - Ordered data - Rank order only	- Quantitative data - Ordered data - Equal intervals between values
Examples	Gender, school, curriculum type, hair color	1st, 2nd, 3rd place, ranked preferences	Age, height, good test scores, good rating scales
Frequency Distribution	Redhead - III Blond - IIII Brunette - II	Best - II Better - III Good - III	5 - I 4 - II 3 - III 2 - III 1 - II
Frequency Polygon/ Histogram	No	Yes	Yes
Bar Graph or Chart	Yes	Yes	Yes
Central Tendency			
Mean	No	Mean Rank	Yes
Median	No	Yes	Yes
Mode	Yes	Yes	Yes
Variability			
Standard Deviation	No	of Ranks	Yes
Range	No	Yes, but[1]	Yes
How many categories	Yes	Yes	Yes
Percent in each	Yes	Yes	Yes
Shape			
Skewness	No	No	Yes
Kurtosis	No	No	Yes

---

[1] The range of ordinal data may well be misleading

The Importance of Scales of Measurement for Descriptive Statistics

Table 3.2 provides a review of the concept of levels or scales of measurement of a variable and provides some additional information and examples about the appropriate use of various kinds of descriptive statistics given nominal, ordinal, or interval data. It is *always* important to know the level of measurement of the *dependent variables* in a study. For the associational approach, it also is necessary to know the scale of the independent variable.

Table 3.2 also illustrates whether and how a number of common descriptive statistics would be utilized if the data (i.e., dependent variable) were nominal, ordinal, or interval/ratio. Frequency distributions would look very similar in all three cases, the only difference is that with nominal data the order in which the categories are listed is arbitrary. Thus, we have listed redhead, blond, and then brunette indicating with dit marks that there are three redheads, four blonds, and two brunettes. However, redheads could be put after brunettes, or between blonds and brunettes because the categories are not ordered. In ordinal data you can see that the order would be invariant. With interval or ratio data, the frequency distribution would look similar, but the intervals between the numbers (e.g., between the five and four, four and three, etc.) would be equal.

Frequency distributions indicate how many participants are in each category, whether those be ordered or unordered categories. When making a diagram of a frequency distribution, one has two somewhat different choices, a histogram/frequency polygon or a bar chart, plus lots of variants. As shown in Table 3.2 and Fig. 3.1, the **frequency polygon** which connects the points between the categories can be used with ordinal or interval data. Frequency polygons should not be used with nominal data because there is no necessary ordering of the points. Thus, it is better to make a **bar graph** or chart of the frequency distribution of variables like gender, ethnic group, school curriculum, or other nominal variables because the points that happen to be adjacent in the frequency distribution are not by necessity adjacent (see Fig. 3.2).

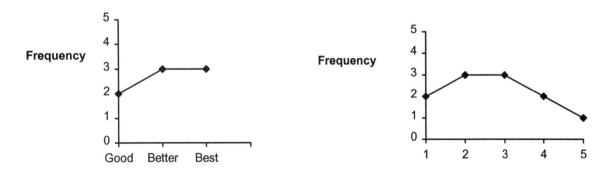

Fig. 3.1. Sample frequency polygons for ordinal and interval level scales.

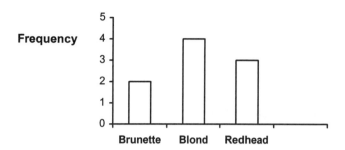

Fig. 3.2. Sample frequency distribution bar chart for the nominal scale of hair color.

Measures of central tendency. Three main measures of the center of a distribution are available: mean, median, and mode. As you can see from Table 3.2, any of them can be used with interval or ratio data while with ordinal data, the mean is usually not appropriate. Only the mode is appropriate for nominal data. The **mean** or arithmetic average takes into account all of the available information in computing the central tendency of a frequency distribution, thus it is usually the statistic of choice assuming that one has interval or ratio data. The **median** or middle score is an appropriate measure of central tendency for ordinal level data. Note from Table 3.2 that one can always use a lower level statistic (e.g., the median) with higher level data (e.g., interval data) but not vice versa. Thus, you will see that the right-hand column (interval data) has all Yes responses. Finally, the **mode**, or most common category, can be used with any kind of data but generally provides the least precise information about central tendency. One would use the mode as the measure of central tendency if there is only one mode, it is clearly identified, and you need a quick noncalculated measure. The median may well be a better measure of central tendency than the mean even if one has interval data under certain circumstances, namely, when the frequency distribution is skewed markedly to one side. For example, the median income in a group with one millionaire is substantially lower and reflects the central tendency of the group better than the average income which would be inflated in both this example and the country as a whole by a few people who very make large amounts of money.

Variability. Variability tells us about the spread or dispersion of the scores. In the extreme if all of the scores in a distribution are the same, there is no variability. If they are all different and widely spaced apart, the variability will be high. You can see from Table 3.2 that the **standard deviation**, the most common measure of variability, is only appropriate when one has interval level data. With nominal or ordinal data one would need to ask questions like how many different categories are there and what the percentages are in each.

Shape. Many statistics assume that the data are normally distributed. That is, their frequency distribution is similar to the **normal curve**, which has five properties:
1. The normal curve is unimodal. It has one "hump," and this hump is in the middle of the distribution. The mode or most frequent value is in the middle.
2. The mean, median, and mode are equal.
3. It is symmetric. If you folded the normal curve in half, the right side would fit perfectly with the left side; that is, it is *not* skewed.
4. It is asymptotic. This means that the extremes never touch the x axis.

5. It is neither too peaked nor too flat, that is, it has zero kurtosis.

Two key statistics are skewness and kurtosis. These indexes are important in determining how much a variable's distribution deviates from the distribution of the normal curve. **Skewness** refers to the lack of symmetry or balance in a frequency distribution. Distributions with a few scores far to the right (high) end, making a long "tail" to the right, have a positive skew and vice versa. **Kurtosis** measures whether the peak of the distribution is taller or shorter than the ideal normal curve and also whether the tails are shorter or longer than the normal curve. Very peaked curves have a positive kurtosis. If a frequency distribution of a variable has a large (plus or minus) skewness and/or kurtosis relative to their standard error, that variable is said to deviate from normality.

Conclusions About Interval Versus Ordinal Data and the Use of Statistics

Chapter 7 provides examples of how the level or scale of measurement affects the type of *inferential statistic* that one can use to test a null hypothesis. One conclusion is that where possible one should attempt to measure especially the dependent variables on interval level scales. This will make it more likely that it will be appropriate to use the more familiar and powerful parametric statistics such as the Pearson correlation and analysis of variance.

However, most psychological measurements are not clearly interval level data, as discussed above. When developing an instrument (rating scales, questionnaire items, etc.) one can avoid the more obvious and clearly ordinal scales by not asking subjects to *rank* (first, second, third) their preferences for certain categories, but instead asking them to *rate* each from very low to very high. Also, it is advisable from the point of view of scaling not to include intermediate categories, especially ones that could clearly make the intervals on the rating scale unequal. Remember our earlier examples about frequency of use in which the categories were clearly much broader at one end of the scale than the other.

However, many social scientists treat all rating scales as if they were, or at least approximated, equal interval scales. When looking through the social science and education literature, one finds many examples of correlations and analysis of variance or similar parametric statistics and few examples of nonparametric techniques like those appropriate for ordinal level data. This is true even when the data appear to be more like an ordinal scale than a true equal interval scale. Thus, while conservative statisticians and researchers would argue that much psychological data is only ordinal level data and that nonparametric statistics should be used, in practice this assumption appears to be widely overlooked or ignored in part because most of the parametric statistics are said to be *robust*, or not much affected, by violations of assumptions.

Nevertheless, we issue two caveats.
1. Always use the appropriate nominal statistics when one has nominal data with three or more categories.
2. If the data are clearly ordinal (i.e., not approximately interval), especially if other assumptions of parametric statistics are violated, it is wise to use nonparametric, ordinal type statistics.

CHAPTER 4

Data Entry, Checking Data, and Descriptive Statistics

Before using statistics to help answer your research questions, you should get a good feel for the data and check carefully for errors. Assignments A and B will help you do this for the HSB data.

You should check your raw data as you collect it even before it is entered into the computer. Make sure that the participants marked their score sheets or questionnaires appropriately; check things such as double answers (when only one is expected) or marking between two ratings. If this sort of thing happens, you need to have a rule (e.g., "use the lower one") that you can apply consistently. Thus, you should "clean up" your data, making sure it is clear, consistent, and readable, before entering it into a data file like that shown in Table 2.1.

After the data are entered into the **SPSS Data Editor**,[1] you will compute some basic descriptive statistics, as demonstrated in Assignments A and B. Certain kinds of errors will be noticeable from Output 4.1, basic descriptive statistics, in Problem 1 of this assignment. To spot these errors, you will need to examine it in conjunction with the possible ranges of values for each variable, which are found in chapter 1 and Appendix D.

Also, you should at least browse the SPSS tutorial on the **Help** menu to get an extended overview of the program.

Problems/Research Questions[2]

1. What are the mean, standard deviation, minimum, and maximum scores for all 75 participants/cases on all variables?

2. Are there any errors in the data that can be spotted by comparing the above output with the codebook? Correct the errors and rerun the basic descriptive statistics.

3. You will learn how to enter new data into the SPSS Data Editor and run the descriptive statistics for that new variable, *visual2*.

---

[1] In the chapters with lab assignments we have identified the SPSS variable names using italics (e.g., *visual2*) and have put in bold the terms used on the SPSS windows (e.g., **SPSS Data Editor**) to help you.

[2] This section near the beginning of each chapter introduces the problems/questions to be answered with SPSS. Questions 1, 2, and 3 here correspond to Problems 1, 2, and 3 of the Lab Assignment in this chapter and to Outputs 4.1, 4.2, and 4.3 at the end of the chapter.

Lab Assignment A

Logon and Get Data

Get/Retrieve the **hsbdata** file from your diskette. There are several ways to do this. The easiest way is:

- Double click on the **SPSS** icon in Windows.
- Then click on **File => Open** after the SPSS application activates (see Fig. 4.1 and 4.2).

 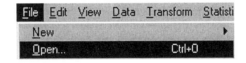

Fig. 4.1. SPSS icon.   **Fig. 4.2. File open menu.**

However, if an SPSS icon is not easily visible, you should begin at the **Start** button (bottom left of screen). Holding down the mouse, scroll to **Programs,** then **SPSS 7.5 for Windows** (see Fig. 4.3). Note, you may have to scroll into further submenus depending on how your computer is set up.

Fig. 4.3. Start menu.

Eventually, you should get a window looking like Fig. 4.4a or Fig. 4.4b.

For **Windows 95:**
- Go to the **Look in** box.
- Select the **3 ½ Floppy (A:).** The file **hsbdata** should appear in the window below **Look in**.
- Then click on **Open** (see Fig. 4.4a).

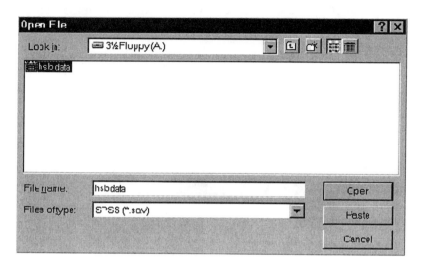

Fig. 4.4a. Windows 95 open data file.

For **Windows NT:**
- Select **Drive a:**.
- Then choose **hsbdata.sav** in the **File name**
- Click on **OK** (see Fig. 4.4b).

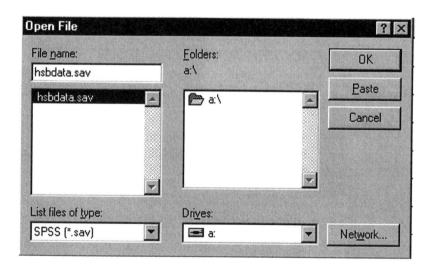

Fig. 4.4b. Windows NT open data file.

- After a few moments, you should get a data file looking like Fig. 4.5. The full data file is shown in Table 2.1.

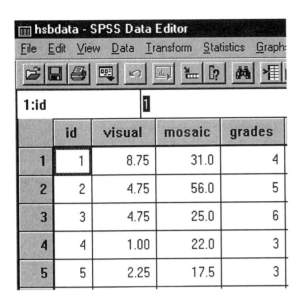

Fig. 4.5. SPSS data editor.

Important: Before doing anything else, follow these commands so that your output will show useful commands that SPSS calls a **syntax** or **log**.
- Click on **Edit => Options** to get Fig. 4.6.
- Click on the **Navigator** tab near the top left of the window.
- Check **Display commands in log** on the lower left of the window.
- Leave the other defaults as is.
- Click on **OK**.

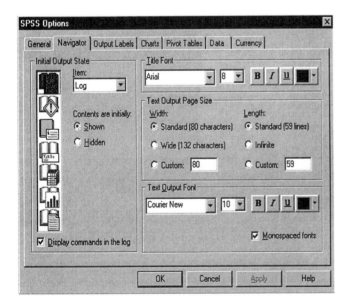

Fig. 4.6. Navigator tab options for syntax/log displays.

Problem 1: Descriptives for All Subjects

To compute the basic descriptive statistics for all subjects you will need to do these steps:
- Select **Statistics**, then **Summarize**, and finally **Descriptives** (see Fig. 4.7).

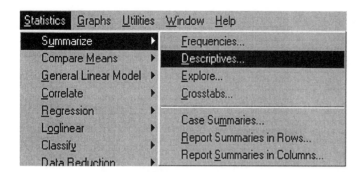

Fig. 4.7. Statistics menu.

After selecting **Descriptives**, you will be ready to compute the mean, standard deviation, minimum, and maximum for all participants/cases on all variables in order to examine the data.

- Now *highlight* all the variables. To highlight, begin at the top of the left box and hold the left mouse button down while you scroll downward until *all* the variables listed turn blue.
- Click on the **arrow** button pointing right. When you finish, the **Descriptives** dialog box should look like Fig. 4.8.

Standardized Scores

Note that if you intended to combine variables with markedly different means and standard deviations, you should standardize (make *z* scores) those variables by checking that box (bottom left) in Fig. 4.8. If variables to be combined in a given study did not use the same metric, some scores would have more weight unless we standardized the variables before combining them. With the HSB data, we only will combine scores that are on the same scale (1=very atypical to 4=very typical) so we will not make and **save standardized values as variables**.

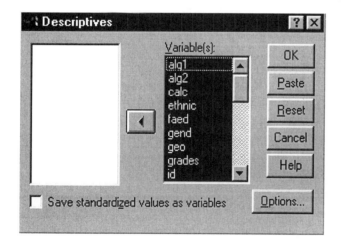

Fig. 4.8. Descriptives.

- Be sure that all the variables have moved out of the left window. If your screen looks like Fig. 4.8, then click on **Options**. You will get Fig. 4.9.

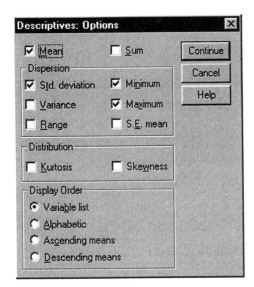

Fig. 4.9. Descriptives: Options.

Follow these steps:
- Ensure that the **Variable list** bubble is highlighted in the **Display Order** section. *Note*: You can also click on **Ascending or Descending means** if you want your variables listed in order of the means. In our case, all the variables are already listed alphabetically so you would get the same output if you checked on **Alphabetic**.
- Notice that the **mean, standard deviation, minimum,** and **maximum** were already checked. At this time, we will not request more descriptive statistics because we will do them in Assignment B, and with only these checked, we will get a compact, easy-to-read output.
- Now, click on **Continue**, which will bring you back to the main **Descriptives** dialog box.
- Then click on **OK** to run the program.

You should get an output like Fig. 4.10. The complete Output 4.1 is appended to this assignment at the end of this chapter. Compare your syntax and output to Output 4.1. If it looks the same you have done the steps correctly. Note that above the output in the back of this chapter we have provided a brief interpretation in a gray box. On the output itself, we have pointed out some of the key things by circling them and making some comments in gray boxes, which are known as callout boxes. Of course, these circles and information boxes will not show up on your printout.

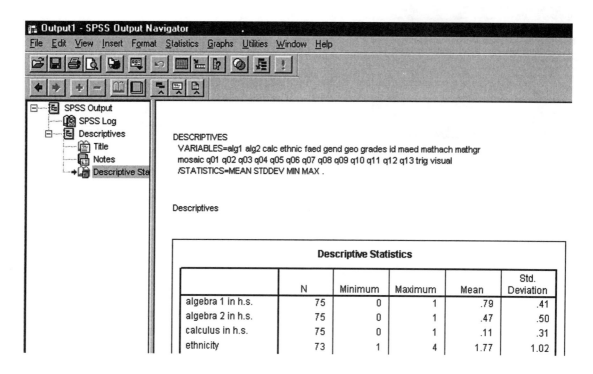

Fig. 4.10. Output navigator window.

The left side of Fig. 4.10 shows the various parts of your output. Every time you run analyses, the commands that you made, with dialog box selections, are recorded in the **SPSS log** or syntax which are the words at the top of the right side of the screen. You can click on any item on the left (e.g., **Descriptive Statistics**) to activate the output for that item, and then you can edit it.

Editing Your Output

Let's talk for a moment about editing your output file. Your output file may look different from ours with some labels wrapped onto two or three lines. You can widen or narrow certain columns to make them look better. To do this, **double click** on the output box (the one with all the statistics in it) or click on the corresponding section on the left to highlight the output that you want to edit. A thick gray line will form a box around that part of the output. Next, move your arrow to the column lines and notice the change it makes into a double arrow (i.e., ←→). Click once (continue to hold it down) with your mouse on the column line and move the columns to the left or right. Also you can edit titles or add text, such as your name. Finally, click once anywhere outside the box to cancel the editing condition. The output item that you selected will return to normal.

Problem 2: Correct Errors and Rerun Descriptives

Now click on **hsbdata,** at the bottom of your screen, to get back to the **SPSS Data Editor** so that you can correct the errors before proceeding. To make the corrections, you must find the participants whose data are in error. *Look at the data file (Table 2.1).* In this example, Participant 1 had a 10 for q01 and Participant 2 had a 40 in q02. Neither of those can be correct because q01 to q13 are ratings on a 4-point scale, varying from 1 to 4. Assume that the 10 should be a 1 and the 40 should be a 4. (In your study, you would check the questionnaires to see what these participants had answered.) It is, of course, wise to check *all* the data against the original answer sheets because the method of checking shown here will only pick up errors when the recorded number is outside the acceptable range. This type of error can, however, distort the means and standard deviation quite seriously, as in this example.

To correct the errors, *highlight* the box/cell (in the data editor) with the error by clicking on it. Then correct it. That is, highlight the q01 for Subject 1, delete the 0, and press enter. Do the same for Subject 2 in q02.

Rerun the basic descriptive statistics by repeating the steps in Problem 1. This should be easy since the variables will already be in the correct (right) box unless you pressed **Reset.**

Problem 3: Entering New Data

Let's enter some new data:
- Click on a *blank column* in the far right side of the data matrix. **The column should turn black (except the first cell) because it is highlighted.**
- First, go to the menu bar and click on **Data =>Define.**
- Type *visual2* in the highlighted box (see Fig. 4.11), but make sure you are not typing over one of your current variables such as ID (identification number).

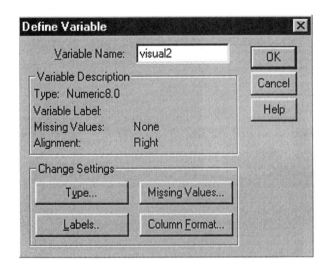

Fig. 4.11. Define variable.

- Next, click on **Labels** and a new screen called **Define Labels** (see Fig. 4.12) will appear.
- Type *Visualization retest* in the **Variable Label** box.
- Under **Value Labels**, define the lowest and highest values (0 and 9) by typing *0* in the **Value** box, and typing *Lowest* in the **Value Label** box, and then clicking **add.** Next, do the procedure again to define the highest value as **9.** Check to see if your screen looks like Fig. 4.12.
- Click on **Continue** then **OK** back in Fig. 4.11.

Note: You can also change the column width and number of decimal places by clicking on **Type** (lower left of Fig. 4.11). A new screen called **Define Variable Type** will appear (see Fig. 4.13).

Then enter the appropriate number of decimal places under **Decimal Places.** In this case, we use 0 for the *decimal places* and leave 8 for the *column width*, so there is enough space at the top of the data column for the variable name.

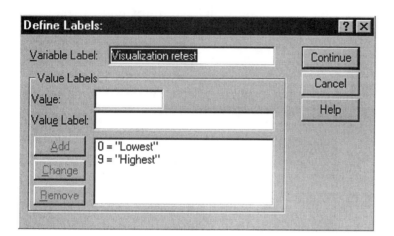

Fig. 4.12. Define labels.

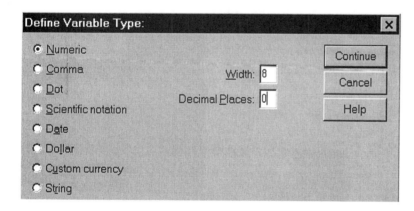

Fig. 4.13. Define variable type.

The next step is to enter the data for *visualization retest*. Ensure your **Data** file is showing.
- It is not already highlighted, click on the far right column, which should say *visual2*.
- To enter the data into this highlighted column simply *type* the number and press **Enter**. For example, type 7 (the number will show up in the blank space above of the row of variable names) and then press **Enter**; the number will be entered into the new variable column (see Fig. 4.14).

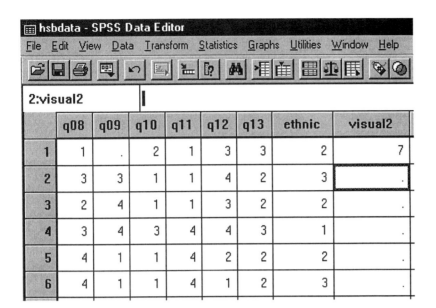

Fig. 4.14. Data entry.

Now repeat the procedure to enter the following data into the highlighted column, which has 75 participants. We have written the *visual2* scores in 5 columns of 15 preceded by the ID number. First enter the data in the left column for participants 1 through 15; then the second column for participants 16 through 30, and so on.

1 - 7	16 - 9	31 - 8	46 - 0	61 - 8
2 - 4	17 - 0	32 - 9	47 - 0	62 - 2
3 - 3	18 - 5	33 - 9	48 - 4	63 - 0
4 - 1	19 - 9	34 - 5	49 - 4	64 - 3
5 - 2	20 - 9	35 - 2	50 - 4	65 - 4
6 - 0	21 - 1	36 - 8	51 - 2	66 - 0
7 - 2	22 - 6	37 - 3	52 - 4	67 - 4
8 - 3	23 - 5	38 - 3	53 - 4	68 - 8
9 - 2	24 - 5	39 - 5	54 - 8	69 - 7
10 - 3	25 - 8	40 - 6	55 - 9	70 - 1
11 - 9	26 - 7	41 - 0	56 - 7	71 - 9
12 - 4	27 - 5	42 - 5	57 - 3	72 - 9
13 - 1	28 - 2	43 - 3	58 - 6	73 - 3
14 - 0	29 - 1	44 - 6	59 - 3	74 - 9
15 - 4	30 - 8	45 - 1	60 - 5	75 - 7

*If you make a mistake, correct it by **clicking on the cell** (the cell will be highlighted instead of the whole column), type the correct score, and press **Enter**.*

Problem 4: Descriptives for Visual2

Try running descriptive statistics for *Visual2* on your own just like you did in Problem 1. Hint: After selecting **Statistics** => **Summarize** => **Descriptives**, click on the **Reset** button and then move *Visual2* over to the **Variable(s)** box. Follow the rest of the steps provided in Problem 1. Does your output look like Output 4.4?

Printing

We recommend that you print the whole output for this assignment as shown below. However, many outputs are rather lengthy, and all are in this book. Therefore, it may not be necessary to print them every time. In your own study, you probably will print most or all outputs. To **Print** your **Output,** ensure the desired file is fully showing (i.e., output box shows on screen) by clicking on the **Output1 - SPSS Output Navigator** at the very bottom of your screen (see Fig. 4.15).

*   Then go to **File** => **Print**. You will get a window like Fig. 4.16.
*   Choose **All visible output** if you want to print everything in your output.
*   Choose **Selection** if you want to print only selected tables and charts. Note: you must highlight those areas in your output file first (see Fig. 4.17).
*   Click on **OK**.

Fig. 4.15. Window bars.

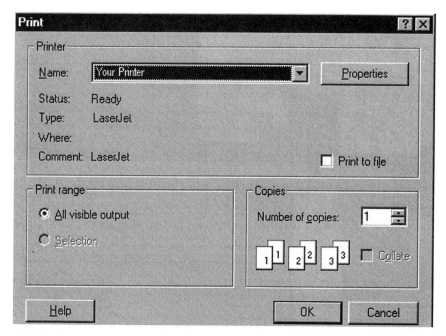

Fig. 4.16. Print.

Saving

You have two types of files: **Data (hsbdata**, see Fig. 4.5) and **Output** (see Fig. 4.10). You will probably want to save all or part of both types at the end of each lab. The reason to **Save** the **SPSS log** or syntax file at the end of each assignment is that you can use the syntax commands to rerun the analysis with or without variations. Because the whole output file may take a lot of space, it will not be possible to save many of them on a floppy disk. Thus, if you save them, you may want to save them to your hard drive or a network drive, assuming you have access to one. Or better yet, you may want to save only the SPSS log portion of the output file, after deleting the rest.

Saving Only the SPSS Log

To save the SPSS log/syntax file, first *make sure you are in the output file by clicking once on the Output icon at the bottom of the screen* (see Fig. 4.15). To save only SPSS log files, highlight everything except the SPSS log (see Fig. 4.17). In this example, click on the **Descriptives** part of the listing and it will highlight everything below it. **Warning**: *Avoid highlighting SPSS output or SPSS log.* You may accidentally delete it. Now just hit the **Delete** button and the highlighted areas will disappear. You should still have the SPSS logs showing. Follow the **Save As** steps below.

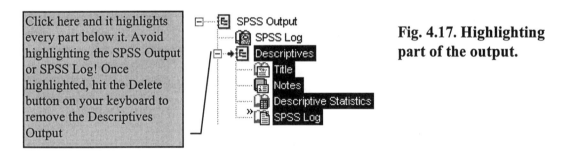

Click here and it highlights every part below it. Avoid highlighting the SPSS Output or SPSS Log! Once highlighted, hit the Delete button on your keyboard to remove the Descriptives Output

Fig. 4.17. Highlighting part of the output.

Note: If you choose to delete everything but the SPSS logs, refer to Appendix C on how to use them as syntax files. Syntax files allow you to get all the information you deleted (chart, tables, etc.) and rebuild it quickly. Yes, somewhere in all that SPSS log verbiage is your chart, table, and everything else you did.

To save your output files follow these steps:
- Click on the **Output1 - SPSS Output Navigator** button at the very bottom of your screen.
- Click **File => Save As**.
- In the **File Name** box type **hsblogA** (see Fig. 4.18). This name assumes that you have deleted all except the SPSS log. If you saved the whole output then you would probably want to give it a different name (e.g., output1).
- Make sure your **Save in** box indicates **3 ½ Floppy (A:)** so you can save it to a disk for future reference (or you can also save it on your own hard drive, C:, or a network drive if you have the capabilities).
- Now click on the **Save** button and your output file is saved!

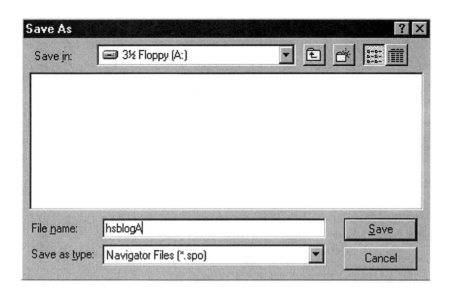

Fig. 4.18. Save as.

Saving the Data file

You should *always* save your data file if you made any changes to it. In this case, we corrected two errors. It is generally a good idea to be safe and save the data at the end of each session so you do not forget to do it when you make new variables. To do this, first:

- Click on the **hsbdata - SPSS Data** button at the bottom of your screen (see Fig. 4.15).
- Then click **File => Save As**.
- Go ahead and rename your data file as **hsbdataA**.
- Make sure you select **Drive A:** (or use C: or a network drive if you have the capability).
- Complete the saving procedure by clicking on **OK**.
- In this case, we corrected two errors so it would be wise to delete **hsbdata,** saving the corrected file.

Exit

Follow these steps:
- Click on **File => Exit**. Note: If you get asked to save anything, return to the saving steps listed previously because it was not done.
- Congratulations on finishing your first assignment!

Optional Problem

If you have time you should do the (Select Cases) **Filter** exercises in Appendix B. That assignment produces descriptive statistics for parts of the sample, first, for those with high math grades and then for those with low math grades.

Interpretation Questions

Examine the printouts for the descriptive statistics.

1. Using Output 4.1, look for any obvious errors or problems in the data. What will you look for?

2. Name the nominal variables in Output 4.2. Can you interpret the mean and standard deviation? Explain.

3. Using Output 4.2: a) How many participants are there all together? b) How many have complete data (nothing missing)? c)What percentage took algebra 1 in high school? d) What is the range of father's education scores? Does this agree with the codebook?

Outputs and Interpretations

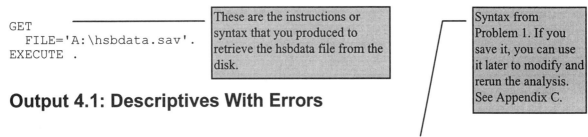

```
GET
  FILE='A:\hsbdata.sav'.
EXECUTE .
```

These are the instructions or syntax that you produced to retrieve the hsbdata file from the disk.

Syntax from Problem 1. If you save it, you can use it later to modify and rerun the analysis. See Appendix C.

Output 4.1: Descriptives With Errors

<u>Syntax for the mean, standard deviation, minimum, and maximum for all variables</u>

```
DESCRIPTIVES
  VARIABLES=alg1 alg2 calc ethnic faed gend geo grades id maed mathach mathgr
  mosaic q01 q02 q03 q04 q05 q06 q07 q08 q09 q10 q11 q12 q13 trig visual
  /STATISTICS=MEAN STDDEV MIN MAX .
```

Interpretation of Output 4.1

The Output provides the number of subjects (*N*), the lowest and highest score, mean or average, and standard deviation for each variable. At the beginning of your data analysis, check to make sure that all means seem reasonable (given the information in your codebook), and check to see that the minimum and maximum are within the appropriate range for each variable. For example, note in the codebook that *alg1* has to be **0 = not taken** or **1 = taken** so the minimum should be 0 and maximum 1. If not, you have an error to correct before proceeding. Did you find the two errors in the data? You will correct them in **Problem 2**. Note, from the bottom of Output 4.1 that the valid number (*N*) of observations/subjects (listwise) is 67, rather than 75, the number of participants in the data file. This is because the listwise *N* only includes the persons with *no* missing data on any variable. Notice that several variables (e.g., ethnicity) each have a few participants missing.

Descriptive Statistics

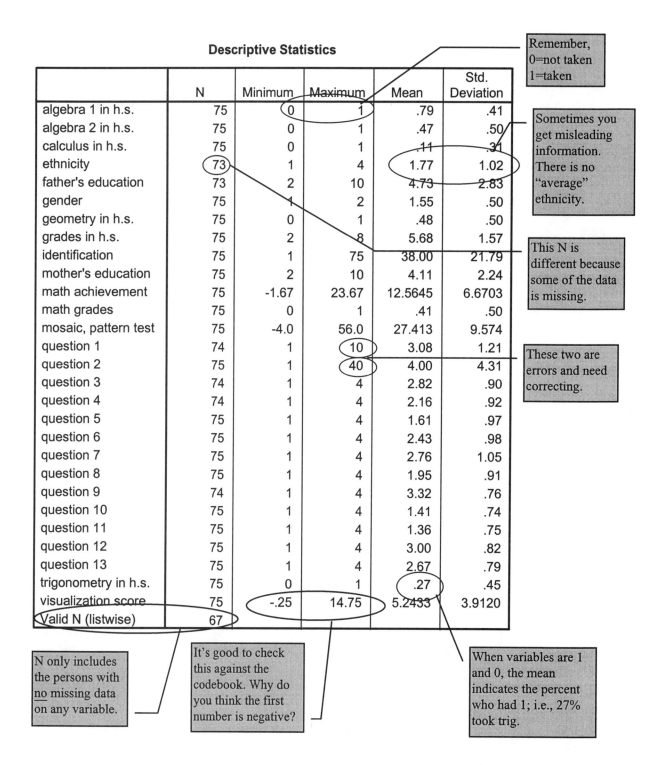

	N	Minimum	Maximum	Mean	Std. Deviation
algebra 1 in h.s.	75	0	1	.79	.41
algebra 2 in h.s.	75	0	1	.47	.50
calculus in h.s.	75	0	1	.11	.31
ethnicity	73	1	4	1.77	1.02
father's education	73	2	10	4.73	2.83
gender	75	1	2	1.55	.50
geometry in h.s.	75	0	1	.48	.50
grades in h.s.	75	2	8	5.68	1.57
identification	75	1	75	38.00	21.79
mother's education	75	2	10	4.11	2.24
math achievement	75	-1.67	23.67	12.5645	6.6703
math grades	75	0	1	.41	.50
mosaic, pattern test	75	-4.0	56.0	27.413	9.574
question 1	74	1	10	3.08	1.21
question 2	75	1	40	4.00	4.31
question 3	74	1	4	2.82	.90
question 4	74	1	4	2.16	.92
question 5	75	1	4	1.61	.97
question 6	75	1	4	2.43	.98
question 7	75	1	4	2.76	1.05
question 8	75	1	4	1.95	.91
question 9	74	1	4	3.32	.76
question 10	75	1	4	1.41	.74
question 11	75	1	4	1.36	.75
question 12	75	1	4	3.00	.82
question 13	75	1	4	2.67	.79
trigonometry in h.s.	75	0	1	.27	.45
visualization score	75	-.25	14.75	5.2433	3.9120
Valid N (listwise)	67				

Remember, 0=not taken 1=taken

Sometimes you get misleading information. There is no "average" ethnicity.

This N is different because some of the data is missing.

These two are errors and need correcting.

N only includes the persons with no missing data on any variable.

It's good to check this against the codebook. Why do you think the first number is negative?

When variables are 1 and 0, the mean indicates the percent who had 1; i.e., 27% took trig.

Output 4.2: Descriptives Corrected

<u>Syntax for the mean, standard deviation, minimum, and maximum for all variables</u>

```
DESCRIPTIVES
  VARIABLES=alg1 alg2 calc ethnic faed gend geo grades id maed mathach
  mathgr mosaic q01 q02 q03 q04 q05 q06 q07 q08 q09 q10 q11 q12 q13 trig
  visual
  /STATISTICS=MEAN STDDEV MIN MAX .
```

Descriptive Statistics

	N	Minimum	Maximum	Mean	Std. Deviation
algebra 1 in h.s.	75	0	1	.79	.41
algebra 2 in h.s.	75	0	1	.47	.50
calculus in h.s.	75	0	1	.11	.31
ethnicity	73	1	4	1.77	1.02
father's education	73	2	10	4.73	2.83
gender	75	1	2	1.55	.50
geometry in h.s.	75	0	1	.48	.50
grades in h.s.	75	2	8	5.68	1.57
identification	75	1	75	38.00	21.79
mother's education	75	2	10	4.11	2.24
math achievement	75	-1.67	23.67	12.5645	6.6703
math grades	75	0	1	.41	.50
mosaic, pattern test	75	-4.0	56.0	27.413	9.574
question 1	74	1	4	2.96	.93
question 2	75	1	4	3.52	.91
question 3	74	1	4	2.82	.90
question 4	74	1	4	2.16	.92
question 5	75	1	4	1.61	.97
question 6	75	1	4	2.43	.98
question 7	75	1	4	2.76	1.05
question 8	75	1	4	1.95	.91
question 9	74	1	4	3.32	.76
question 10	75	1	4	1.41	.74
question 11	75	1	4	1.36	.75
question 12	75	1	4	3.00	.82
question 13	75	1	4	2.67	.79
trigonometry in h.s.	75	0	1	.27	.45
visualization score	75	-.25	14.75	5.2433	3.9120
Valid N (listwise)	67				

Output 4.3: Syntax for entering Visual2

Syntax for visualization retest

```
FORMATS visual2 (F8).
VARIABLE LABELS visual2 "Visualization retest".
VALUE LABELS visual2
 .000000000000000 "Lowest"
 9.00000000000000 "Highest"
.
```

A syntax is useful because it tells you what you did and allows you to check your work. It is also helpful when you use advanced SPSS analysis. See Appendix C.

Syntax for saving hsbdata data

```
SAVE OUTFILE='A:\hsbdataA.sav'
   /COMPRESSED.
```

Output 4.4: Descriptives for Visual2

Syntax for descriptive statistics for Visual2

```
DESCRIPTIVES
  VARIABLES=visual2
  /STATISTICS=MEAN STDDEV MIN MAX .
```

Descriptive Statistics

	N	Minimum	Maximum	Mean	Std. Deviation
Visualization retest	75	0	9	4.47	2.93
Valid N (listwise)	75				

CHAPTER 5

More Descriptive Statistics and Checking the Normal Distribution

This assignment includes more descriptive (see chapter 3) statistics and three ways to examine your data to see if the variables are approximately normally distributed, an assumption of most of the inferential statistics that we will use. Two key statistics are skewness and kurtosis. These indexes determine how much a variable's distribution deviates from the distribution of the normal curve. **Skewness** refers to the lack of symmetry in a frequency distribution. Distributions with a long "tail" to the right have a positive skew and vice versa. **Kurtosis** measures whether the peak of the distribution is taller or shorter than the ideal normal curve and also whether the tails are higher or lower than the normal curve. Very peaked curves have a positive kurtosis. If a frequency distribution of a variable has a large (plus or minus) skewness and/or kurtosis relative to their standard error, that variable is said to deviate from normality. As a rule of thumb, we say that if the skewness and/or kurtosis measure is more than 2.5 times its standard error the assumption of normality has been violated. In this assignment, we examine this assumption for several key variables. However, many of the inferential statistics that we will use are robust or quite insensitive to violations of normality.

Also, you should browse more of the SPSS tutorial, on the **Help** menu, so that you will have a better idea of the range of things that you can do with SPSS.

Problems/ Research Questions

1. What are the percentages of males and females and for each ethnic group for the clearly nominal variables of *gend* and *ethnic*?

2. What are the percentages in each category for the dichotomous variables: *mathgr, alg1, alg2, calc, geo,* and *trig*?

3. What are the frequency distributions for the approximately interval scale variables: *visual, mosiac, grades, mathach*? Are those variables normally distributed?

4. What are the descriptive statistics and distributions separately for the male and female math achievement scores?

Lab Assignment B

Logon and Get Data

Open the **hsbdataA** data file you saved from the last assignment (see Lab Assignment A on how to open files).

Problem 1: Frequency Distributions

Let's determine frequencies for your nominal categorical variables.
- Click on **Statistics => Summarize => Frequencies**.
- Holding down the Control key on your keyboard, click on the variables *gend* and *ethnic*. (Note: holding down the control key allows you to highlight two or more variables.)
- Now click on the **arrow** button to move them over. Does it look like Fig. 5.1?

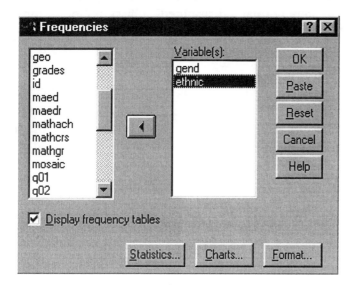

Fig. 5.1. Frequencies.

- Click on **OK** to see your syntax and output file. Does it look like Output 5.1?

Problem 2: More Frequencies on Your Own

Now try it again by doing **Frequencies** for the two-category, ordered variables: *mathgr, alg1, alg2, geo, trig,* and *calc*. Hint: Don't forget to move *gend* and *ethnic* back to the left box by clicking on **Reset** before moving *mathgr,* etc. to the **Variables** box. You should get syntax and outputs that look like those in Output 5.2.

Problem 3: Frequencies, Statistics, and Histograms

Now let's take a look at some histograms along with the frequency distributions for several approximately interval scale variables. Follow these commands:
- **Statistics => Summarize => Frequencies**.
- Don't forget to **Reset**!
- Let's do the variables *visual, mosaic, grades,* and *mathach*. Highlight each and then click on the **arrow** button. It should look like Fig. 5.2.

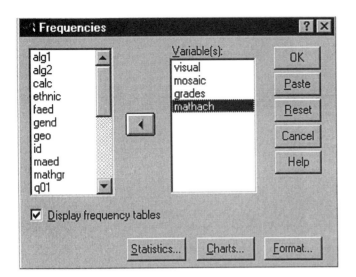

Fig. 5.2. Frequencies.

Follow these steps to get more statistics:

- Now, click on **Statistics** and select **Mean, Median, Mode, Kurtosis, Skewness, Standard Deviation, Variance, Range, and Percentile(s)** (see Fig. 5.3).
- <u>Note</u>: to obtain, specifically, the 33rd and 67th percentiles: type **33** in the box, click on **Add**, type **67** and click on **Add**. (You could instead click on **Cut points for** and type 3).
- Click on **Continue**.

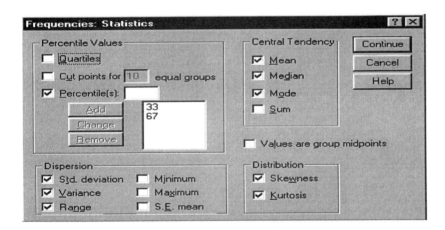

Fig. 5.3. Frequencies: Statistics.

Continue with these steps:

- Next, click on **Charts** (see Fig. 5.2).
- Select **Histogram[s]** and **With normal curve**. Does it look like the example in Fig. 5.4?
- Click on **Continue**.
- Finally, click on **OK** to get a syntax and output file. Does it look like Output 5.3?

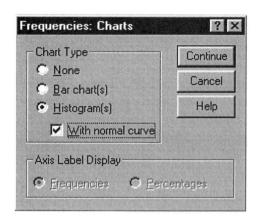

Fig. 5.4. Frequencies: Charts.

Problem 4: Box Plots and Descriptive Statistics

Now let's make a box plot comparing males and females on math achievement. Do the following commands:

- **Statistics => Summarize => Explore**. See Fig. 5.5.
-

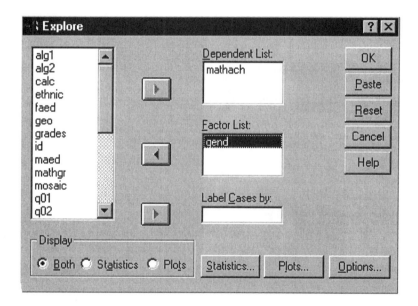

Fig. 5.5. Explore.

- Click on *mathach* and move it to the **Dependent List**.
- Next, click on *gend* and move it to the **Factor** (or independent variable) **List.**
- Finally, click on the **Plots** button (*not the plots under display*). Compare to Fig. 5.6.

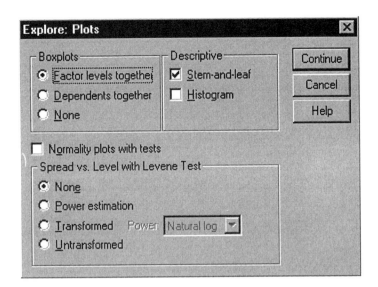

Fig. 5.6. Explore: Plots.

- Do not add or change this window. That is, leave the defaults alone!
- Click on **Continue** and you will be back to the original menu.
- Click on **OK**.

You will get an output file complete with syntax, statistics, and box plots. See Output 5.4 and compare it to your own output and syntax. As with most SPSS subprograms, we could have requested a wide variety of other statistics, but chose not to.

Print, Save, and Exit

- Print your output file if you so desire: **File => Print**. Don't forget to choose **All visible output** and click on **OK**.

Remember to save SPSS log files, which take less disk space than the whole output life. To do so highlight everything except the SPSS logs (see Lab Assignment A, Fig. 4.15) and delete the charts and tables but keep the SPSS logs. The commands are:
- **File => Save As.**
- Name your file **hsblogB**. Note: Refer to Appendix C on how to use syntax files and SPSS log files appropriately.

Now for the final steps:
- Save your data file as **hsbdataB (File => Save As)**.
- **File => Exit** are your last commands to exit the system.

Note: If you get any messages about saving your output, chart, or data, then it is not saved. You can choose to save it or not. We suggest you save the syntax files as a minimum.

Interpretation Questions

1. Using Output 5.2: a) Did any participants have missing data on the variables? b) What percent of students have a valid (nonmissing) math grade of mostly A-B? c) How many participants had low (less A-B) math grades? d) What percent and valid percent took algebra? Why are these the same?

2. Using Output 5.3, note that you have many statistics including skewness and kurtosis, frequency distributions, and histograms for each of the four variables: a) Is the skewness statistic more than 2.5 times its standard error for any of these four variables? b) Is the kurtosis statistic more than 2.5 times its standard error for any of these four variables? c) Why are the answers to (a) and (b) important? d) Do the distributions of visualization, mosaic, grades, and math achievement scores seem to be approximately normal from looking at the histograms? Does this agree with what you found from examining the skewness and kurtosis scores divided by their standard errors? e) What is the mean visualization score? f)What percentage of students have grades of mostly B or less? g) What percentage of students have mostly A grades?

3. Using Output 5.4: a) What can you say about the normality of the male and female math achievement scores by examining the skewness and kurtosis statistics in the descriptive tables? b) What are the average male and female math achievement scores? c) How many males have math achievement scores of 5? d) What did you learn from examining the box plot? Were the highest scores for males and females different? How about the lowest scores?

Outputs and Interpretations

Syntax for getting hsbdataA file

```
GET FILE
"A:\hsbdataA.sav".
EXECUTE.
```

Output 5.1: Frequencies

Syntax for gender and ethnic

```
FREQUENCIES
  VARIABLES=gend ethnic .
```

Interpretation of Output 5.1

The first table, titled statistics, provides only the number of participants for whom we have valid gender and ethnicity data and the number with missing data (0 for gender and 2 for ethnicity). We did not request any other statistics because almost all of them (e.g., median, range, standard deviation) are not appropriate to use with nominal data. (See Table 3.2). The other two tables are frequency distributions -- one for gender and one for ethnicity. The left-hand column shows the **valid** categories/levels/values, **missing** values, and **totals**. The frequency column gives the number of participants who had each value. The **percent** column is the percent who had each value, including missing values. For example, in the ethnicity table, 97.3% had a valid ethnic group and 2.7% were missing. The **valid percent** shows the percent of those with nonmissing data at each value; e.g., 56.2% of the 73 students with a listed ethnic group were Euro-Americans. Finally, **cumulative** percent is the percent of subjects in a category *plus* the categories listed above it. This last column is not very useful with nominal data, but can be quite informative in frequency distributions with many ordered categories. For example, in the distributions of mosaic scores in Output 5.3, 56% of the students had mosaic scores of 27 *or less*.

Statistics

The number of persons with usable data

	N	
	Valid	Missing
gender	75	0
ethnicity	73	2

gender

		Frequency	Percent	Valid Percent	Cumulative Percent
Valid	male	34	45.3	45.3	45.3
	female	41	54.7	54.7	100.0
	Total	75	100.0	100.0	
Total		75	100.0		

Male and female are valid values, categories or levels of the variable gender.

ethnicity

		Frequency	Percent	Valid Percent	Cumulative Percent
Valid	Euro-Amer	41	54.7	56.2	56.2
	African-Amer	15	20.0	20.5	76.7
	Hispanic-Amer	10	13.3	13.7	90.4
	Asian-Amer	7	9.3	9.6	100.0
	Total	73	97.3	100.0	
Missing	9	2	2.7		
	Total	2	2.7		
Total		75	100.0		

The percent of participants in this category plus the categories listed above it.

The number 9 is an arbitrary label that indicates missing data. Blank or no number is the typical missing value.

There were 10 Hispanics and 7 Asians in the study.

9.3% listed their ethnicity as Asian-American.

2.7% did not indicate ethnicity.

This shows the percent of those with nonmissing data at each value.

Output 5.2: Frequencies

Syntax for frequencies

```
FREQUENCIES
  VARIABLES=mathgr alg1 alg2 geo trig calc.
```

Statistics

	N	
	Valid	Missing
math grades	75	0
algebra 1 in h.s.	75	0
algebra 2 in h.s.	75	0
geometry in h.s.	75	0
trigonometry in h.s.	75	0
calculus in h.s.	75	0

math grades

		Frequency	Percent	Valid Percent	Cumulative Percent
Valid	less A-B	44	58.7	58.7	58.7
	most A-B	31	41.3	41.3	100.0
	Total	75	100.0	100.0	
Total		75	100.0		

algebra 1 in h.s.

		Frequency	Percent	Valid Percent	Cumulative Percent
Valid	not taken	16	21.3	21.3	21.3
	taken	59	78.7	78.7	100.0
	Total	75	100.0	100.0	
Total		75	100.0		

algebra 2 in h.s.

		Frequency	Percent	Valid Percent	Cumulative Percent
Valid	not taken	40	53.3	53.3	53.3
	taken	35	46.7	46.7	100.0
	Total	75	100.0	100.0	
Total		75	100.0		

geometry in h.s.

		Frequency	Percent	Valid Percent	Cumulative Percent
Valid	not taken	39	52.0	52.0	52.0
	taken	36	48.0	48.0	100.0
	Total	75	100.0	100.0	
Total		75	100.0		

trigonometry in h.s.

		Frequency	Percent	Valid Percent	Cumulative Percent
Valid	not taken	55	73.3	73.3	73.3
	taken	20	26.7	26.7	100.0
	Total	75	100.0	100.0	
Total		75	100.0		

calculus in h.s.

		Frequency	Percent	Valid Percent	Cumulative Percent
Valid	not taken	67	89.3	89.3	89.3
	taken	8	10.7	10.7	100.0
	Total	75	100.0	100.0	
Total		75	100.0		

Output 5.3: Frequencies, Statistics, and Histograms

Syntax for the frequency distribution, descriptive statistics, and histograms

```
FREQUENCIES
  VARIABLES=mosaic visual grades mathach
  /PERCENTILES= 33 67
  /STATISTICS=STDDEV VARIANCE RANGE MEAN MEDIAN MODE SKEWNESS SESKW KURTOSIS
  SEKURT
  /HISTOGRAM  NORMAL.
```

Interpretation of Output 5.3

The output file provides all the requested statistics for the four variables as a group. Then the four frequency distributions and four histograms with the normal curve superimposed over them are given individually so you can visualize whether the frequency distribution (histogram) looks normal. However, visual inspection can be deceiving because distributions need only be approximately normal. In the statistics tables, note columns for the skewness and kurtosis of the four variables. Divide each of the statistics by its standard error. If the result is not more than 5.5 (which is approximately the .01 level) that skewness or kurtosis is *not* significantly different from normal. Note that, using this measure, none of the four variables is markedly skewed, but the distribution of the *mosaic* scores is too peaked; i.e., it has a positive kurtosis almost six times its standard error. You can see this visually in the histogram.

Notice also the 33rd and 67th percentile columns in the statistic tables. You could use these percentiles if you wanted to divide your participants into three approximately equal size groups such as low, medium, and high. You can see from Output 5.3 that the 33rd and 67th percentiles for *mosaic* are 24.04 and 29.50. Thus, the low mosaic group would have scores from lowest to 24.04, the medium group from 24.04 to 29.50, and the high achievement group from 29.50 to highest. This could be done using the **Recode** command described in Assignment C.

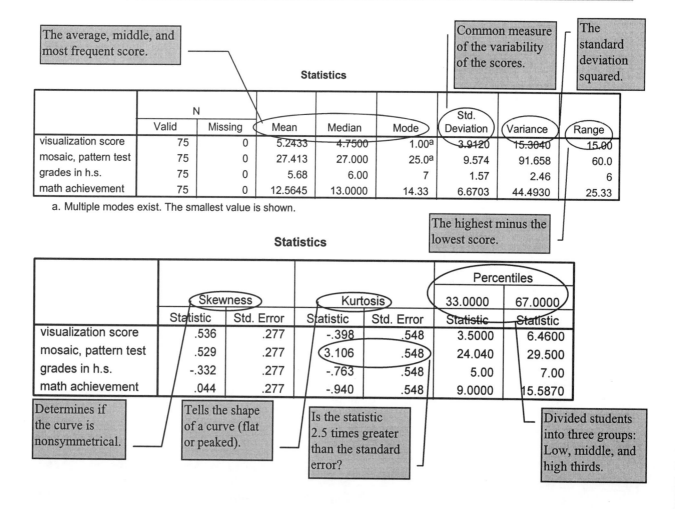

The average, middle, and most frequent score.

Common measure of the variability of the scores.

The standard deviation squared.

Statistics

	N		Mean	Median	Mode	Std. Deviation	Variance	Range
	Valid	Missing						
visualization score	75	0	5.2433	4.7500	1.00a	3.9120	15.3040	15.00
mosaic, pattern test	75	0	27.413	27.000	25.0a	9.574	91.658	60.0
grades in h.s.	75	0	5.68	6.00	7	1.57	2.46	6
math achievement	75	0	12.5645	13.0000	14.33	6.6703	44.4930	25.33

a. Multiple modes exist. The smallest value is shown.

The highest minus the lowest score.

Statistics

	Skewness		Kurtosis		Percentiles	
					33.0000	67.0000
	Statistic	Std. Error	Statistic	Std. Error	Statistic	Statistic
visualization score	.536	.277	-.398	.548	3.5000	6.4600
mosaic, pattern test	.529	.277	3.106	.548	24.040	29.500
grades in h.s.	-.332	.277	-.763	.548	5.00	7.00
math achievement	.044	.277	-.940	.548	9.0000	15.5870

Determines if the curve is nonsymmetrical.

Tells the shape of a curve (flat or peaked).

Is the statistic 2.5 times greater than the standard error?

Divided students into three groups: Low, middle, and high thirds.

mosaic, pattern test

		Frequency	Percent	Valid Percent	Cumulative Percent
Valid	-4.0	1	1.3	1.3	1.3
	-4.0	1	1.3	1.3	2.7
	11.0	1	1.3	1.3	4.0
	13.0	1	1.3	1.3	5.3
	13.5	1	1.3	1.3	6.7
	16.0	1	1.3	1.3	8.0
	17.5	1	1.3	1.3	9.3
	18.0	1	1.3	1.3	10.7
	20.0	1	1.3	1.3	12.0
	20.5	2	2.7	2.7	14.7
	22.0	4	5.3	5.3	20.0
	22.5	2	2.7	2.7	22.7
	23.0	4	5.3	5.3	28.0
	23.5	2	2.7	2.7	30.7
	24.0	2	2.7	2.7	33.3
	24.5	3	4.0	4.0	37.3
	25.0	5	6.7	6.7	44.0
	26.0	3	4.0	4.0	48.0
	26.5	1	1.3	1.3	49.3
	27.0	5	6.7	6.7	56.0
	27.5	1	1.3	1.3	57.3
	28.0	3	4.0	4.0	61.3
	28.5	1	1.3	1.3	62.7
	29.0	2	2.7	2.7	65.3
	29.5	2	2.7	2.7	68.0
	30.0	2	2.7	2.7	70.7
	30.5	2	2.7	2.7	73.3
	31.0	4	5.3	5.3	78.7
	32.0	1	1.3	1.3	80.0
	32.5	1	1.3	1.3	81.3
	33.0	3	4.0	4.0	85.3
	34.0	1	1.3	1.3	86.7
	35.0	1	1.3	1.3	88.0
	35.5	1	1.3	1.3	89.3
	36.0	1	1.3	1.3	90.7
	37.0	1	1.3	1.3	92.0
	41.0	1	1.3	1.3	93.3
	44.0	1	1.3	1.3	94.7
	51.5	1	1.3	1.3	96.0
	53.0	1	1.3	1.3	97.3
	56.0	2	2.7	2.7	100.0
	Total	75	100.0	100.0	
Total		75	100.0		

Do you know what this means?

Histogram

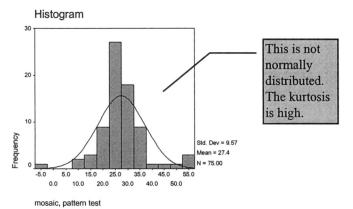

Std. Dev = 9.57
Mean = 27.4
N = 75.00

mosaic, pattern test

This is not normally distributed. The kurtosis is high.

visualization score

		Frequency	Percent	Valid Percent	Cumulative Percent
Valid	-.25	7	9.3	9.3	9.3
	1.00	10	13.3	13.3	22.7
	2.25	5	6.7	6.7	29.3
	2.50	1	1.3	1.3	30.7
	3.50	7	9.3	9.3	40.0
	3.75	2	2.7	2.7	42.7
	4.75	10	13.3	13.3	56.0
	5.00	2	2.7	2.7	58.7
	6.00	6	8.0	8.0	66.7
	6.50	1	1.3	1.3	68.0
	7.25	5	6.7	6.7	74.7
	8.50	2	2.7	2.7	77.3
	8.75	2	2.7	2.7	80.0
	9.50	1	1.3	1.3	81.3
	9.75	6	8.0	8.0	89.3
	11.00	4	5.3	5.3	94.7
	13.50	2	2.7	2.7	97.3
	14.75	2	2.7	2.7	100.0
	Total	75	100.0	100.0	
Total		75	100.0		

Histogram

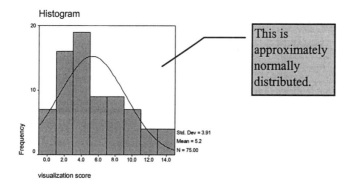

This is approximately normally distributed.

Std. Dev = 3.91
Mean = 5.2
N = 75.00

visualization score

grades in h.s.

		Frequency	Percent	Valid Percent	Cumulative Percent
Valid	mostly D	1	1.3	1.3	1.3
	half CD	8	10.7	10.7	12.0
	mostly C	8	10.7	10.7	22.7
	half BC	16	21.3	21.3	44.0
	mostly B	15	20.0	20.0	64.0
	half AB	18	24.0	24.0	88.0
	mostly A	9	12.0	12.0	100.0
	Total	75	100.0	100.0	
Total		75	100.0		

Histogram

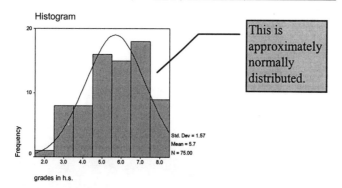

This is approximately normally distributed.

Std. Dev = 1.57
Mean = 5.7
N = 75.00

grades in h.s.

math achievement

		Frequency	Percent	Valid Percent	Cumulative Percent
Valid	-1.67	1	1.3	1.3	1.3
	1.00	2	2.7	2.7	4.0
	2.33	1	1.3	1.3	5.3
	3.67	3	4.0	4.0	9.3
	4.00	2	2.7	2.7	12.0
	5.00	5	6.7	6.7	18.7
	5.33	1	1.3	1.3	20.0
	6.33	2	2.7	2.7	22.7
	6.67	1	1.3	1.3	24.0
	7.67	4	5.3	5.3	29.3
	8.00	1	1.3	1.3	30.7
	9.00	4	5.3	5.3	36.0
	9.33	1	1.3	1.3	37.3
	10.33	4	5.3	5.3	42.7
	10.67	1	1.3	1.3	44.0
	11.67	2	2.7	2.7	46.7
	12.00	2	2.7	2.7	49.3
	13.00	3	4.0	4.0	53.3
	14.33	9	12.0	12.0	65.3
	14.67	1	1.3	1.3	66.7
	15.67	2	2.7	2.7	69.3
	17.00	5	6.7	6.7	76.0
	18.33	1	1.3	1.3	77.3
	18.67	1	1.3	1.3	78.7
	19.67	3	4.0	4.0	82.7
	20.33	1	1.3	1.3	84.0
	21.00	3	4.0	4.0	88.0
	22.33	2	2.7	2.7	90.7
	22.67	1	1.3	1.3	92.0
	23.67	6	8.0	8.0	100.0
	Total	75	100.0	100.0	
Total		75	100.0		

Histogram

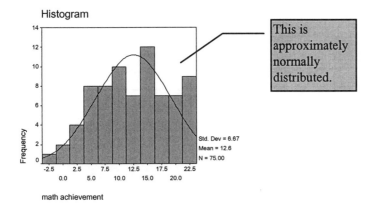

This is approximately normally distributed.

Std. Dev = 6.67
Mean = 12.6
N = 75.00

math achievement

Output 5.4: Explore and Box Plots

Syntax for explore and box plots

```
EXAMINE
  VARIABLES=mathach BY gend
  /PLOT BOXPLOT STEMLEAF
  /COMPARE GROUP
  /STATISTICS DESCRIPTIVES
  /CINTERVAL 95
  /MISSING LISTWISE
  /NOTOTAL.
```

Interpretation of Output 5.4

The first two tables provide descriptive statistics like those in Output 5.3, but for males and females separately. The next table includes **stem-and-leaf** plots for each gender. They are sort of like histograms turned on the side. For middle-sized groups like the 34 males and 41 females, they give a visual impression of the distribution, and they show each person's score on the dependent variable. Each number under the "leaf" heading represents one person's score on math achievement, so it might have been better to have commas between numbers. Each "stem" tells you what number to put in front of the leaf to know what the math achievement score was. Thus, for the males, the 3 to the right of the zero stem means a score of 03 or 3, and the three 1s beside the stem of 2 are three males with scores of 21.

Box plots are a graphical representation of the distribution of scores on a variable, with the whole group divided on the basis of another variable, in this case gender. Each "box" represents the middle 50% of the cases and the "whiskers" at the top and bottom of the box indicate the "expected" top and bottom 25%. However, there may be outliers (shown with "O"s) and really extreme scores (shown with asterisks), above or below the end of the whiskers. Notice that there are not any Os or *s in the box plot in Output 5.4. Thus, box plots can be useful for identifying variables with extreme scores, which can make the distribution skewed (i.e., nonnormal). Check the raw data or score sheet to be sure there is not a coding error.

gender

Case Processing Summary

| | | Cases | | | | | |
| | | Valid | | Missing | | Total | |
	gender	N	Percent	N	Percent	N	Percent
math achievement	male	34	100.0%	0	.0%	34	100.0%
	female	41	100.0%	0	.0%	41	100.0%

Descriptives

	gender			Statistic	Std. Error
math achievement	male	Mean		14.7550	1.0344
		95% Confidence Interval for Mean	Lower Bound	12.6505	
			Upper Bound	16.8595	
		5% Trimmed Mean		14.8454	
		Median		14.3330	
		Variance		36.379	
		Std. Deviation		6.0315	
		Minimum		3.67	
		Maximum		23.67	
		Range		20.00	
		Interquartile Range		10.0005	
		Skewness		-.156	.403
		Kurtosis		-.963	.788
	female	Mean		10.7479	1.0458
		95% Confidence Interval for Mean	Lower Bound	8.6344	
			Upper Bound	12.8615	
		5% Trimmed Mean		10.6454	
		Median		10.3330	
		Variance		44.838	
		Std. Deviation		6.6961	
		Minimum		-1.67	
		Maximum		23.67	
		Range		25.33	
		Interquartile Range		10.5000	
		Skewness		.331	.369
		Kurtosis		-.698	.724

Stem-and-Leaf Plots

```
math achievement Stem-and-Leaf Plot for
GEND= male

  Frequency    Stem &  Leaf

      1.00       0 .  3
      7.00       0 .  5557799
     11.00       1 .  01123444444
      7.00       1 .  5578899
      8.00       2 .  11123333

 Stem width:    10.00
 Each leaf:       1 case(s)

math achievement Stem-and-Leaf Plot for
GEND= female

  Frequency    Stem &  Leaf

      1.00      -0 .  1
      7.00       0 .  1123344
     12.00       0 .  555666778999
     11.00       1 .  00002334444
      5.00       1 .  77779
      5.00       2 .  02233

 Stem width:    10.00
 Each leaf:       1 case(s)
```

Box plot of math achievement for males and females

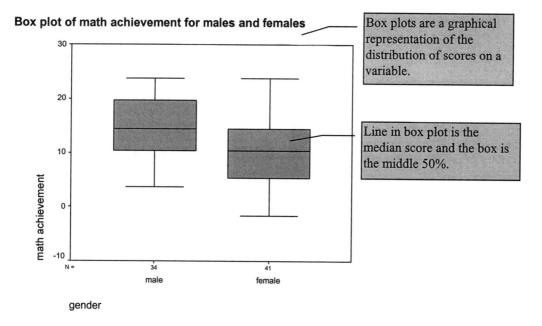

Box plots are a graphical representation of the distribution of scores on a variable.

Line in box plot is the median score and the box is the middle 50%.

CHAPTER 6

Data Transformations: Count, Recode, Compute

In this assignment, you will do several data transformations to get your data in the form needed to answer the research questions. This aspect of data analysis is sometimes called file management and can be quite time consuming. That is especially true if you have a lot of questions/items that need to be reversed (because they were negatively worded) and/or combined to compute the summated or composite variables that you want to use in later analyses.

This is a somewhat mundane and tedious aspect of research, but it is important to do it carefully so you do not introduce errors into your data. The SPSS tutorial has some information on **data transformations** so we suggest you review it.

The three items used for the math attitude scale called *pleasure* were chosen *conceptually*, because they all seemed to be measuring that aspect of attitudes regarding mathematics. In Assignment F, we will use the **factor analysis** program to group the 13 math attitude items empirically (i.e., based on a computer analysis of the subjects' ratings of the 13 items). SPSS will help us decide which items to combine to form scale scores. Then we will have to make a judgment about whether to use our conceptual analysis or the computer's empirical (factor) analysis (see the introduction to Assignments F and G for more discussion of *summated scales* and *internal consistency reliability*).

In Problem 5, you will check, like you did in chapter 5, Assignment B, whether the new composite variables are normally distributed. You should review chapter 3 on descriptive statistics including skewness and kurtosis to help you understand the material.

Problems/Research Questions

1. How many math courses (*mathcrs*) did each of the 75 participants take in high school? The courses are *alg1, alg2, calc, geo,* and *trig*. **Label** your new variable.

2. **Recode** *maed* and *faed* (mother's and father's education) so that those with no postsecondary education have a value of 1, those with some postsecondary have a value of 2, and those with a bachelor's degree or more have a value of 3. **Label** the new variables and values.

3. **Compute** the average pleasure scale score from *q02, q06,* and *q10* **after** reversing (**Recoding**) *q06* and *q10*. **Label** the new computed variable as pleasure and its highest and lowest values.

4. **Compute** the *competence* and *motivation* scale scores. **Label** the new variables and values.

5. Are the data for the computed variables (*mathcrs, pleasure, motivatn,* and *competnc*) distributed normally?

Lab Assignment C

Logon and Get Data

Get/retrieve **hsbdataB** from your disk. (See the **Get Data** step in Lab Assignment A for reference).

Problem 1: Transform (with count), Label, and Check Variables

If the hsbdataB file is not showing, click on the hsbdataB bar at the bottom of your screen until you see your data showing. Now, let's count the number of math courses (*mathcrs*) that each of the 75 participants took in high school.
- First, click on **Transform => Count**. You will see a menu like Fig. 6.1 below.
- Now, type *mathcrs* in the **Target (or new) Variable** box.
- Next, type **math courses taken** in the **Target Label** box.
- Then, highlight *alg1, alg2, calc, geo,* and *trig* and click on the **arrow** button to move them over to the **Numeric Variables** box.

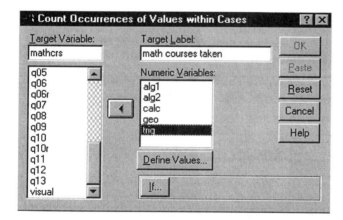

Fig. 6.1. Count.

- Click on **Define Values.** You will get a picture looking like Fig. 6.2.
- Type **1** in the **Value** box and click on **Add**. This sets up the computer to count how many 1's (or courses taken) each participant had.
- Now click on **Continue** to return to the dialog box in Fig. 6.1.
- Finally, click on **OK**.

If you want to delete the decimal places for your new data, highlight the variable *mathcrs* on far right:
- Then click on **Data => Define Variable**.
- Click on **Type**.
- Enter 0 in the **Decimal Places** box.

The first 10 numbers of your **Data**, under *mathcrs* file, should look like Fig. 6.3.

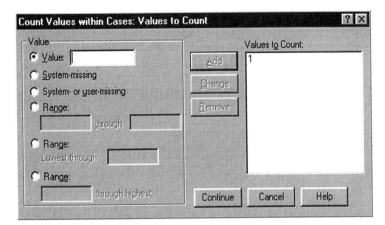

Fig. 6.2.
Count values.

Fig. 6.3.
Data column.

Checking Your Counts

Check your syntax. Is it exactly like the one in Output 6.1? If you did not have this book, you could check your count statement by examining your data file. Look at the first participant (ID = 1) and notice participant one has zeroes in the *alg1, alg2, geo, trig,* and *calc* columns. The same is true for participants 2 and 3. Thus, they have taken no (0) math courses. They should and do have zeros in the *mathcrs* column. Also, it would be good to check a few participants who took several math courses just to be sure the count worked correctly.

Notice that there are no tables or figures for this output, just syntax.

Problem 2: Recode, Relabel, and Check

We will **Recode** *maed* and *faed* so that those with no postsecondary education (2s and 3s) have a value of **1**, those with some postsecondary will have **2** and those with a bachelor's degree or more will have a value of **3**.

Explanation

It is usually *not* desirable to dichotomize or trichotomize a good, approximately interval scale variable. However, these variables have a flaw in the categories/values (and we needed another independent variable with a few levels or categories to demonstrate certain analyses later). The flaw can be seen in the codebook. A value of 5 is given for students who had a parent with 2 years of vocational college (presumable an A.S. degree), but a 6 is given to a parent with less than 2 years of (a 4-year) college. Thus, a parent who went 1 week (or 1 credit) to a 4-year college would be rated as having more education than a parent with an associate's degree. This makes the variable not fully ordered so we have recoded it. Recodes also are used to combine two or more small groups/categories of a variable so that group size will be large enough to perform statistical analyses. For example, one might have only a few "widowed" or "single" parents that might be combined with "divorced" parents and called "not married" to compare to a larger group of "married" parents.

Follow these steps:
- Click on **Transform => Recode => Into Different Variables** and you should get Fig. 6.4.
- Now click on *maed* then the **arrow** button.
- Click on *faed* and the **arrow** to move them to the **Numeric Variables => Output** box.
- Now highlight *faed* in the **Numeric Variable** box so that it turns blue.
- Click on the **Output Variable Name** box and type *faedr*.
- Click on the **Label** box and type **Father's educ rev**.
- Click on **Change**. Did you get *faed =>faedr* in the **Numeric Variable** box as in Fig. 6.4?

Now repeat these procedures with *maed*.
- Highlight *maed*.
- Click on **Output Variable Name**, type *maedr*.
- Click **Label**, type **Mother's educ rev**, and click **Change**.
- Then click on **Old and New Values** to get Fig. 6.5.

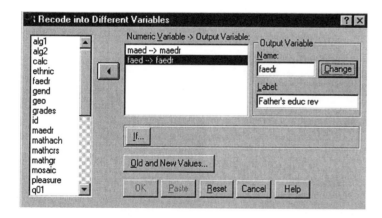

Fig. 6.4. Recode into different variables.

- Click on **Range** and type **2** in the first box and **3** in the second box.
- Click on **Value** (part of New Value on the right) and type **1**.
- Then click on **Add**.
- Repeat these steps to change old values **4** through **7** to a new **Value** of **2.** Then **Range: 8** through **10** to **Value: 3**. Does it look like Fig. 6.6?
- If it does, click on **Continue**.
- Finally, click on **OK**.

Check your **Data** file to see if *faedr* and *maedr* with numbers ranging from 1 to 3 have been added on the far right side. To be extra careful, check the data file for a few participants to be sure the recodes were done correctly. For example, the first participant had 10 for *faed* which should be 3 for *faedr*. Is it? Check a few more to be sure; or compare your syntax file with the one in Output 6.2.

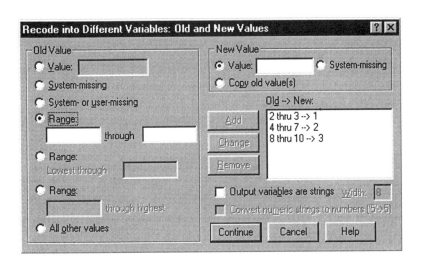

Fig. 6.5. Recode.

- Now, we will **label** the new (1, 2, 3) values.
- Go to your Data file and click on *faedr* (the whole column should highlight).
- Now click on **Data => Define Variables => Labels**. You should get something like Fig. 6.6.
- Now, type **Father's educ rev** in the **Variable Label** box.
- Click on the **Value** box and type **1**.
- Click on the **Value Label** box and type **HS grad or less**.
- Click on **Add**.
- Then click on the **Value** box again and type **2**.
- Click on the **Value Label** box and type **Some College**.
- Click on **Add**.
- Click once more on the **Value** box and type **3**.
- Click on the **Value Label** box and type **BS or More**.
- Now click on **Add**. Does it look like Fig. 6.6?
- Click on **Continue** then **OK**.

Important: You have only done *faedr (*father's education revised). You need to repeat these steps for *maedr*. Do **Value Labels** for *maedr* on your own.

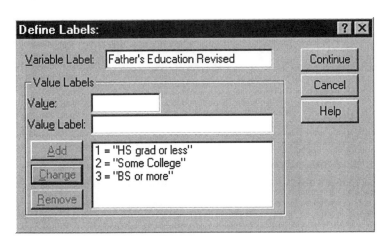

Fig. 6.6. Define labels.

Problem 3: Recode and Compute Pleasure Scale Score

Now let's **Compute** the average pleasure with math scale score (*pleasure*) from *q02, q06,* and *q10* **after** reversing (**Recoding**) *q06* and *q10* which are negatively worded items (see the codebook). We will keep both the new *q06r* and *q10r* and old (*q06* and *q10*) variables to check the recodes and to play it safe. Then, we will **Label** the new computed **variable** (*pleasure*) and **values**.

- Click on **Transform => Recode => Into Different Variables**.
- Click on **Reset** to clear the window of old information as a precaution.
- Click on *q06*.
- Click on the **arrow** button.
- Click on **Output Variable Name** and type *q06r*.
- Click on **Label** and type **q06 reversed**.
- Finally click on **Change**.
- Now repeat these steps for *q10*. Does it look like Fig. 6.7?

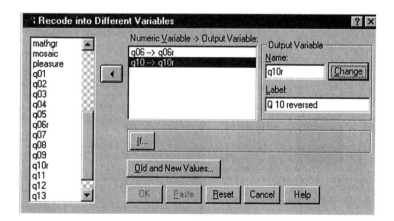

Fig. 6.7. Recode.

- Click on **Old and New Values** to get Fig. 6.8.
- Now click on the **Value** box (under **Old Value**) and type **4**.
- Click on the **Value** box for the **New Value** and type **1**.
- Click on **Add**.

This is the first step in recoding. You have told the computer to change values of 4 to 1. Now do these steps over to recode the values **3** to **2, 2** to **3,** and **1** to **4**. If you did it right, the screen will look like Fig. 6.8 in the **Old => New** box. *Check your box carefully to be sure the recodes are exactly like Fig. 6.8.*

- Click on **Continue** and then **OK**.

Now check your **Data** file to see if there is a *q06r* and a *q10r* in the last two columns with numbers ranging from 1 to 4. To double check the recodes, compare the *q06* and *q10* columns on your data file with the *q06r* and *q10r* columns for a few subjects. Also, you should check your syntax file with the one in **Output 6.3**.

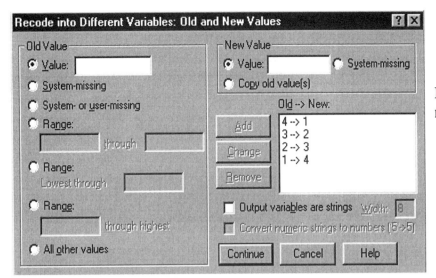

Fig. 6.8. Recode: Old and new values.

Now let's try computing **pleasure** (*q02, q06r,* and *q10r*).
- Click on **Transform => Compute**.
- In the **Target Variable** box of Fig. 6. 9, type *pleasure*.

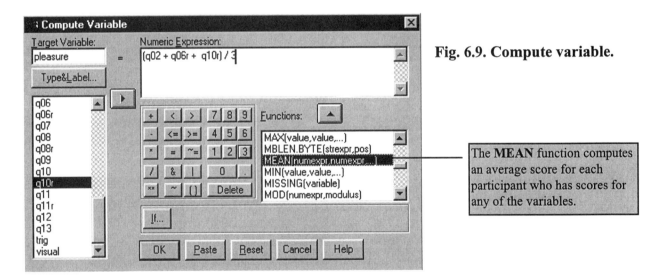

Fig. 6.9. Compute variable.

The **MEAN** function computes an average score for each participant who has scores for any of the variables.

- Click on **Type & Label** and give it the name **Pleasure scale** (see Fig. 6.10).
- Click on **Continue** to return to Fig. 6.9.
- In the **Numeric Expression** box type **(*q02+q06r+q10r*)/3**.

An Alternative Method to Compute a Mean of a Summated Scale
The method we used to compute summated or composite scales will not compute an average score for a participant if he or she is missing data for any of the questions. (The computed score will be missing). This can result in a sizable decrease in subjects who have composite scores if a number of participants did not answer even one or a few questions. In this circumstance one might choose to use the MEAN function, shown in the callout box beside Fig. 6.9, because it utilizes all of the available data.

In the method we used, the computer added questions 2, 6r, and 10r and divided the sum by three, giving the result a new name, *"pleasure."* Be sure your formula is *exactly* like the one shown. For example, *you must have the parentheses, and you must have zero (not the letter O) in front of 2 and 6r.* It is slower, but safer to click on ( ), then move *q02* to the right, then click on +, etc., because you are less likely to make a mistake than if you type the formula in the **Numeric Expression** box.

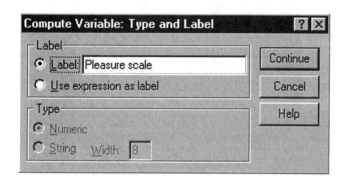

Fig. 6.10. Compute variable: Type and label.

- Finally, click on **OK**.

Check your data file to see if pleasure has been added. You should also *calculate the pleasure score by hand for a few participants to be sure it was done correctly.* The computer will not make calculation mistakes but sometimes you may not tell it exactly what you intended. Check your syntax with the one in Output 6.3.
- Now label the *pleasure* variable as "Pleasure Scale," and provide value labels: 1 = very low, 4 = very high. See Fig. 6.6 if you need help.

Problem 4: Computing Competence and Motivation Summated Scale Scores

Start by reversing (using **recode**) questions 4, 5, 8, and 11 as you did for *question 6 and 10* above. Refer to the steps above if you need help. You should then move on to **compute** the *competence scale* and the *motivation scale*, using commands similar to those that you used before to compute the summated scale for pleasure. You will need these new math attitude scale scores in Assignment D. Note that the **Target Variable** names, competence and motivation, have to be shortened because SPSS variable names cannot be longer than eight characters. The **labels**, competence scale and motivation scale, can be longer. The formulas are:

Competnc = (q03+q05r+q09+q11r)/4
Motivatn = (q01+q04r+q07+q08r+q12+q13)/6
Hints:
- Be sure to reverse *q04, q05, q08,* and *q11* by recoding (1 = 4, 2 = 3, etc.) **before** computing the motivation and competence math attitude scale scores.
- Don't forget to **label** your new variables as "competence scale" and "motivation scale." Also add value labels as you did for the pleasure scale.
- Examine your data file to be sure that the competence and motivation scales were computed correctly.

- Note that your syntax should say **EXECUTE** at the end or you forgot to check **OK**.
- Check your syntax with the one in Output 6.5.

Problem 5: Doing Frequencies and Checking Normality for the Computed Variables

Using Fig. 5.1 to 5.4 in chapter 5 as a guide, run the same descriptive statistics (skipping percentiles in Fig. 5.3), and do histograms with a normal curve superimposed (Fig. 5.4) for the computed variables: *mathcrs, pleasure, motivatn,* and *competnc.* However, to save space, after selecting the appropriate statistics, uncheck the **Display Frequency Tables** box in Fig. 5.2. Note: If you uncheck the **Display Frequency Tables** first, you may get an error message. Did you get a syntax and output like 6.5?

Print, Save, and Exit

- Print any outputs if you like (**File => Print**).
- Save your data file as **hsbdataC (File => Save As)**.
- Save the SPSS Log/Syntax as **hsblogC**.
- **Exit** SPSS. To Exit: **File => Exit.**

Interpretation Questions

1. Using your initial HSB data file (or the file in chapter 2), compare the original data to your new variables: a) How many math courses did participant (ID) number 11 take? b) Why did you recode father's and mother's education? What should *faedr* be for participants 2, 5, and 8? c) What should be the pleasure scale score for participant 1? d) Why is comparing a few initial scores to transformed scores important?

2. Why did you reverse questions 6 and 10?

3. In Output 6.5, do the motivation scale scores differ markedly from the normal distribution? How do you know? What about the competence scale scores?

Outputs and Interpretations

Output 6.1: Counting Math Courses Taken

Syntax for counting math courses with values of 1

```
COUNT
  mathcrs = alg1 alg2 calc geo trig  (1)  .
VARIABLE LABELS mathcrs 'Math courses taken' .
EXECUTE .
```

Output 6.2: Recoding Mother's and Father's Education

<u>Syntax for recoding father's and mother's education</u>

```
RECODE
  faed maed
  (2 thru 3=1)  (4 thru 7=2)  (8 thru 10=3)  INTO  faedr  maedr .
VARIABLE LABELS faedr "Father's educ rev" /maedr "Mother's educ rev".
EXECUTE .
VALUE LABELS faedr
 1.00000000000000 "HS grad or less"
 2.00000000000000 "Some College"
 3.0 "BS or More"
 .
VALUE LABELS maedr
 1.00000000000000 "HS grad or less"
 2.00000000000000 "Some College"
 3.0 "BS or More"
 .
```

Output 6.3: Compute Pleasure Scale

<u>Syntax for reversing questions 6 and 10</u>

```
RECODE
  q06 q10
  (4=1)  (3=2)  (2=3)  (1=4)  INTO  q06r  q10r .
VARIABLE LABELS q06r 'q06 reversed' /q10r 'q10 reversed'.
EXECUTE .
```

<u>Syntax for computing Pleasure scale</u>

```
COMPUTE Pleasure = (Q02+Q06R+Q10R)/3 .
EXECUTE .
VARIABLE LABELS pleasure "Pleasure scale".
VALUE LABELS pleasure
 1.00000000000000 "Lowest"
 4.00000000000000 "Highest"
 .
```

Output 6.4: Recoding the Reversed Math Attitude Questions

<u>Syntax for recoding four reversed math attitude variables</u>

```
RECODE
  q04 q05 q08 q11
  (1=4)  (2=3)  (3=2)  (4=1)  INTO  q04r  q05r  q08r  q11r .
VARIABLE LABELS q04r 'Q6 reversed' /q05r 'Q05 reversed' /q08r 'Q 8 reversed'
 /q11r 'Q 11 reversed'.
EXECUTE .
FORMATS q04r (F8).
FORMATS q05r (F8).
FORMATS q08r (F8).
FORMATS q11r (F8).
```

<u>Syntax for computing competence scale score</u>

```
COMPUTE competnc = (q03+q05r+q09+q11r)/4 .
VARIABLE LABELS competnc 'Competence scale' .
EXECUTE .
VALUE LABELS pleasure
 1.00000000000000 "Lowest"
 4.00000000000000 "Highest"
```

Syntax for computing motivation scale score

```
COMPUTE motivatn = (q01+q04r+q07+q08r+q12+q13)/6 .
VARIABLE LABELS motivatn 'Motivation scale' .
EXECUTE .
VALUE LABELS pleasure
 1.00000000000000 "Lowest"
 4.00000000000000 "Highest"
```

Output 6.5: Statistics and Histograms

Syntax for statistics and histograms for four computed variables

```
FREQUENCIES
  VARIABLES=mathcrs pleasure motivatn competnc   /FORMAT=NOTABLE
  /STATISTICS=STDDEV VARIANCE RANGE MEAN MEDIAN MODE SKEWNESS SESKW KURTOSIS
  SEKURT
  /HISTOGRAM  NORMAL .
```

Interpretation of Output 6.5

The first table in Output 6.5 provides a similar wide variety of descriptive statistics as in Assignment B. Note that the skewness and kurtosis and their standard errors are provided for each of the computed variables (*mathcrs, pleasure, motivatn,* and *comptenc*). With this information you can decide whether these variables are distributed normally as you did in Assignment B. The skewness and kurtosis should not be more than 2.5 times the standard error. The competence scale seriously violates the assumption of normality, and the skewness of the pleasure scale is a little more than 2.5 times its standard error. Thus, it would be prudent to select a nonparametric statistic when competence and, perhaps, pleasure are used as dependent variables in an analysis. However, most parametric statistics are very robust if there are violations of normality so nonparametric statistics are not essential here.

The remaining parts of this output are histograms with the normal curve superimposed for each of the four computed variables. Note that although none of the distributions look exactly normal, the competence histogram is the most deviant.

Statistics

| | N | | | | | Std. | |
	Valid	Missing	Mean	Median	Mode	Deviation	Variance
Math course taken	75	0	2.11	2.00	0[a]	1.67	2.80
Pleasure scale	75	0	3.2267	3.3333	3.33	.6300	.3969
Motivation scale	73	2	2.8744	2.8333	2.83	.6382	.4072
Competence scale	73	2	3.2945	3.5000	3.75	.6645	.4416

a. Multiple modes exist. The smallest value is shown.

Statistics

	Skewness		Kurtosis		Range
	Statistic	Std. Error	Statistic	Std. Error	Statistic
Math course taken	.325	.277	-1.145	.548	5
Pleasure scale	-.732	.277	-.216	.548	2.33
Motivation scale	-.570	.281	-.034	.555	2.83
Competence scale	-1.634	.281	3.037	.555	3.00

To be normally distributed, the skewness and kurtosis should not be more than 2.5 times the standard error.

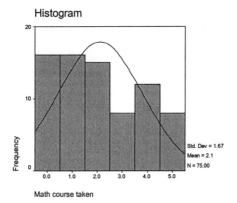

Histogram — Math course taken
Std. Dev = 1.67
Mean = 2.1
N = 75.00

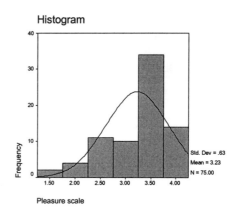

Histogram — Pleasure scale
Std. Dev = .63
Mean = 3.23
N = 75.00

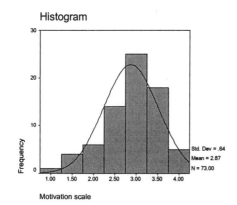

Histogram — Motivation scale
Std. Dev = .64
Mean = 2.87
N = 73.00

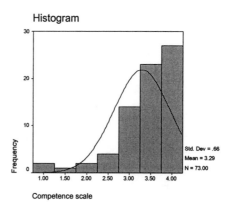

Histogram — Competence scale
Std. Dev = .66
Mean = 3.29
N = 73.00

CHAPTER 7

Selecting and Interpreting Inferential Statistics

General Design Classifications for Difference Questions

Within the randomized experimental, quasi-experimental, and also comparative approaches, all designs must fit into one of three categories that we call the general design classification. Understanding this classification is essential in order to determine the proper statistical analysis for difference questions.

Between Groups Designs

Between groups designs are defined as designs where each participant in the research is in *one and only one* condition or group. For example, in a study investigating the effects of teaching style on student satisfaction, there may be three groups (or conditions or levels) of the independent variable, teaching style. These conditions could be authoritarian, participatory, and a combination of the two. In a between groups design, each participant receives only one of the three conditions or levels. If the investigator wished to have 20 participants in each group, then 60 participants would be needed to carry out the research.

Within Subjects or Repeated Measures Designs

Within subjects designs are conceptually the opposite of between groups designs. In these designs, each participant in the research *receives or experiences all of the conditions* or levels of the independent variable in order to complete the study. Using the above example of the investigation of the effects of the independent variable, teaching style, on the dependent variable, student satisfaction, there still would be three conditions or levels to the independent variable, teaching style. These conditions are authoritarian teaching style, participatory teaching style, and a combination of the two. In a within subjects design, each participant would experience and be measured for student satisfaction on all three conditions or levels of the independent variable. If the researcher wished to have 20 participants for each condition, only 20 participants would be needed to carry out the research, since each participant undergoes all three conditions of the independent variable in the research. Since each participant is assessed more than once; i.e., for each condition, these designs are also referred to as *repeated measures* designs. Within subjects designs have appeal due to the smaller number of participants needed and reduction in error variance. However, they may be less appropriate than between groups designs in applied settings because of the possibility of *carryover* or *practice effects*. If the purpose of the study is to investigate conditions that may result in a long-term or permanent change, such as learning, it is not possible for a participant to be in one condition, and then "unlearn" that condition to be in the same previous state to start the next condition. Within subjects designs may be appropriate, if the effects of order of presentation are negligible, when participants are asked, for example, to evaluate several topics. Order effects can be controlled by presenting the conditions to participants in different orders (e.g., in random orders or counterbalanced so that, for example, half receive Condition A first and half receive Condition B first). Within subjects designs also are used when there is a pretest and a posttest.

Mixed Designs

Mixed designs have at least *one between groups independent variable* and at least *one within subjects independent variable*; thus, they have a minimum of two independent variables. A between groups independent variable is any independent variable that sets up between groups conditions. A within subjects independent variable is any independent variable that sets up within subjects conditions. Let's return to our example of investigating the effect of the independent variable, teaching style, on the dependent variable, student satisfaction. If teaching style is a within subjects independent variable, as in the second example above, we would additionally need a second independent variable that is a between groups independent variable in order to complete the criteria for a mixed design. The second independent variable for this example could be the gender of the instructor. Gender is a between groups independent variable, with two levels, female and male. Therefore, this example satisfies the criteria for a mixed design: two independent variables, with one a within subjects variable (teaching style) and the other independent variable a between groups variable (gender).

Classification of Designs for Difference Questions

The information in this section is important for knowing how to enter data into a computer database or spreadsheet so that the appropriate statistical analysis can be done. Also it is crucial for knowing which difference inferential statistic to choose for the analysis.

Other Design Considerations

Change or trials as an independent variable. Consider the following example. Participants are randomly assigned to one of two groups, an intervention group which receives a new curriculum and a control group which receives the old curriculum. Participants are measured prior to the intervention and after the intervention (perhaps at the end of the semester). This is a pretest-posttest control group design. It is a mixed design because there are two independent variables, one a between groups independent variable, and the other a within subjects independent variable. The independent variable, type of curriculum, is a between groups independent variable because each participant experiences only one of the two curriculums. The other independent variable in this study, "change," is a within subjects independent variable because participants within each group were measured more than once in the study. This independent variable is referred to as change because what we are interested in is the difference or change between the first measurement period and the second. Change is considered a third type of variable, rather than an active independent variable, because you could not actively manipulate it.

Data Format

The data format for between groups, within subjects, and mixed designs can be illustrated to help visualize what is happening in the research. This method *depicts how the data are entered into the computer* for statistical analyses. Data for each participant are placed in a single horizontal row.

Between group designs. Suppose that we have a between groups design with two independent variables, teaching style and gender. Each independent variable has two levels (teaching style, authoritarian or participatory; and gender, male or female). The data would be entered as follows, assuming 12 participants were assigned (3 each) to the four groups. Of course, most studies would have many more participants.

Participant Number	Teaching Style	Gender	Math Achievement	Key
				Value, Teaching Style
1	1	1	DV	1 Authoritarian
2	1	1	DV	2 Participatory
3	1	1	DV	Gender
4	1	2	DV	1 Male
5	1	2	DV	2 Female
6	1	2	DV	
7	2	1	DV	Math Achievement
8	2	1	DV	DV = a score, or value on
9	2	1	DV	the dependent variable,
10	2	2	DV	math achievement
11	2	2	DV	
12	2	2	DV	

In this example, each participant in each group is observed/measured once on the dependent variable, a measure of math achievement. Four columns are seen in this example. The first column is a participant identification number. The next two columns represent the two independent variables. The last column is for the dependent variable. The order of the columns is not important when using SPSS.

Within subjects/repeated measures designs. In contrast to between groups designs, no columns are used to identify the *independent variables* in within subjects designs. Rather the dependent variable (math achievement) is measured several times and each measurement is placed in a separate column. Suppose that we have a study which uses a within subjects design, with two independent variables, both within subjects independent variables. The first independent variable is time, with two levels, pretest and posttest. The second independent variable is our teaching style independent variable, with two levels, authoritarian and participatory. However, since both independent variables are within subject independent variables, each participant must undergo all conditions of the experiment.

Note that the dependent variable (math achievement) scores are what go in each column. The data are entered as follows:

Participant Number	Pretest Participatory	Pretest Authoritarian	Posttest Participatory	Posttest Authoritarian
	(Condition 1)	(Condition 2)	(Condition 3)	(Condition 4)
1	DV	DV	DV	DV
2	DV	DV	DV	DV
3	DV	DV	DV	DV

The 12 participants in the between groups design could be reduced to 3 with this design. However, each participant must undergo all four conditions. Note that the posttest variables must have different SPSS variable names than the corresponding pretest variables.

Mixed design. This type of design is illustrated by combining both the between groups design and the within subjects design. A common example of a mixed design would be a research study to evaluate the effects of a new curriculum. The between groups independent variable would be the curriculum, with two levels, new curriculum and old curriculum. The within subjects independent variable would be time, with two levels, before the evaluation and after the evaluation. Because the diagram is relatively simple, we have included the variable name as well as the levels.

Participant Number	Type of Curriculum	Pretest	Posttest
1	1	DV	DV
2	1	DV	DV
3	1	DV	DV
4	2	DV	DV
5	2	DV	DV
6	2	DV	DV

Notice that each participant is in only one group, but all participants in each group are measured before the intervention and after the intervention. This design requires twice as many participants as the within subjects design.

Classifying the Design

It is helpful to have a brief descriptive label for a research design that identifies the design for other researchers. The labels we use, called **design classifications**, also guide us toward the proper statistics to use. We do not have classifications for the descriptive or associational approaches so this section applies to difference questions and the randomized experimental, quasi-experimental, and comparative approaches. Designs are usually classified in terms of the *overall type of design* (between groups, within subjects, or mixed), the *number of independent variables*, and the *number of levels within each* independent variable.

Single factor designs. If the design has one independent variable only (either a between groups design or a within subjects design), then it should be described as a *single factor design*. (Factor is another name for independent variable). For example, a between groups design with one independent variable and four levels would be described as a single factor design with four levels. If the same design was a within subjects design with four levels, then it would be described as a single factor repeated measures design with four levels. Note that "between groups" is not stated directly in the first example but is implied because there is no mention in that example of repeated measures.

Between groups factorial designs. When there is more than one independent variable, then the levels of *each* independent variable become important in the description of the design. For example, suppose a design has three between groups independent variables, and the first independent variable has two levels, the second independent variable has three levels, and the third independent variable has two levels. The design is written as a 2 x 3 x 2 factorial design (factorial means two or more independent variables or factors). Notice again that between groups is not explicitly mentioned but is implied because there is no mention of repeated measures, as in a within subjects design description. Since the design is a between groups design, the number of groups needed to carry out the study is 2 multiplied by 3 multiplied by 2, or 12 groups.

Within subjects factorial designs. On the other hand, if the design is a within subjects design with two independent variables, each with two levels, then it is described as a 2 x 2 within subjects design or, more commonly, a 2 x 2 design with repeated measures on both factors.

Mixed design. Such a design might have two between groups independent variables with three and four levels, respectively, and one within subjects independent variable with two levels. It would be described as a 3 x 4 x 2 factored design with repeated measures on the third factor.

Remember, when describing a design, that *each* independent variable is given one number, the number of *levels* for that variable. Thus a design description with three numbers (e.g., 2 x 3 x 4) has *three* independent variables or factors, which have 2, 3, and 4 levels. A single factor design is described in words, as above, and not with numerals and multiplication signs. The *dependent* variable is *not* part of the design description, so is not considered in this section.

Selection of Inferential Statistics

Now that we have introduced the basic design concepts, it is time to begin thinking about which of the hundreds of possible inferential statistics to use. This section may seem overwhelming at first because a lot of statistical tests are introduced. It is probably wise to come back to this chapter later, from time to time when you have to make a decision about which statistic to use.

We will present six steps that will help in the selection of the proper statistical test for data analysis. In order to utilize these steps, you must remember or review a number of things from chapter 1 and the first part of this chapter. In chapter 1, we presented a discussion of five broad approaches to research. The first three (experimental, quasi-experimental, and comparative) all compare groups and test difference hypotheses or questions. These three approaches utilize the same types of statistics, which we called difference inferential statistics (see Fig. 1.1). These statistics (e.g., *t* test and analysis of variance) will be computed in chapters 14 - 18 and are shown here in Fig. 7.1 and 7.3.

The associational approach to research utilizes what we called associational inferential statistics and will be computed in chapters 8 - 13. The statistics in this group examine the association or relationship between two or more variables and are shown in Fig. 7.2 and 7.4.

Also it is necessary for you to remember or review the concepts of: independent and dependent variables (chapter 1); between groups, within subjects, and mixed designs (this chapter); and nominal, ordinal, and interval scales of measurement (chapter 3).

It is worth noting that there may be more than one appropriate statistical analysis. One might assume, since the statistical formulas are precise mathematically, that this precision generalizes to the choice of a statistical test. As we shall see, that is not always true.

Using Tables 7.1 to 7.4 to Select Statistics

As with research questions/hypotheses discussed in chapter 1, we divide inferential statistics into two kinds: basic and complex. For *basic* statistics there is *one* independent and *one* dependent variable. For complex difference and associational statistics there are three or more variables. We call them *complex* rather than multivariate because there is not unanimity about the definition of multivariate, and several such complex statistics (e.g., factoral ANOVA) are not usually classified as multivariate.

The statistics shown in Tables 7.1 to 7.4 are each discussed in the remaining chapters in this book, and assignments and outputs are given demonstrating how to compute them using SPSS 7.5. There are other statistics, but these tables include most of the inferential statistics that you will encounter in reading research articles.

Fig. 7.1 is a decision tree to help you use these four tables.

1.   Decide whether your research question or hypothesis is a *difference* one (i.e., compares groups) or an *associational* one (relates variables). Our rule of thumb is that if the independent/predictor variable has five or more ordered levels/values, the question should be considered an associational one.[1] The former leads you to Tables 7.1 or 7.3 and the latter to Tables 7.2 or 7.4.

---

[1] The exception is that if you want to assess the strength of the association between a nominal independent variable with fewer than five levels, you would use the appropriate nominal associational statistic (i.e., phi or Cramer's V).

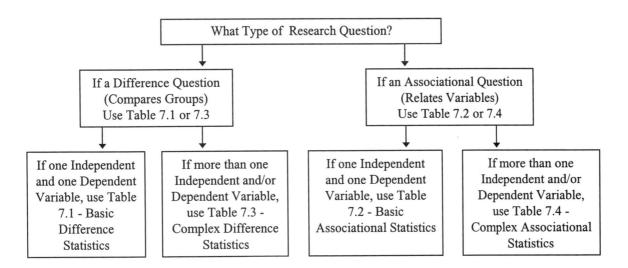

Fig. 7.1. A decision tree to decide how to select the appropriate statistic from Tables 7.1 to 7.4.

2.   Decide how many variables there are in your question. If there is only one independent and one dependent variable, use Tables 7.1 or 7.2. If there is *more* than one independent and/or one dependent variable to be used in this analysis, use Tables 7.3 and 7.4.

3.   If your question involves a *basic* two variable *difference question*, you must determine: (a) the scale of the *dependent* variable and whether assumptions are markedly violated, (b) how many values/levels/groups/samples in your independent variable, and (c) whether the design is between groups or within subjects. The answers to these questions lead to a specific box and statistic in Table 7.1.

4.   Or, if you ask a *basic* two variable *associational question*, use Table 7.2. Which row you use depends on whether *both* variables are interval, ordinal, or nominal. At this point, you can identify an appropriate basic associational statistic.

5.   Or, if you ask a *complex difference question* (3 or more variables) appropriate statistics are identified using Table 7.3.

6.   Or, if you ask a *complex associational question* (3 or more variables) appropriate statistics are identified using Table 7.4.

Table 7.1. *Selection of an Appropriate Inferential Statistic for Basic, Two Variable, Difference Questions or Hypotheses (for Experimental, Quasi-Experimental, and Comparative Approaches)*[†]

	Scale of Measurement of **Dependent Variable** ↓	COMPARE ↓	One Factor or Independent Variable with 2 Categories or Levels/Groups/Samples		One Independent Variable 3 or more Categories or Levels or Groups	
			Independent Samples or Groups (Between)	Repeated Measures or Related Samples (Within)	Independent Samples or Groups (Between)	Repeated Measures or Related Samples (Within)
Parametric Statistics	Dependent Variable Approximates **Interval** or Ratio Data and Assumptions Not Markedly Violated	MEANS	INDEPENDENT SAMPLES *t* TEST or ONE-WAY ANOVA ch. 14	PAIRED SAMPLES *t* TEST ch. 14	ONE-WAY ANOVA ch. 15	GLM REPEATED MEASURES ANOVA ch. 17
Nonparametric Statistics	Dependent Variables Clearly **Ordinal** (or Ranked) Data or ANOVA Assumptions Markedly Violated	MEDIANS OR RANKS	MANN-WHITNEY ch. 14	WILCOXON ch. 14	KRUSKAL-WALLIS ch. 15	FRIEDMAN ch. 17
	Dependent Variable **Nominal** (Categorical) Data	COUNTS	CHI-SQUARE ch. 14	MCNEMAR	CHI-SQUARE	COCHRAN Q TEST

Table 7.2. *Selection of an Appropriate Inferential Statistic for Basic, Two Variable, Associational Questions or Hypotheses (for the Associational Approach)* [†]

Level (scale) of Measurement of **Both Variables** ↓	RELATE ↓	Two Variables or Scores for the Same or Related Subjects
Variables are Both Interval Data and assumption not markedly related	SCORES	PEARSON (r) ch. 9
Both Variables at least Ordinal Data or assumptions markedly violated	RANKS	KENDALL TAU or SPEARMAN (Rho) ch. 9
One variable is Interval and One Nominal Data		ETA ch. 8
Both Variables are Nominal (categorical) Data	COUNTS	PHI or CRAMER'S V ch. 8

[†] It is acceptable to use statistics which are in the box(es) **below** the appropriate statistic, but there is usually some loss of information and power. **It is not acceptable to use statistics above the appropriate box.**

Table 7.3. *Selection of the Appropriate Complex (More than One Independent and/or Dependent Variable) Statistic to Answer Difference Questions/Hypotheses (for the Experimental, Quasi-Experimental, and/or Comparative Approaches)*

Dependent Variable(s) ↓	Two or More Independent Variables		
	All Between Groups	**All Within Subjects**	**Mixed (Between & Within)**
One Dependent Variable Interval scale	Factorial ANOVA ch. 16	Factorial ANOVA with Repeated Measures on all Factors	Factorial ANOVA with Repeated Measures on some Factors- ch. 17
Ordinal Dependent Variable	None Common	None Common	None Common
Nominal Dependent Variable	LOG LINEAR	None Common	None Common
Several Dependent Variables Interval Scale	MANOVA ch. 18	MANOVA with Repeated Measures on all Factors	MANOVA with Repeated Measures on some Factors

Table 7.4. *Selection of the Appropriate Complex Associational Statistic for the Purpose of Predicting a Single Dependent/Outcome Variable from Several Independent Variables*

One Dependent Variable ↓	Several Independent Variables		
	All Interval	**Some Interval Some "Dummy" (2 category)**	**All Dummy**
Interval (Continuous)	MULTIPLE REGRESSION ch. 12	MULTIPLE REGRESSION ch. 12	MULTIPLE REGRESSION ch. 12
Nominal Categories	DISCRIMINANT ANALYSIS ch. 13	LOGISTIC REGRESSION ch. 13	LOGISTIC REGRESSION ch. 13

Something that is not obvious from Table 7.1 and 7.2 or the decision tree is that the broad question *of whether there is a relationship between variables X and Y can be answered two ways.*[2] If both the independent variable and dependent variable provide approximately interval level data with five or more levels, the best statistic (based on Fig. 7.1 and Table 7.2) to use is

---

[2] As discussed in chapter 1, difference and associational questions are subcategories of the general relationship question. This is consistent with the argument by statisticians that all parametric inferential statistics are relational. However, we think it is helpful to students to make the distinction between different questions (and statistics) and associational questions (and statistics).

the Pearson correlation, and that would be our recommendation. However, some researchers choose to divide the independent variable into two or several categories or groups such as low, medium, and high and then do a one-way ANOVA. Conversely, others who start with an independent variable that has only a few (say two through four ordered categories) may choose to do a correlation instead of a one-way ANOVA. While these choices are not necessarily wrong, they are uncommon, and we do not think they are the best practice.

Interpreting the Results of a Statistical Test

The rationale, calculations, and interpretation of each of these specific statistics, is presented in the following chapters in some detail. For each statistic (i.e., t, F, χ^2, r, etc.) the calculations produce a number or *calculated value* based on the specific data in your study. See the left side of Fig. 7.2 for *approximate* values when the study has about 50 participants or is a 2 x 2 chi-square.

To interpret that calculated value, it is compared to *critical values* found in a table or stored in the computer's memory, taking into account the degrees of freedom which is usually based on the number of participants. The middle column of Fig. 7.2 shows how to interpret any inferential test once you know the probability level (p) from the computer or whether the calculated value is greater than the critical value. In general, if the calculated value of the statistics (t, F, etc.) is relatively large, the probability or p is small, e.g., .05, .01, .001. If the probability is *less than* the critical level (usually .05), we can say that the results are *statistically significant* or that they are significant at the .05 level or that $p < .05$. We can also reject the null hypothesis of no difference or no relationship. We do not usually state it, but we could think about the level of confidence (1-p) in the results as shown on the right side of Fig. 7.2.

Note that computer printouts such as those from SPSS make interpretation of the various statistics quite easy by printing the actual significance or probability level (p) so you do not have to look up a critical value in a table. This translates all of the common inferential statistics into a common metric, the significance level or **sig**. This level is also the probability of a Type I error or the probability of rejecting the null hypothesis when it is actually true. Thus, regardless of what specific statistic you use, if the sig. or p is small (usually less than .05) the finding is *statistically* significant and you reject the null hypothesis. We will see, however, that statistical significance is not the same as *practical* significance or importance. With large samples we can find statistical significance even when the differences or associations are quite small/low. Thus, in addition to statistical significance, we will, in many of the assignments, examine measures of the effect size or how much variance in the dependent variable can be predicted from the independent variable. We will see that it is quite possible to have a statistically significant result that is quite weak; i.e., has a low effect size. Remember that the null hypothesis is that there is *no* difference or *no* association. A significant result with a low effect size means that we can be very confident that there is *some* difference or association, but it is small, maybe not of practical importance.

APPROXIMATE CALCULATED VALUE OF THE STATISTIC[1]				INTERPRETATION	SIGNIFICANCE LEVEL[2] (p, Probability, Sig.)	LEVEL OF CONFIDENCE[3]
t	F	χ^2	r		Sig.	$1 - p$
			±1.00			
↑	↑	↑	↑			
± 5.0	25.0	20.0	±0.44		0.001	99.9% Confident
				• STATISTICALLY SIGNIFICANT at $p < 0.01$ • Reject Null Hypothesis • Results probably not due to chance		
± 2.68	7.17	6.63	±0.36 ←	Critical Values	0.01	99% Confident
				• SIGNIFICANT at $p<0.05$		
± 2.01	4.03	3.84	±0.28 ←	Critical Values	0.05	95% Confident
					0.10	
				• NOT SIGNIFICANT • Do NOT reject Null Hypothesis • Results could be due to chance.		Too low to be confident
					0.50	Almost surely due to chance
0	0	0	0		1.00	

[1] For these examples, $df = 50$ for t test; $df = 1, 50$ for F (ANOVA); $df = 1$ for χ^2; $df = 50$ for r (Pearson Correlation).

[2] This is the probability that the results are due to chance, i.e., probability of a *Type I Error*.

[3] This is the probability or level of confidence that the results are not due to chance.

Note: When the output indicates that the probability or significance = 0.000, you should state that $p<0.001$ in your paper because there is always some small probability of a Type I error.

Fig. 7.2. Interpreting inferential statistics.

Now you should be ready to study each of the above statistics in order to learn more about computation and interpretation. Good luck. Study hard. It may be tough going at times, but hopefully this overview has given you a good foundation. It would be wise for you to review the sections on the decision tree (Fig. 7.1), Tables 7.1 - 7.4, and this section from time to time. If you do, you will have a good grasp of how the various statistics fit together, when to use them, and how to interpret the results.

CHAPTER 8

Cross-Tabulation and Nonparametric Association

This assignment will produce cross-tabulation tables and several of the nonparametric measures of association mentioned in chapter 7: Kendall's tau, eta, phi, and Cramer's *V*. Chi-square also is computed using the **Crosstabs** menu that we will use in this assignment. Chi-square can be used to determine if there is a relationship between two categorical variables, but it does not indicate the strength of the association, as do the other nonparametric statistics mentioned above. Thus, we will wait to compute chi-square until chapter 14.

Problems/Research Questions

1. Is there a significant association/relationship between gender and math grades? If so, how strong is it? Begin by cross-tabulating (**Crosstabs**) math grades and gender.

2. Is there a significant association between father's education and math grades? If so, how strong is it? Cross-tabulate math grades and father's education revised.

3. Is there an association between gender and grades in high school? How strong is the association?

4. Is there an association between gender and math achievement? How strong is the association?

Lab Assignment D

Logon and Get Data

- Get your data file **hsbdataC**.

Problem 1 : Cross-Tabulate Math Grades and Gender

To do **crosstabs** follow these steps:
- Click on **Statistics => Summarize => Crosstabs**.
- Put *mathgr* in the **Rows** box using the arrow key and put *gend* in the **Columns** box (see Fig. 8.1). It is arbitrary which variable is put in rows and which in columns.
- Next, click on **Statistics** and select **Phi and Cramer's *V*** (see Fig. 8.2).
- Click on **Continue**.
- Once you return to the Crosstabs menu, click on **Cells**.
- Now, click on **Expected** and **Total**; ensure that **Observed** is also checked (see Fig. 8.3).
- Click on **Continue** then **OK**. Compare your syntax and output to Output 8.2.

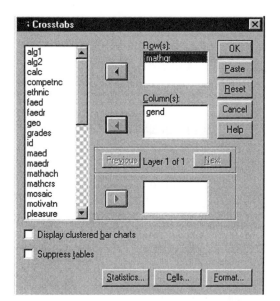

Fig. 8.1. Crosstabs.

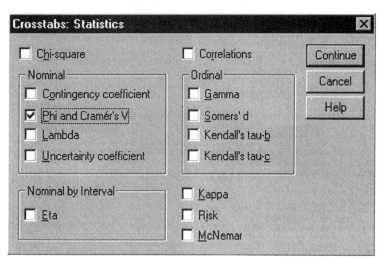

**Fig. 8.2.
Crosstabs: Statistics.**

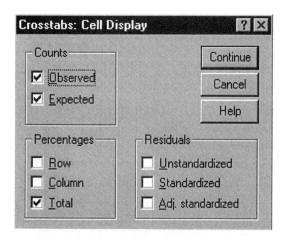

Fig. 8.3. Crosstabs: Cell display.

Problem 2: Cross-Tabulate Math Grades and Father's Education Revised

Now try an exercise yourself. Cross-tabulate (**Crosstabs**) math grades (***Rows***) and father's education revised *(Columns)*. Click on **Cells** and ask that the **Observed and Expected** cell counts and **Total** percentages be printed in the table. In addition, request the following **Statistics**: **Phi/Cramer's** *V* and **Kendall's ta i-b** coefficient for ordinal data. Compare your syntax and output to Output 8.2.

Problem 3: Cross Tabulate Grades and Gender—Compute Eta

There is an important associational statistic, eta, that is used when one variable is nominal and the other is interval (see Fig. 8.2). We will use this statistic to indicate the association between gender and grades (an approximately interval level variable with eight values). Eta squared will be an important statistic in later chapters when we interpret the *effect size* of various ANOVAs. Follow these steps:
- Click on **Statistics => Summarize => Crosstabs**.
- Put *grades* in the **Rows** box using the arrow key and put *gend* in the **Columns** box (see Fig. 8.1).
- Next, click on **Statistics** and select **Eta** (see Fig. 8.2).
- Click on **Continue**.
- Now, click on **Cells** and select **Expected** and **Observed** (see Fig. 8.3).
- Click on **Continue**.
- Click on **OK**. Compare your syntax and output to Output 8.3.

Problem 4: Cross-Tabulate Math Courses Taken and Gender—Compute Eta

Now try a cross-tabulation on your own. Use Problem 3 as a guide but this time use *mathcrs* and *gend*. Check your output against Output 8.4.

Print, Save, and Exit

- **Print** your output file, if necessary.
- Save your data file as hsbdataD (**File => Save As**).
- Save the SPSS log files as **hsblogD**.
- **Exit** SPSS.

Interpretation Questions

1. Compare the observed and expected counts or frequencies in the cross-tabulation table in Output 8.2. How does this difference in counts affect statistical significance?

2. In Output 8.2, if you assumed that *faedr* and *mathgr* were nominal scale data, should you use phi or Cramer's *V* to examine the strength of the relationship? Explain the results of the phi or Cramer's *V* test.

3. If we assumed (as is true) that *faedr* and *mathgr* were at least ordinal data, which of the statistics used in Output 8.2 is usually the most appropriate to measure the *strength* of the relationship: phi, Cramer's *V*, or Kendall's tau-b? Interpret the results.

4. In Output 8.4, what is the value of the appropriate eta? Do you think it is high or low? How would you describe the results?

Outputs and Interpretations

```
GET
  FILE='A:\hsbdataC.sav'.
EXECUTE .
```

Output 8.1: Crosstabs and Nonparametric Associational Statistics

Syntax for Crosstabs math grades by gender

```
CROSSTABS
  /TABLES=mathgr  BY gend
  /FORMAT= AVALUE TABLES
  /STATISTIC= PHI
  /CELLS= COUNT EXPECTED TOTAL .
```

Interpretation of Output 8.1 and 8.2

The case processing summary table indicates that there are no missing data. Note, in the second (cross-tabulation) table, that the **expected count** of the number of male students with grades less than A or B is 19.9 and the observed or actual **count** is 24. Thus, there are somewhat more (4.1) males with low grades than would be expected by chance, given the **totals** shown in the table. There are also discrepancies between observed and expected counts in the other three cells of the table. A question answered by the chi-square test is whether these discrepancies between observed and expected counts are bigger than one might expect by chance.

There are several nonparametric measures of association that we could have chosen in Fig. 8.2. All of them except chi-square attempt, in different ways, to measure the *strength* of the association between two variables on the same -1 to +1 scale used by the Pearson correlation (see chapter 9). If both variables are nominal and you have a 2 x 2 table, like the one in Output 8.2, **phi** is the appropriate statistic.

For larger tables with nominal data (like the 3 x 2 factorial in Problem 3 and Output 8.3), **Cramer's *V*** is the appropriate statistic. In Problem 3, we also requested **Kendall's tau-b** because both math grades and father's education can be considered to be ordered variables and ordinal data. If the association between variables is weak, the value of the statistic will be close to zero and the significance level (sig.) will be greater than .05, the usual cutoff to say that an association is statistically significant.

Case Processing Summary

	Cases					
	Valid		Missing		Total	
	N	Percent	N	Percent	N	Percent
math grades * gender	75	100.0%	0	.0%	75	100.0%

math grades * gender Crosstabulation

			gender		Total
			male	female	
math grades	less A-B	Count	24	20	44
		Expected Count	19.9	24.1	44.0
		% of Total	32.0%	26.7%	58.7%
	most A-B	Count	10	21	31
		Expected Count	14.1	16.9	31.0
		% of Total	13.3%	28.0%	41.3%
Total		Count	34	41	75
		Expected Count	34.0	41.0	75.0
		% of Total	45.3%	54.7%	100.0%

There are 4.1 more males with low grades than expected by chance.

Symmetric Measures

		Value	Approx. Sig.
Nominal by Nominal	Phi	.220	.056
	Cramer's V	.220	.056
N of Valid Cases		75	

Use phi to measure the strength of the association if one or both variables are nominal and you have a **2 x 2** table as in this case.

Output 8.2: Crosstabs and Nonparametric Associational Statistics

Syntax for Crosstabs, Crosstabs tables and statistics math grades by father's education revised

```
CROSSTABS
  /TABLES=mathgr  BY faedr
  /FORMAT= AVALUE TABLES
  /STATISTIC= PHI BTAU
  /CELLS= COUNT EXPECTED TOTAL .
```

Case Processing Summary

	Cases					
	Valid		Missing		Total	
	N	Percent	N	Percent	N	Percent
math grades * Father's ed rev	73	97.3%	2	2.7%	75	100.0%

math grades * Father's ed rev Crosstabulation

			Father's ed rev			
			hs grad or less	some college	BS or more	Total
math grades	less A-B	Count	23	9	11	43
		Expected Count	22.4	9.4	11.2	43.0
		% of Total	31.5%	12.3%	15.1%	58.9%
	most A-B	Count	15	7	8	30
		Expected Count	15.6	6.6	7.8	30.0
		% of Total	20.5%	9.6%	11.0%	41.1%
Total		Count	38	16	19	73
		Expected Count	38.0	16.0	19.0	73.0
		% of Total	52.1%	21.9%	26.0%	100.0%

Symmetric Measures

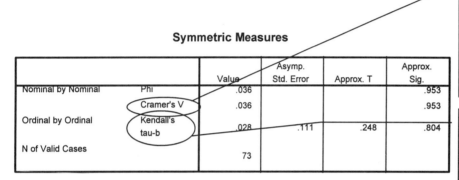

		Value	Asymp. Std. Error	Approx. T	Approx. Sig.
Nominal by Nominal	Phi	.036			.953
	Cramer's V	.036			.953
Ordinal by Ordinal	Kendall's tau-b	.028	.111	.248	.804
N of Valid Cases		73			

> Measures the *strength* of a relationship of two nominal variables when one or both have three or more levels/values.

> Measures the strength of the association if both variables are ordinal.

Output 8.3: Crosstabs and Eta

Syntax for Crosstabs, Crosstabs tables and statistics math grades by gender

```
CROSSTABS
  /TABLES=grades  BY gend
  /FORMAT= AVALUE TABLES
  /STATISTIC=ETA
  /CELLS= COUNT EXPECTED .
```

Interpretation of Output 8.3

The second table shows the actual **counts** and the **expected counts** of the number of persons in each cell. If there are big positive discrepancies between the actual and expected counts in the upper left and negative discrepancies in the lower right or vice versa, that would indicate that there is an association between the two variables. Like most measures of association, eta can vary from about -1.0 through zero to +1.0. High positive or negative values of eta indicate a strong association. In this case eta is .105 a low value, indicating a weak, undoubtedly nonsignificant association. With 75 subjects, an eta of .33 would be statistically significant, indicating there is some association. However, eta squared would be only .11, indicating that the two variables share only 11% common variance. We will see eta squared again when interpreting the size of the "effect" in analysis of variance.

Case Processing Summary

	Cases					
	Valid		Missing		Total	
	N	Percent	N	Percent	N	Percent
grades in h.s. * gender	75	100.0%	0	.0%	75	100.0%

grades in h.s. * gender Crosstabulation

			gender		Total
			male	female	
grades in h.s.	mostly D	Count	1	0	1
		Expected Count	.5	.5	1.0
	half CD	Count	4	4	8
		Expected Count	3.6	4.4	8.0
	mostly C	Count	4	4	8
		Expected Count	3.6	4.4	8.0
	half BC	Count	8	8	16
		Expected Count	7.3	8.7	16.0
	mostly B	Count	5	10	15
		Expected Count	6.8	8.2	15.0
	half AB	Count	9	9	18
		Expected Count	8.2	9.8	18.0
	mostly A	Count	3	6	9
		Expected Count	4.1	4.9	9.0
Total		Count	34	41	75
		Expected Count	34.0	41.0	75.0

Note that the discrepancies between counts and expected are quite small. This indicates that there is no association.

Directional Measures

			Value
Nominal by Interval	Eta	grades in h.s. Dependent	.105
		gender Dependent	.201

Grades is the dependent or interval scale variable so we use this value for eta.

Output 8.5: Eta for Math Courses Taken and Gender

Syntax for Eta of math courses by gender

```
CROSSTABS
  /TABLES=mathcrs  BY gend
  /FORMAT= AVALUE TABLES
  /STATISTIC=ETA
  /CELLS= COUNT EXPECTED .
```

Case Processing Summary

	Cases					
	Valid		Missing		Total	
	N	Percent	N	Percent	N	Percent
Math course taken * gender	75	100.0%	0	.0%	75	100.0%

Math course taken * gender Crosstabulation

			gender		Total
			male	female	
Math course taken	No taken	Count	4	12	16
		Expected Count	7.3	8.7	16.0
	1	Count	3	13	16
		Expected Count	7.3	8.7	16.0
	2	Count	9	6	15
		Expected Count	6.8	8.2	15.0
	3	Count	6	2	8
		Expected Count	3.6	4.4	8.0
	4	Count	7	5	12
		Expected Count	5.4	6.6	12.0
	All math courses	Count	5	3	8
		Expected Count	3.6	4.4	8.0
Total		Count	34	41	75
		Expected Count	34.0	41.0	75.0

Directional Measures

			Value
Nominal by Interval	Eta	Math course taken Dependent	.328
		gender Dependent	.419

CHAPTER 9

Correlation and Scatterplots

In this assignment, you will learn about how to compute the basic associational statistics. The Pearson correlation is a parametric statistic used when both variables are at least interval scale. When you have ranked data or when other assumptions (such as normality of the data) are markedly violated, one should use a nonparametric equivalent of the Pearson correlation coefficient (such as Spearman's rho or Kendall's tau). The Kendall's tau is said to deal with ties in a better way than the Spearman rho. Here we ask you to compute all three correlations and compare them.

Chapter 7 is important background because it will help you understand when to compute/choose associational statistics, and it will remind you about what the significance test means and how to interpret it.

Problems/Research Questions

1. What is the association between grades in high school and math achievement? You will compute three bivariate (2 variable) **correlations** (Pearson, Spearman, and Kendall's tau-b) of *grades* and *mathach*.

2. What are the correlations among all of the variables, *mathach, visual, mosaic, mathcrs, pleasure, comptnc,* and *motivatn,* using Pearson correlations.

3. In this problem, you will compare **pairwise** and **listwise** exclusion of missing data.

4. Using the Graphs menu, you will request **Scatterplots** with the linear, quadratic, and cubic regression lines and r^2 printed on the scatterplot for *grades* and *mathach* and for some of the other correlations.

Lab Assignment E

Logon and Get Data

*   Retrieve **hsbdataD** from your **Data** file.

Problem 1: Correlate Grades and Math Achievement

To do Pearson, Kendall, and Spearman correlations follow these commands:
*   **Statistics => Correlate => Bivariate**.
*   Move *mathach* and *grades* to the **Variables** box.
*   Next, ensure that the **Pearson, Kendall's tau-b, and Spearman** boxes are checked.

- Make sure that the **Two-tailed** (under **Test of Significance**) and **Flag significant correlations** are checked (see Fig. 9.1).
- Now click on **Options** to get that dialog box.
- Click on **Means and standard deviations** and note that **Exclude cases pairwise** is checked. Does your screen look like Fig. 9.2?
- Click on **Continue** then on **OK**. What does your output file look like? Compare Output 9.1 to your output and syntax.

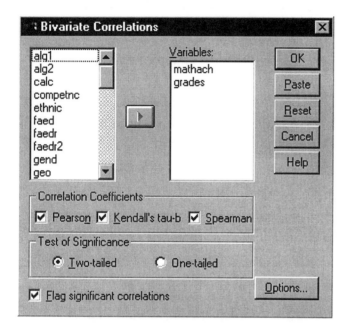

Fig. 9.1. Bivariate correlations.

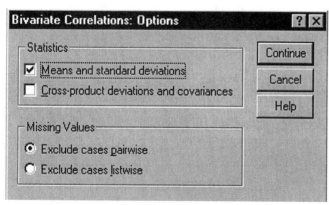

Fig. 9.2. Bivariate correlations: Options.

Problem 2: Correlation Matrixes for Several Interval Scale Variables

Now, on your own, compute a **Pearson** correlation among all the following variables: *mathach, visual, mosaic, mathcrs, pleasure, competnc*, and *motivatn*. Follow similar procedures outlined previously except:

- Click *off* **Kendall's tau-b** and **Spearman** (under **Correlation Coefficients**).

It is usually best, except in exploratory research with small samples, to use two-tailed tests. The 'flag" puts an asterisk beside the correlation coefficients that are statistically significant so that they can be identified quickly. The output also prints the exact significance level (*p*) which is redundant with the asterisk so you wouldn't report both in a thesis or paper.

- For **Options,** obtain **Means and standard deviations,** and **Exclude cases pairwise**.

This will produce Output 9.2, which was reduced in size to fit on the page. To see if you are doing the work right, compare your own syntax file and output to Output 9.2.

Problem 3: Correlations With Pairwise Exclusions

Next, rerun the same analysis, except:
- Click *off* **Means and standard deviation** (in the **Options** window).
- Change **Exclude cases pairwise** to **Exclude cases listwise** (under **Missing Values).**

Now, compare the correlations in Output 9.3 (listwise exclusion of participants with any missing data) to the Pearson correlations in Output 9.2 (pairwise deletion). Are they the same?

Problem 4: Scatterplots - Mathach With Grades

Let's now work on developing a scatterplot of the correlations of *mathach* with *grades*. Follow these commands:
- **Graphs => Scatter**. This will give you Fig. 9.3.
- Click on **Simple** then **Define** which will bring you to Fig. 9.4.

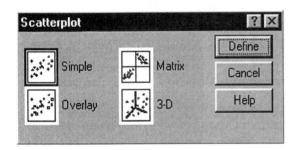

Fig. 9.3. Scatterplot.

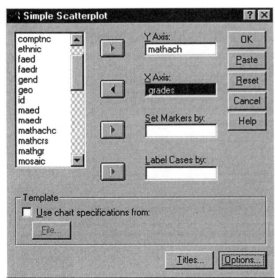

Fig. 9.4. Simple scatterplot.

- Now, move *mathach* to the **Y** axis and *grades* to the **X** axis (*the dependent variable goes on the Y axis*).
- Click on **Options** and make sure **Exclude cases listwise** is highlighted (see Fig. 9.5).
- Click on **Continue**.
- Next, click on **Titles** (in Fig. 9.4) and type "**Correlation of math achievement with high school grades**" (see Fig. 9.6).
- Click on **Continue** then on **OK**. You will get an output chart which looks like Fig. 9.7.

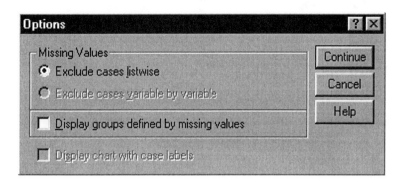

Fig. 9.5. Options.

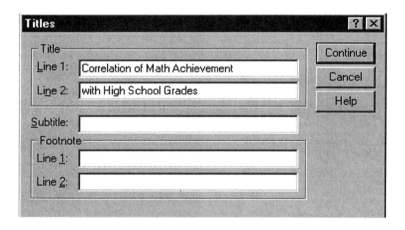

Fig. 9.6. Titles.

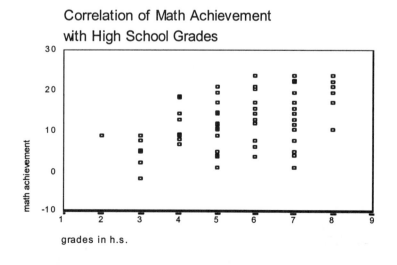

Fig. 9.7. Scatterplot output.

Now let's put the regression lines on the scatterplot so we can get a better sense of the correlation and how much scatter or deviation from the line there is.

- *Double click* on the chart in the output file. You will see a dialog box like Fig. 9.8.
- Select **Chart => Options** until you see Fig. 9.9.
- Click on **Total** in the **Fit Line** box and **Show sunflowers**; there is no need to change the **Sunflower Options**. The sunflowers indicate, by the number of petals, how many participants had essentially the same point on the scatterplot.
- Next, click on the **Fit Options** button, which will give you Fig. 9.10.
- Ensure that the **Linear Regression** box is highlighted.
- Then check the **Individual** box and **Display R-Square in legend** box. Check to be sure your window is like Fig. 9.10.
- Click on **Continue** then **OK**.

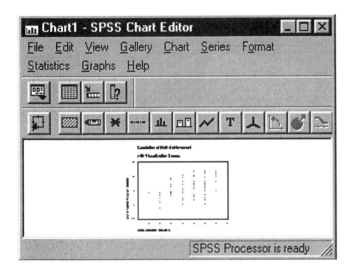

Fig. 9.8. SPSS chart editor.

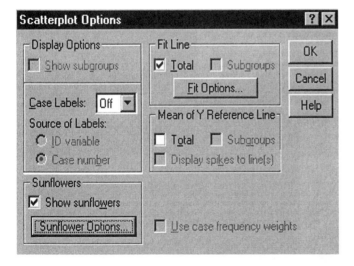

Fig. 9.9. Scatterplot options.

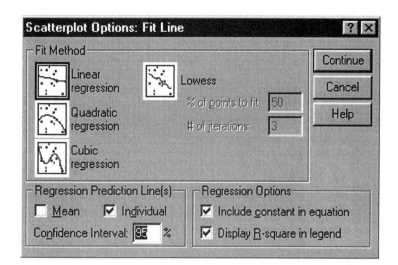

Fig. 9.10. Chart: Scatterplot.

Now, if the points on the scatterplot do not lie close to the regression line, it could be that the data were curvilinear (better fit a curved line). If so, you could (in Fig. 9.10) click on **Quadratic** and possibly the **Cubic regression** boxes (one at a time) to and see what the fit and r^2 look like. If the quadratic and/or cubic r^2 are quite a bit higher, a linear Pearson correlation is not the best statistic to use. Output 9.4 shows the quadratic and cubic regression lines as well as the linear chart. Check your syntax and output against Output 9.4.

Now try the following scatterplots by doing the same steps as Problem 3. Don't forget to *change the title* before you run each scatterplot.

1. *Mosaic* (X) with *mathach* (Y).
2. *Mathcrs* (X) with *mathach* (Y).

Do your syntax and output look like the ones in Output 9.5 and 9.6?

Print, Save, and Exit

- Print your output if you want.
- Save your data file as **hsbdataE** (**File => Save As**).
- Save the SPSS log files as **hsblogE**.
- **Exit** SPSS.

Interpretation Questions

1. In Output 9.1: a) What do the correlation coefficients tell us? b) What is r^2 for the Pearson correlation? What does it mean? c) Compare the Pearson, Kendall, and Spearman correlations on both correlation size and significance level. d) When should you use which type?

2. In Output 9.2, how many of the Pearson correlation coefficients are significant?

3. In Output 9.3: a) How many Pearson correlations are there? b) How many are significant?

4. Write an interpretation of a) one of the significant and b) one of the nonsignificant correlations in Output 9.3. Include whether or not the correlation is significant, your decision about the null hypothesis, *and* a sentence or two describing the correlations in nontechnical terms.

5. What is the difference between the pairwise and listwise correlation matrixes?

6. Using Outputs 9.5, and 9.6, inspect the scatterplots. a) What is r^2? b) Is the linear relationship as good as a curvilinear (quadratic) one? c) Why should one do scatterplots?

Outputs and Interpretations

```
GET
FILE='A:\hsbdataD.sav'.
EXECUTE .
```

Output 9.1: Pearson, Spearman, and Kendall's Tau-b Correlations

Syntax for Pearson correlation of math achievement with grades in h.s.

```
CORRELATIONS
  /VARIABLES=mathach grades
  /PRINT=TWOTAIL SIG
  /STATISTICS DESCRIPTIVES
  /MISSING=PAIRWISE .
```

Interpretation of Output 9.1

The first table provides **descriptive statistics** for the variables to be correlated, in this case math achievement and grades. The two **correlations** tables are the key. Each has three parts, with the information in matrix form which, unfortunately, means that every number is presented twice. We have provided callout boxes to help you.

The Pearson correlation coefficient is .504; the significance level or *p* is .000 and the number of participants with both variables (*mathach* and *grades*) is 75. In a report, this would usually be written as: $r(73) = .50, p < .001$. Note that the degrees of freedom ($N-2$ for correlations) is put in parentheses after the statistic (*r* for Pearson correlation) which is usually rounded to two decimal places. The significance or *p* value follows and is stated as less than .001 rather than .000. Note that the correlation values for Kendall's tau-b and Spearman's rho are different from *r*, but in this case they have the same significance level ($p < .001$).

This correlation is significant, because the "sig" is less than .05, ($p < .05$) so we can reject the null hypothesis of no association and state that there *is an association* between grades and math achievement. Because the correlation is positive, students who have high grades generally have high math achievement scores and vice versa. This means that high grades generally are *associated* with high achievement, medium with medium, and low with low. If the correlation is significant and *negative* (e.g., -.50), high grades would be associated with low achievement and vice versa. If the correlation was not significant, there would be *no* systematic association between a student's grades and achievement. In that case you could not predict anything about math achievement from knowing someone's grades.

103

Descriptive Statistics

	Mean	Std. Deviation	N
math achievement	12.5645	6.6703	75
grades in h.s.	5.68	1.57	75

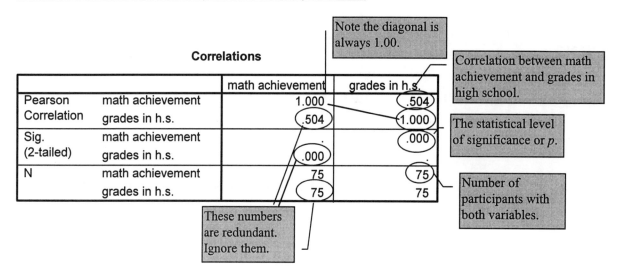

Correlations

		math achievement	grades in h.s.
Pearson Correlation	math achievement	1.000	.504
	grades in h.s.	.504	1.000
Sig. (2-tailed)	math achievement		.000
	grades in h.s.	.000	
N	math achievement	75	75
	grades in h.s.	75	75

Note the diagonal is always 1.00.

Correlation between math achievement and grades in high school.

The statistical level of significance or *p*.

Number of participants with both variables.

These numbers are redundant. Ignore them.

Syntax for Kendall's Tau-b and Spearman Rho correlations of math achievement with grades in h.s.

```
NONPAR CORR
  /VARIABLES=mathach grades
  /PRINT=BOTH TWOTAIL NOSIG
  /MISSING=PAIRWISE .
```

Nonparametric Correlations

Correlations

			math achievement	grades in h.s.
Kendall's tau-b	Correlation Coefficient	math achievement	1.000	.370**
		grades in h.s.	.370**	1.000
	Sig. (2-tailed)	math achievement	.	.000
		grades in h.s.	.000	.
	N	math achievement	75	75
		grades in h.s.	75	75
Spearman's rho	Correlation Coefficient	math achievement	1.000	.481**
		grades in h.s.	.481**	1.000
	Sig. (2-tailed)	math achievement	.	.000
		grades in h.s.	.000	.
	N	math achievement	75	75
		grades in h.s.	75	75

**. Correlation is significant at the .01 level (2-tailed).

Output 9.2: Pearson Correlation Matrix (Pairwise Exclusion)

Syntax for Pearson correlation matrixes (pairwise exclusion of missing data)

```
CORRELATIONS
  /VARIABLES=mathach visual mosaic mathcrs pleasure competnc motivatn
  /PRINT=TWOTAIL NOSIG
  /STATISTICS DESCRIPTIVES
  /MISSING=PAIRWISE .
```

Interpretation of Output 9.2

Notice that after the descriptive statistics table, there is a large **correlations** table divided into three sections: Pearson correlation coefficients, significance, and N. These numbers are, as in Output 9.1, each given twice so you have to be careful in reading them. It is a good idea to look only at the numbers below the diagonal (1.00 as in the coefficients section, dots in the significance section, and 75s in the N section). There are 21 different correlations in the table. In the first column, there is the correlation of each of the other six variables with math achievement. In the second column, each of the other six variables is correlated with visualization score, but note that the .423 for *visual* and *mathach* is the same as the correlation of *mathach* and *visual* in the first column, so ignore it. The Pearson correlations on this table are interpreted similarly to the one in Output 9.1. However, because there are 21 correlations, the odds are that at least one could be statistically significant by chance (i.e., .05= 1/20). Thus, it would be prudent to use the .01 level of significance. The Bonferroni correction (.05/21= .002) would be a conservative approach designed to keep the significance level at .05 for the whole study.

Descriptive Statistics

	Mean	Std. Deviation	N
math achievement	12.5645	6.6703	75
visualization score	5.2433	3.9120	75
mosaic, pattern test	27.413	9.574	75
Math course taken	2.11	1.67	75
Pleasure scale	3.2267	.6300	75
Competence scale	3.2945	.6645	73
Motivation scale	2.8744	.6382	73

Correlations with math achievement.

Correlations with visualization score.

Use correlations above or below line.

Correlations

		math achievement	visualization score	mosaic, pattern test	Math course taken	Pleasure scale	Competence scale	Motivation scale
Pearson Correlation	math achievement	1.000	.423**	.213	.794**	.094	.332**	.316**
	visualization score	.423**	1.000	.030	.399**	-.160	.007	.047
	mosaic, pattern test	.213	.030	1.000	-.059	.085	.111	.083
	Math course taken	.794**	.399**	-.059	1.000	-.006	.309**	.298*
	Pleasure scale	.094	-.160	.085	-.006	1.000	.431**	.305**
	Competence scale	.332**	.007	.111	.309**	.431**	1.000	.570**
	Motivation scale	.316**	.047	.083	.298*	.305**	.570**	1.000
Sig. (2-tailed)	math achievement	.	.000	.067	.000	.421	.004	.006
	visualization score	.000	.	.798	.000	.171	.954	.695
	mosaic, pattern test	.067	.798	.	.616	.466	.349	.487
	Math course taken	.000	.000	.616	.	.958	.008	.010
	Pleasure scale	.421	.171	.466	.958	.	.000	.009
	Competence scale	.004	.954	.349	.008	.000	.	.000
	Motivation scale	.006	.695	.487	.010	.009	.000	.
N	math achievement	75	75	75	75	75	73	73
	visualization score	75	75	75	75	75	73	73
	mosaic, pattern test	75	75	75	75	75	73	73
	Math course taken	75	75	75	75	75	73	73
	Pleasure scale	75	75	75	75	75	73	73
	Competence scale	73	73	73	73	73	73	71
	Motivation scale	73	73	73	73	73	71	73

**. Correlation is significant at the 0.01 level (2-tailed).

*. Correlation is significant at the 0.05 level (2-tailed).

Output 9.3: Pearson Correlation Matrix (Listwise Exclusion)

Syntax for Pearson correlation matrix

```
CORRELATIONS
  /VARIABLES=mathach visual mosaic mathcrs pleasure competnc motivatn
  /PRINT=TWOTAIL NOSIG
  /MISSING=LISTWISE .
```

Interpretation of Output 9.3

In this table there is not a separate section for N because, with **listwise** exclusion, only the same 71 subjects who have scores on all seven variables are used for all correlations. Note that the correlations are slightly different from those in Output 9.2 where the N's varied depending on how many subjects had each pair of variables. Factor analysis, Cronbach's alpha, and multiple regression (Assignments F, G, and H) all use listwise deletion, so if you have one or more variables with quite a bit of missing data the N may be dramatically reduced.

Correlations[a]

		math achievement	visualization score	mosaic, pattern test	Math course taken	Pleasure scale	Competence scale	Motivation scale
Pearson Correlation	math achievement	1.000	.434**	.246*	.804**	.101	.335**	.316**
	visualization score	.434**	1.000	.035	.429**	-.191	.010	.047
	mosaic, pattern test	.246*	.035	1.000	.000	.067	.104	.083
	Math course taken	.804**	.429**	.000	1.000	.005	.318**	.301*
	Pleasure scale	.101	-.191	.067	.005	1.000	.443**	.309**
	Competence scale	.335**	.010	.104	.318**	.443**	1.000	.570**
	Motivation scale	.316**	.047	.083	.301*	.309**	.570**	1.000
Sig. (2-tailed)	math achievement	.	.000	.038	.000	.400	.004	.007
	visualization score	.000	.	.773	.000	.111	.931	.695
	mosaic, pattern test	.038	.773	.	.999	.576	.386	.489
	Math course taken	.000	.000	.999	.	.964	.007	.011
	Pleasure scale	.400	.111	.576	.964	.	.000	.009
	Competence scale	.004	.931	.386	.007	.000	.	.000
	Motivation scale	.007	.695	.489	.011	.009	.000	.

**. Correlation is significant at the 0.01 level (2-tailed).

*. Correlation is significant at the 0.05 level (2-tailed).

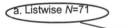

a. Listwise N=71

Cases with missing values for any variable are excluded from all correlations using listwise.

Output 9.4: Scatterplots, Grades With Math Achievement

Syntax for Scatterplot of grades with math achievement with linear, quadratic (curved), and cubic (2 bend) regression

```
GRAPH
  /SCATTERPLOT(BIVAR)=grades WITH mathach
  /MISSING=LISTWISE
  /TITLE= 'Correlation of math achievement' 'with high school grades'.
```

Interpretation of Output 9.4

The three scatterplots shown in Output 9.4 are the same except that the first shows the best fit for a straight (linear) regression line (i.e., it minimizes the squared differences between the points and the line), and the second is the best fit for a line with one curve (quadratic) and the third is the best fit for a line with two bends or curves (cubic). To the right of each scatterplot is the r^2 which indicates the percentage of variance in the dependent variable (*mathach*) that can be predicted from the independent variable (*grades*). Note that the r^2 (.2541) for the linear (first) scatterplot means that $r=.504$, which is what Output 9.1 had for the same correlation.

Note also that the r^2 for the quadratic (.2581) and the r^2 for the cubic regression (.2817) are quite similar to that (.2541) for the linear regression line. Thus, there is little improvement in fit over the linear regression, which is what is used in computing the Pearson and Kendall correlations.

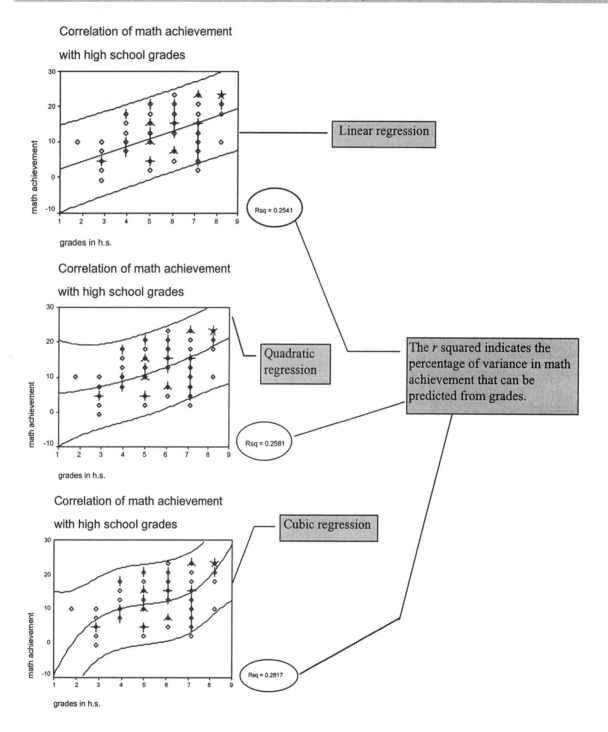

Output 9.5: Scatterplot, Mosaic With Math Achievement

Syntax for Scatterplots mosaic with mathach

```
GRAPH
  /SCATTERPLOT(BIVAR)=mosaic WITH mathach
  /MISSING=LISTWISE
  /TITLE= 'correlation of mosaic scores' 'with math achievement scores'.
```

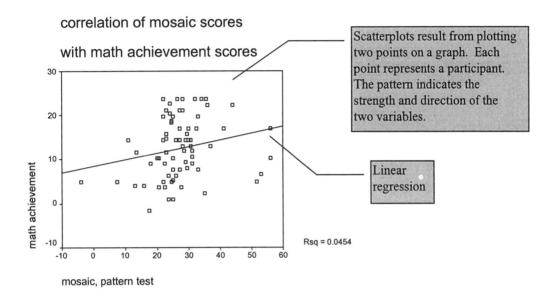

Scatterplots result from plotting two points on a graph. Each point represents a participant. The pattern indicates the strength and direction of the two variables.

Linear regression

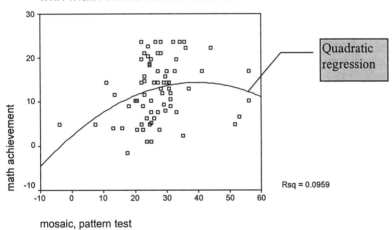

Quadratic regression

Output 9.6: Scatterplots Math Courses Taken With Math Achievement

Syntax for Scatterplots mathcrs with mathach

```
GRAPH
  /SCATTERPLOT(BIVAR)=mathcrs WITH mathach
  /MISSING=LISTWISE
  /TITLE= 'correlation of math courses' 'with math achievement scores'.
```

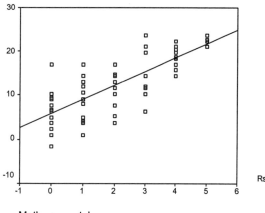

Rsq = 0.6306

Math course taken

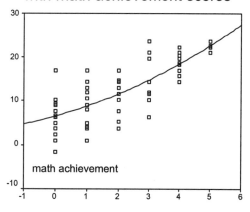

Rsq = 0.6380

Math course taken

CHAPTER 10

Factor Analysis: Data Reduction With Principal Components Analysis

Factor analysis, a complex associational technique, is used for several purposes, but the main one is data reduction.[1] When you have a number of questions about the same general topic (e.g., attitudes about mathematics), you may want to ask whether the questions could be grouped into a smaller number of composite variables. Table 10.1 shows that *either* factor analysis or conceptual analysis (i.e., thinking based on theory and/or literature) can be used to reduce the number of variables to a more manageable and meaningful number of summated scales. The table also shows that you should check the internal consistency reliability of these new scales with Cronbach's alpha (see Assignment G) before actually computing the scales. You may want to check your conceptual analysis with factor analysis as well as Cronbach alphas. That is what we are doing here for our conceptualization of the three math attitude scales.

Table 10.1. *Two Strategies for Reducing Many Related Items to Fewer Composite Variables*

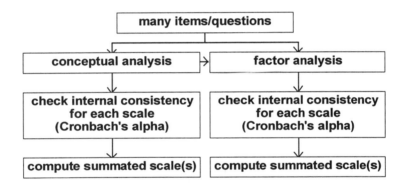

After doing your conceptual or factor analysis, you have several decisions:

1. If you identify only one conceptual scale or one factor and it is supported by an alpha above .70, compute one overall summary scale score. However,
2. If there is more than one conceptual scale or more than one factor and they have good alphas, compute the several summated scale scores. Also, compute an overall scale score *if* it makes sense conceptually. However,
3. If the factor analysis results do not make good conceptual sense, do not use them. In this case, use the conceptual factors, rethink the conceptualization, or use each item separately

---

[1] Statisticians call what we have done in this chapter principal components analysis (PCA) rather than exploratory factor analysis (EFA). In SPSS, principal components analysis is done with the factor analysis program using the **principal components extraction** method. This is consistent with common usage, but there are technical differences between PCA and EFA (see Grimm & Yarnold, 1994).

Problems/ Research Questions

1. Can variables *q01* to *q13* be grouped into a smaller number of composite variables called components or factors? Using the principal components extraction method of the factor analysis program, you will have the computer sort the variables and suppress printing of values if the factor loading is less than .30. You will use a Varimax rotation and allow all factors with eigenvalues over 1.00 to be computed.

2. Rerun the factor analysis but specify that you want the number of factors to be three because our conceptualization is that there are three math attitude scales or factors: motivation, competence, and pleasure.

3. Run a factor analysis to see how the four "achievement" variables, *mathach, visual, mosaic,* and *grades*, cluster or factor.

Lab Assignment F

Logon and Get Data

- Retrieve your most recent data file: **hsbdataE.**

Problem 1: Factor Analysis on Math Attitude Variables

To begin factor analysis use these commands:
- **Statistics => Data Reduction => Factor** to get Fig. 10.1.
- Next select the variables *q01* through *q13*. *Do not* include q04r or any of the other reversed questions.

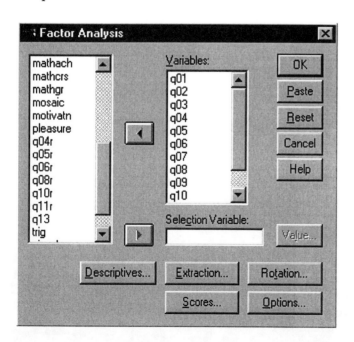

Fig. 10.1. Factor analysis.

Now click on **Descriptives** to produce Fig. 10.2.

- Then click on the following: **Initial solution** (under **Statistics**), **Coefficients, Determinant, KMO and Bartlett's test of sphericity** (under **Correlation Matrix**).
- Click on **Continue**.

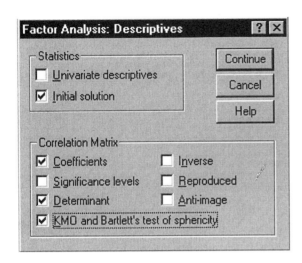

Fig. 10.2. Factor analysis: Descriptives.

- Next, click on **Extraction** at the bottom of Figure 10.1. This will give you Fig. 10.3.
- Make sure **Eigenvalues over 1** is checked.

This default setting will allow the *computer to decide* how many math attitude factors to compute; i.e., as many as have eigenvalues (a measure of variability explained) greater than 1.0. If you have a clear theory or conceptualization about how many factors or scales there should be, you can set the **number of factors** to that number, as we will in Problem 2.

- *Unclick* display **Unrotated factor solution**.
- Click on **Continue**.

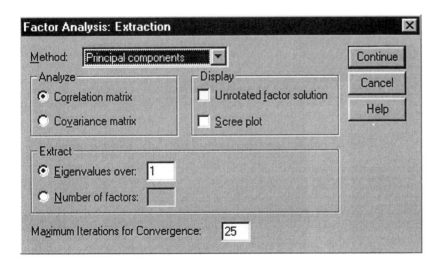

Fig. 10.3. Extraction method to produce principal components analysis (PCA).

- Now click on **Rotation,** which will give you Fig. 10.4.
- Click on **Varimax**.
- Then click on **Continue**.

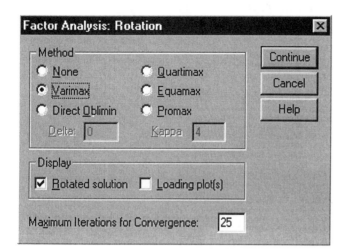

Fig. 10.4. Factor analysis: Rotation.

- Next, click on **Options** which will give you Fig. 10.5.
- Then click on **Sorted by size**.
- Click on **Suppress absolute values less than** and type **.3** (point 3) in the box (see Fig. 10.5). Suppressing small factor loadings makes the output easier to read.
- Click on **Continue** then **OK**. Compare Output 10.1 to your output and syntax.

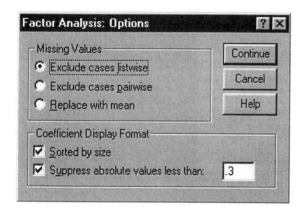

Fig. 10.5. Factor analysis: Options.

Problem 2: Factor Analysis on Math Attitude Variables With Three Factors Specified

Now try doing factor analysis yourself with the same variables, rotation, and options. This time, however, *click off* everything on the descriptive screen except **Initial solution**. Also, use a different **Extraction** subcommand; click on **Extract Number of factors** and then type **3** because our conceptualization is that there are 3 factors. Compare Output 10.2 to your output and syntax. Note that the **Initial Statistics** table is the same, but the **Rotated Component Matrix** now shows three somewhat different factors.

Problem 3: Factor Analysis on Achievement Variables

Now try doing another factor analysis yourself on the "achievement variables," *mathach, visual, mosaic,* and *grades.*
- First press **Reset**.
- Use the default settings (i.e., the boxes that are already checked) for **Extraction**.
- In addition, under **Rotation**, check **Varimax**, display **Rotated solution**, and **Loading plots**.
- Under **Descriptives** check **Univariate descriptives, Initial solution, Coefficients, Determinant**, and **KMO** and **Bartlett's test of sphericity**.

We have requested a more extensive, less simplified output for contrast with the earlier ones. Compare Output 10.3 to your syntax and output.

Print, Save, and Exit

- **Print** your lab assignment results if you want.
- **Save** your data file as **hsbdataF** (**File** => **Save As**).
- **Save** the SPSS log files as **hsblogF**.
- **Exit** SPSS.

Interpretation Questions

1. Using Output 10.1: a) Make a table of the five highest correlations and the five lowest. Indicate whether the variables for the highest and lowest correlations are in the same or in different conceptual clusters (i.e., competence, motivation, and pleasure) as indicated on page 19 for each question. b) What might you name each component or factor in the rotated factor matrix? c) How do these statistical components differ from the three conceptual math attitude composite variables (competence, motivation, and pleasure) computed in Assignment C and shown in chapter 2 and the codebook (Appendix D)?

2. Using Output 10.2: a) How do the rotated components in Output 10.2 differ from those in Output 10.1? b) Are the factors in Output 10.2 closer to the conceptual composites in the codebook? c) How might you name the three factors in Output 10.2?

3. Using Output 10.3: a) Are the assumptions that were tested violated? Explain. b) How many components or factors are there with eigenvalues greater than 1.0, and what total/cumulative percent of variance is accounted for by them? c) Describe the main aspects of the correlation matrix, rotated component matrix, and plot in Output 10.3.

Outputs and Interpretations

```
GET
  FILE='A:\hsbdataE.sav'.
EXECUTE .
```

Output 10.1: Factor Analysis for Math Attitude Questions

Syntax for factor analysis of math attitude questions

```
FACTOR
  /VARIABLES q01 q02 q03 q04 q05 q06 q07 q08 q09 q10 q11 q12 q13   /MISSING
  LISTWISE /ANALYSIS q01 q02 q03 q04 q05 q06 q07 q08 q09 q10 q11 q12 q13
  /PRINT INITIAL CORRELATION DET KMO ROTATION
  /FORMAT SORT BLANK(.3)
  /CRITERIA MINEIGEN(1) ITERATE(25)
  /EXTRACTION PC
  /CRITERIA ITERATE(25)
  /ROTATION VARIMAX
  /METHOD=CORRELATION .
```

Interpret Output 10.1

The factor analysis program generates a number of tables depending on which options you have chosen. The first table in Output 10.1 is a **correlation matrix** showing how each of the 13 questions is associated with each of the other 12. Note some of the correlations are high (e.g., + or - .60 or greater) and some are low (i.e., near zero). The high correlations indicate that two items are associated and will probably be grouped together by the factor analysis.

Next, several assumptions are tested. The **determinant** (located under the correlation matrix) should be more than .00001. For instance, 2.316E-3 is the same as .002316 so this assumption is met. The **KMO** should be greater than .70, and is inadequate if less than .50. The **Bartlett** test should be significant (i.e., significance less than .05); these assumptions also are met.

The **Total Variance Explained** table shows how the variance is divided among the 13 possible components/factors. Note that four factors have **eigenvalues** (a measure of explained variance) greater than 1.0, which is a common criterion for a factor to be useful. Thus, unless you specify otherwise, as we will in Problem 2, the computer will look for the best four-factor solution.

In this case, the computer tried seven iterations before converging on the solution shown in the **Rotated Component Matrix** table. This table is the key one for understanding the results of the analysis. Note that the computer has sorted the 13 math attitude questions (Q01 to Q13) into four groups of 5, 3, 3, and 2 items, respectively. Within each component, the items are sorted from the one with the highest factor weight or loading (i.e., Q05 for factor 1, with a loading of -.88) to the one with the lowest (q02) that was still loaded *the most* on that factor. We have enclosed these items in circles for easy identification. Loadings are correlation coefficients of each item with the component so they range from -1.0 through 0 to + 1.0. A negative loading just means that the question needs to be reversed when interpreting that factor.

The investigator should examine the content of the items that load high on each factor to see if they fit together conceptually and can be named. Items 5, 3, and 11 were intended to reflect an

116

attitude or perception of competence at math (see page 19). Item 1 was intended to measure motivation for doing math, but in retrospect one can imagine that the phrase "until I can do them well" could be interpreted as competence. Likewise, Item 2, " I feel happy after solving a hard problem," although intended to measure pleasure at doing math, might also reflect competence at doing math. Every item has a weight or loading on every factor, but in a "clean" factor analysis almost all of the loadings that are not in the circles that we have drawn will be quite low (less than .40). We asked the computer to print only loadings of .30 or above so all the blanks in the table are low loadings. Note that Item 11 and, especially, Item 2 load above .40 on both Components 1 and 4. The latter component could be labeled pleasure at math, which was conceptually composed of Items 2, 6 and 10.

For our purposes, we will ignore the Factor Transformation Matrix; it was used to convert the initial factor matrix into the rotated factor matrix.

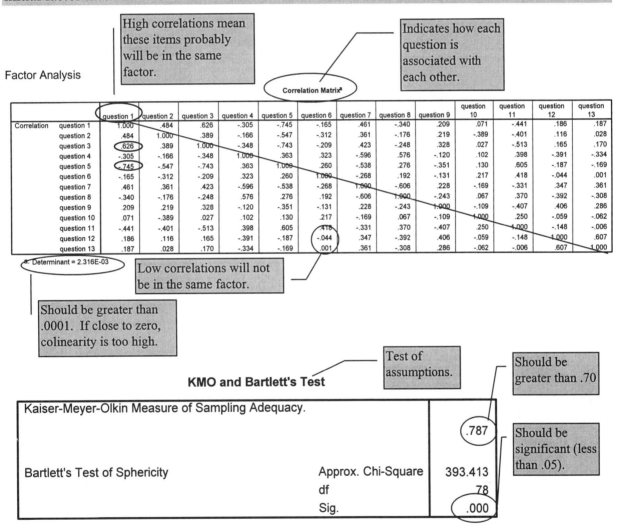

Factor Analysis

High correlations mean these items probably will be in the same factor.

Indicates how each question is associated with each other.

Correlation Matrix[a]

		question 1	question 2	question 3	question 4	question 5	question 6	question 7	question 8	question 9	question 10	question 11	question 12	question 13
Correlation	question 1	1.000	.484	.626	-.305	-.745	-.165	.461	-.340	.209	.071	-.441	.186	.187
	question 2	.484	1.000	.389	-.166	-.547	-.312	.361	-.176	.219	-.389	-.401	.116	.028
	question 3	.626	.389	1.000	-.348	-.743	-.209	.423	-.248	.328	.027	-.513	.165	.170
	question 4	-.305	-.166	-.348	1.000	.363	.323	-.596	.576	-.120	.102	.398	-.391	-.334
	question 5	-.745	-.547	-.743	.363	1.000	.260	-.538	.276	-.351	.130	.605	-.187	-.169
	question 6	-.165	-.312	-.209	.323	.260	1.000	-.268	.192	-.131	.217	.418	-.044	.001
	question 7	.461	.361	.423	-.596	-.538	-.268	1.000	-.606	.228	-.169	-.331	.347	.361
	question 8	-.340	-.176	-.248	.576	.276	.192	-.606	1.000	-.243	.067	.370	-.392	-.308
	question 9	.209	.219	.328	-.120	-.351	-.131	.228	-.243	1.000	-.109	-.407	.406	.286
	question 10	.071	-.389	.027	.102	.130	.217	-.169	.067	-.109	1.000	.250	-.059	-.062
	question 11	-.441	-.401	-.513	.398	.605	.418	-.331	.370	-.407	.250	1.000	-.148	-.006
	question 12	.186	.116	.165	-.391	-.187	-.044	.347	-.392	.406	-.059	-.148	1.000	.607
	question 13	.187	.028	.170	-.334	-.169	.001	.361	-.308	.286	-.062	-.006	.607	1.000

a. Determinant = 2.316E-03

Low correlations will not be in the same factor.

Should be greater than .0001. If close to zero, colinearity is too high.

Test of assumptions.

Should be greater than .70

KMO and Bartlett's Test

Kaiser-Meyer-Olkin Measure of Sampling Adequacy.			.787
Bartlett's Test of Sphericity	Approx. Chi-Square		393.413
	df		78
	Sig.		.000

Should be significant (less than .05).

Communalities

	Initial
question 1	1.000
question 2	1.000
question 3	1.000
question 4	1.000
question 5	1.000
question 6	1.000
question 7	1.000
question 8	1.000
question 9	1.000
question 10	1.000
question 11	1.000
question 12	1.000
question 13	1.000

Extraction Method:
Principal Component
Analysis.

Notice these are greater than one. Eigenvalues refer to the variance explained or accounted for.

Total Variance Explained

Component	Initial Eigenvalues			Rotation Sums of Squared Loadings		
	Total	% of Variance	Cumulative %	Total	% of Variance	Cumulative %
1	4.805	36.963	36.963	3.207	24.666	24.666
2	1.826	14.049	51.011	2.327	17.898	42.564
3	1.333	10.255	61.267	1.887	14.514	57.078
4	1.133	8.718	69.985	1.678	12.907	69.985
5	.883	6.791	76.776			
6	.666	5.120	81.895			
7	.541	4.159	86.055			
8	.453	3.481	89.536			
9	.380	2.920	92.456			
10	.299	2.299	94.755			
11	.285	2.193	96.948			
12	.241	1.853	98.801			
13	.156	1.199	100.000			

Extraction Method: Principal Component Analysis.

Over 2/3 of the variance is accounted for by these four factors.

Component Matrix[a]

a. 4 components extracted.

Percent of variance for each component after rotation.

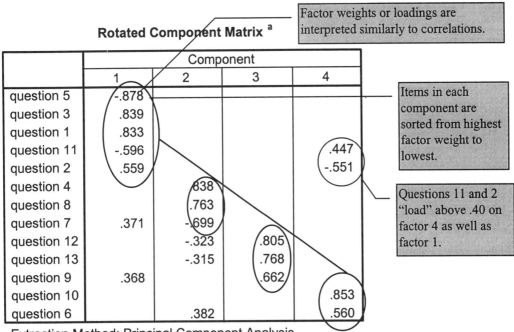

Rotated Component Matrix [a]

	Component			
	1	2	3	4
question 5	-.878			
question 3	.839			
question 1	.833			
question 11	-.596			.447
question 2	.559			-.551
question 4		838		
question 8		.763		
question 7	.371	-699		
question 12		-.323	.805	
question 13		-.315	.768	
question 9	.368		.662	
question 10				.853
question 6		.382		.560

Factor weights or loadings are interpreted similarly to correlations.

Items in each component are sorted from highest factor weight to lowest.

Questions 11 and 2 "load" above .40 on factor 4 as well as factor 1.

Extraction Method: Principal Component Analysis.
Rotation Method: Varimax with Kaiser Normalization.

a. Rotation converged in 7 iterations.

Component Transformation Matrix

Component	1	2	3	4
1	.711	-.540	.343	-.292
2	-.495	-.410	.681	.352
3	.484	.193	.028	.853
4	.123	.709	.647	-.251

Extraction Method: Principal Component Analysis.
Rotation Method: Varimax with Kaiser Normalization.

Output 10.2: Factor Analysis for Math Attitude Questions Limited to Three Factors

Syntax for factor analysis of math attitude questions limited to three factors

```
FACTOR
  /VARIABLES q01 q02 q03 q04 q05 q06 q07 q08 q09 q10 q11 q12 q13  /MISSING
  LISTWISE /ANALYSIS q01 q02 q03 q04 q05 q06 q07 q08 q09 q10 q11 q12 q13
  /PRINT INITIAL ROTATION
  /FORMAT SORT BLANK(.3)
  /CRITERIA FACTORS(3) ITERATE(25)
  /EXTRACTION PC
  /CRITERIA ITERATE(25)
  /ROTATION VARIMAX
  /METHOD=CORRELATION .
```

Factor Analysis

Communalities

	Initial
question 1	1.000
question 2	1.000
question 3	1.000
question 4	1.000
question 5	1.000
question 6	1.000
question 7	1.000
question 8	1.000
question 9	1.000
question 10	1.000
question 11	1.000
question 12	1.000
question 13	1.000

Extraction Method:
Principal Component
Analysis.

Total Variance Explained

Component	Initial Eigenvalues			Rotation Sums of Squared Loadings		
	Total	% of Variance	Cumulative %	Total	% of Variance	Cumulative %
1	4.805	36.963	36.963	3.289	25.300	25.300
2	1.826	14.049	51.011	2.843	21.869	47.169
3	1.333	10.255	61.267	1.833	14.097	61.267
4	1.133	8.718	69.985			
5	.883	6.791	76.776			
6	.666	5.120	81.895			
7	.541	4.159	86.055			
8	.453	3.481	89.536			
9	.380	2.920	92.456			
10	.299	2.299	94.755			
11	.285	2.193	96.948			
12	.241	1.853	98.801			
13	.156	1.199	100.000			

Extraction Method: Principal Component Analysis.

Component Matrix[a]

a. 3 components extracted.

Rotated Component Matrix^a

	Component		
	1	2	3
question 5	-.878		
question 1	.851		
question 3	.845		
question 11	-.598		.484
question 12		.815	
question 13		.786	
question 8		-.682	
question 4		-.651	
question 7	.421	.611	
question 9	.303	.397	
question 10			.807
question 6			.651
question 2	.534		-.537

Extraction Method: Principal Component Analysis.
Rotation Method: Varimax with Kaiser Normalization

a. Rotation converged in 5 iterations.

Component Transformation Matrix

Component	1	2	3
1	.729	.585	-.356
2	-.477	.806	.350
3	.492	-.086	.867

Extraction Method: Principal Component Analysis.
Rotation Method: Varimax with Kaiser Normalization.

Output 10.3: Factor Analysis for Achievement Scores

Syntax for factor analysis of achievement scores

```
FACTOR
  /VARIABLES mathach visual mosaic grades   /MISSING LISTWISE /ANALYSIS
  mathach visual mosaic grades
  /PRINT UNIVARIATE INITIAL CORRELATION DET KMO EXTRACTION ROTATION
  /PLOT ROTATION
  /CRITERIA MINEIGEN(1) ITERATE(25)
  /EXTRACTION PC
  /CRITERIA ITERATE(25)
  /ROTATION VARIMAX
  /METHOD=CORRELATION .
```

Interpret Output 10.3

Compare Output 10.3 to your output and syntax in Output 10.1. Note that in addition to the tables in Output 10.1 you have: a) a table of descriptive statistics for each variable; it also provides the listwise *N* which you would not know otherwise; b) a table of commonalties; c) a component matrix, which is unrotated and is used for purposes beyond the scope of this book;

and d) plots of the factor loadings. Note that the default setting we used does not sort the variables by factors and does not suppress low loadings in the **rotated factor matrix**. Thus, you have to organize the table yourself; i.e., *mathach, grades,* and *visual* in that order are factor 1, and *mosaic* is factor 2.

Factor Analysis

Descriptive Statistics

	Mean	Std. Deviation	Analysis N
math achievement	12.5645	6.6703	75
visualization score	5.2433	3.9120	75
mosaic, pattern test	27.413	9.574	75
grades in h.s.	5.68	1.57	75

Correlation Matrixª

		math achievement	visualization score	mosaic, pattern test	grades in h.s.
Correlation	math achievement	1.000	.423	.213	.504
	visualization score	.423	1.000	.030	.127
	mosaic, pattern test	.213	.030	1.000	-.012
	grades in h.s.	.504	.127	-.012	1.000

a. Determinant = .562

KMO and Bartlett's Test

Kaiser-Meyer-Olkin Measure of Sampling Adequacy.		.468
Bartlett's Test of Sphericity	Approx. Chi-Square	41.414
	df	6
	Sig.	.000

This is not adequate because there is only one score (mosaic) to represent the second component. You should have several for each component.

Communalities

	Initial	Extraction
math achievement	1.000	.801
visualization score	1.000	.401
mosaic, pattern test	1.000	.959
grades in h.s.	1.000	.603

Extraction Method: Principal Component Analysis.

Total Variance Explained

Component	Initial Eigenvalues			Extraction Sums of Squared Loadings			Rotation Sums of Squared Loadings		
	Total	% of Variance	Cumulative %	Total	% of Variance	Cumulative %	Total	% of Variance	Cumulative %
1	1.755	43.873	43.873	1.755	43.873	43.873	1.717	42.928	42.928
2	1.009	25.237	69.110	1.009	25.237	69.110	1.047	26.183	69.110
3	.872	21.795	90.906						
4	.364	9.094	100.000						

Extraction Method: Principal Component Analysis.

Component Matrix [a]

	Component	
	1	2
math achievement	.894	3.309E-02
visualization score	.629	-6.96E-02
mosaic, pattern test	.267	.943
grades in h.s.	.699	-.339

Extraction Method: Principal Component Analysis.

a. 2 components extracted.

Rotated Component Matrix [a]

	Component	
	1	2
math achievement	.864	.234
visualization score	.629	7.393E-02
mosaic, pattern test	4.740E-02	.978
grades in h.s.	.757	-.173

Extraction Method: Principal Component Analysis.
Rotation Method: Varimax with Kaiser Normalization.

a. Rotation converged in 3 iterations.

Refer to the questions at the end of the assignment.

Component Transformation Matrix

Component	1	2
1	.974	.225
2	-.225	.974

Extraction Method: Principal Component Analysis.
Rotation Method: Varimax with Kaiser Normalization.

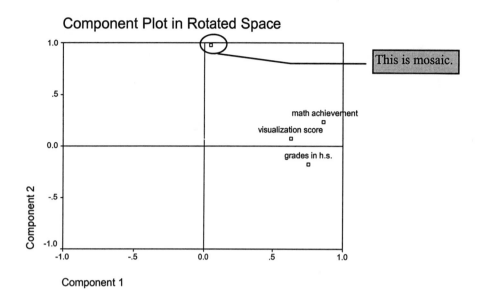

Component Plot in Rotated Space

CHAPTER 11

Several Measures of Reliability

This assignment illustrates several of the methods for computing instrument reliability.

Internal consistency reliability. In this assignment we will compute the most commonly used type of internal consistency reliability, Cronbach's coefficient **alpha**. This measure determines the consistency of a <u>multiple item scale</u>. Note that alpha is only appropriate when you have several items that are summed to make a composite score or summated scale. It is based on the mean or average correlation of each item in the scale with every other item. Alpha is widely used in the social science literature, because it provides a measure of reliability which can be obtained from one testing session or one administration of a questionnaire.

Reliability for one score/measure. Problem 3 computes a correlation coefficient to check the reliability of the visualization score. Three of the four types of reliability can be illustrated by this correlation. If *visual2* was each participant's score from retaking the test a month or so after they initially took it, then the correlation would be a measure of *test-retest reliability*. If *visual2* was a score on an alternative/parallel or equivalent version of the visualization test, then this would be a measure of *equivalent forms reliability*. If the visualization tests were scored by two different raters, the correlation could be an index of *interrater reliability*. This type of reliability is needed when behaviors or answers to questions are not easily scored objectively (e.g., when there are open-ended questions or ratings based on observations).

Reliability for nominal variables. There are several methods of computing interrater or interobserver reliability. Above, we mentioned using a correlation coefficient. Cohen's **kappa** is used to assess interobserver agreement when the data are nominal categories. Imagine that the father's and mother's education variables were based on school records. Now, new variables, *faedr2 and maedr2,* were obtained by asking 20 students to indicate the education of their parents. The question is, how reliable are the parent education classifications?

Problems/Research Questions

1. What is the internal consistency reliability of the conceptual math attitude scale of motivation. Note that you do not actually use the computed motivation scale score. The **Reliability** program uses the individual items to create the scales temporarily.

2. What is the internal consistency reliability of the competence scale?

3. What is the internal consistency reliability of the pleasure scale?

4. What is the internal consistency reliability when the motivation scale is modified as suggested by the factor analysis in Output 10.2?

5. What is the internal consistency of the modified competence scale?

6. What is the reliability of the visualization score? This is an example of any of the three types of reliability mentioned in the third paragraph of the introduction to this lab.

7. You will enter a second father's and mother's education score for the first 20 participants. What is the interrater reliability of the father's education codes?

8. What is the interrater reliability of the mother's education codes?

Lab Assignment G

Logon and Get Data

- First logon and get **hsbdataF**.

Problem 1: Internal Consistency Reliability of the Motivation Math Attitude Scale

- Now let's do reliability analysis for the motivation scale. Click on **Statistics => Scale => Reliability Analysis**. You should get a dialog box like Fig. 11.1.
- Now move the variables *q01, q04r, q07, q08r, q12,* and *q 13* (motivation questions) to the **Items** box. Be sure to use *q04r* and *q08r* (not *q04* and *q08*).
- Click on the **List item labels** box. Be sure the **Model** is **Alpha** (refer to Fig. 11.1).

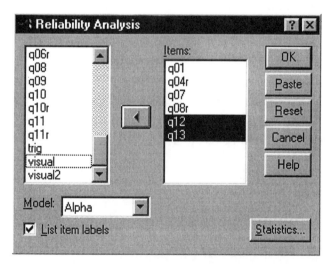

Fig. 11.1. Reliability analysis.

- Click on **Statistics** in the **Reliability Analysis** dialog box and you will see something similar to Fig. 11.2.
- Check the following items: **Item, Scale, Scale if item deleted** (under **Descriptives**), **Correlations** (under **Inter-Item**), **Means,** and **Correlations** (under **Summaries**).
- Click on **Continue** then **OK**. Compare your syntax and output to Output 11.1.

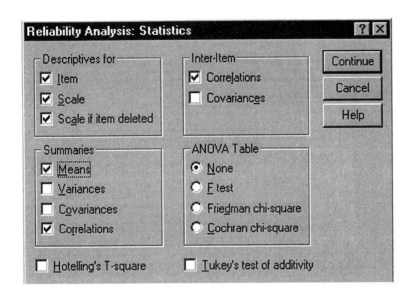

Fig. 11.2. Reliability analysis: Statistics.

Problems 2 and 3: Cronbach Alphas for the Competence and Pleasure Math Attitude Scales

Let's repeat the same steps as before except check the reliability of the following scales and then compare your output to 11.2 and 11.3.

- competence scale *q03, q05r, q09, q11r*
- pleasure scale *q02, q06r, q10r*

Problems 4 and 5: Cronbach Alphas for the Modified Scales

Let's redo the alphas for the motivation and competence scales. To save space click off **Means** and **Correlations** under **Summaries** in the **Statistics** window.

- modified motivation scale *q04r, q07, q08r, q12*, and *q13*
- modified competenc*e* scale *q01, q03, q05r, q11r*

Problem 6: Reliability of One Score Using Correlation

Let's do a Pearson *r* for *visual* and *visual2*.
- Click on **Statistics** => **Correlate** => **Bivariate**.
- Move variables *visual* and *visual2* into the variable box (see Fig. 9.1 and 9.2 for help).
- *Don't* select **flag significant correlations** because reliability coefficients should always be significant. They should also be positive and greater than .70.
- Click on **Options.**
- Click on **Means and Standard deviations.**
- Click on **Continue** and **OK**. Do your syntax and output look like Output 11.6?

Problem 7: Checking Agreement/Reliability With Categorical Data Using Kappa

When we have two categorical variables with the *same* values (usually two raters' observations or scores using the same codes), you can compute Cohen's kappa to check the reliability or agreement between the measures. For Problems 7 and 8 we must enter the data for *faedr2* and *maedr2,* which are as follows for the first 20 subjects.

| *faedr2*: | 3, 1, 1, 2, , 1, 3, 2, 2, , 1, 3, 2, 2, 1, , 1, 3, 1, 3 | blanks= missing |
| *maedr2*: | 3, 1, 1, 1, 1, 1, 2, 2, 1, 1, 1, 3, 1, 1, 1, 1, 1, 3, 1, 1 | |

If you don't remember how to enter data, refer to Assignment A in chapter 4. *Note:* Don't forget to label the new variables, "father's education by student" and "mother's education by student" and their values, 1 = hs grad or less, 2 = some college, 3= bs or more. Refer to chapter 4, Assignment A if you need help with making labels.

Now, to figure the kappa:
- Click on **Statistics** => **Summarize** => **Crosstabs**.
- Move *faedr* to the **Rows** box and *faedr2* to the **Columns** box.
- Click on **Kappa** in the **statistics** dialog box.
- As usual, click on **Continue** and go back to the Crosstabs dialog window.
- Then click on **Cells** and request the **Observed** cell counts and **Total** under **percentages**.
- Click on **Continue** and then **OK**. Compare your syntax and output to Output 11.7.

Problem 8: Checking Agreement/Reliability With Kappa

Try another similar exercise yourself.
- This time we use *maedr* and *maedr2*.
- Compare your syntax and output to Output 11.8.

Print, Save, and Exit

- **Print** assignment as required or desired.
- Save your data as **hsbdataG** (Use **File** => **Save As**).
- Save your SPSS log as **hsblogG**.
- **Exit** SPSS.

Interpretation Questions

1. Using Output 11.1 to 11.5, make a table indicating the mean interitem correlation and the alpha coefficient for each of the scales. Indicate whether these alphas high or low.

2. For the competence scale what item has the *lowest* corrected item-total correlation? What would be the alpha if that item was deleted from the scale?

3. Using Output 11.6: a) What is the reliability coefficient for the visualization score? b) Is it acceptable? c) If this were a measure of interrater reliability, what would be the procedure for measuring *visual* and *visual2*?

4. From Output 11.8, what is the kappa coefficient? What does it mean?

Outputs and Interpretations

```
GET
  FILE='A:\hsbdataF.sav'.
EXECUTE .
```

Output 11.1: Reliability of the Math Attitude Scale for Motivation

Syntax for the reliability of math attitude scale-motivation

```
RELIABILITY
  /VARIABLES=q01 q04r q07 q08r q12 q13
  /FORMAT=LABELS
  /SCALE(ALPHA)=ALL/MODEL=ALPHA
  /STATISTICS=DESCRIPTIVE SCALE CORR
  /SUMMARY=TOTAL MEANS CORR .
```

Interpretation of Output 11.1

The first section lists the items (*q01*, etc.) that you requested be included in this scale and their labels. It was produced by selecting **List items labels** in Fig. 11.1. Next is a table of descriptive statistics for each item, produced by checking **Item** in Fig. 11.2. The third table is a matrix showing the **interitem correlations** of every item in the scale with every other item, and it shows the number of participants with no missing data on these variables (73). Next, there are three one-line tables providing summary descriptive statistics for: a) the **scale** (sum of 6 motivation items), b) the **item means**, produced under summaries, and c) **correlations,** under summaries. The latter two tell you, for example, the average, minimum, and maximum of the item means and of the interitem correlations.

The final table, which we think is the most important, is produced by the **scale if item deleted** check under descriptive. This table, labeled Item-total Statistics, provides five pieces of information for each item in the scale. The two we find most useful are the corrected Item-total correlation and the alpha if item deleted. The former is the correlation of each specific item with the sum/total of the other items in the scales. If this correlation is moderate or high, .40 or above, the item is probably at least moderately correlated with most of the other items and will make a good component of this summated rating scale. Items with lower item-total correlations do not fit into this scale as well, psychometrically. If the item-total correlation is negative or very low, less than .20, it is wise to examine the item for wording problems and conceptual fit. You may want to modify or delete such items. You can tell from the last column what the alpha would be if you deleted an item. Compare this to the alpha for the scale with all 6 items included, which is given at the bottom of the output. Deleting a poor item will usually make the alpha go up, but will make only a small difference in the alpha, unless the scale has only a few items (e.g., less than 5) because alpha is based on the number of items as well as their average intercorrelations.

In general, you will use the unstandardized **alpha**, unless the items in the scale have quite different means and standard deviations. For example, if we were to make a summated scale from *mathach*, *grades,* and *visual,* as suggested by the factor analysis in Output 6.3, we would use the standardized alpha. As with other reliability coefficients, alpha should be above .70; however, it is common to see journal articles where one or more scales have somewhat lower alphas, e.g., in the .60-.69 range, especially if these are only a handful of items in a scale. A very high alpha (e.g., greater than .90) probably means that the items are repetitious or that you have more items in the scale than are really necessary for a reliable measure of the concept.

```
****** Method 2 (covariance matrix) will be used for this analysis ******
    R E L I A B I L I T Y   A N A L Y S I S   -   S C A L E   (A L P H A)

    1.    Q01        question 1
    2.    Q04R       Q4 reversed
    3.    Q07        question 7
    4.    Q08R       Q 8 reversed
    5.    Q12        question 12
    6.    Q13        question 13
```

```
                        Mean         Std Dev        Cases

    1.    Q01          2.9589          .9345         73.0
    2.    Q04R         2.8219          .9181         73.0
    3.    Q07          2.7534         1.0643         73.0
    4.    Q08R         3.0548          .9112         73.0
    5.    Q12          2.9863          .8248         73.0
    6.    Q13          2.6712          .8003         73.0
```

List of items requested and their labels.

Descriptive statistics for each item.

Interitem correlations.

```
              Correlation Matrix

              Q01         Q04R         Q07         Q08R         Q12

Q01         1.0000
Q04R         .2504      1.0000
Q07          .4644       .5514      1.0000
Q08R         .2963       .5763       .5870      1.0000
Q12          .1794       .3819       .3441       .3891      1.0000
Q13          .1674       .3162       .3601       .3108       .6033
```

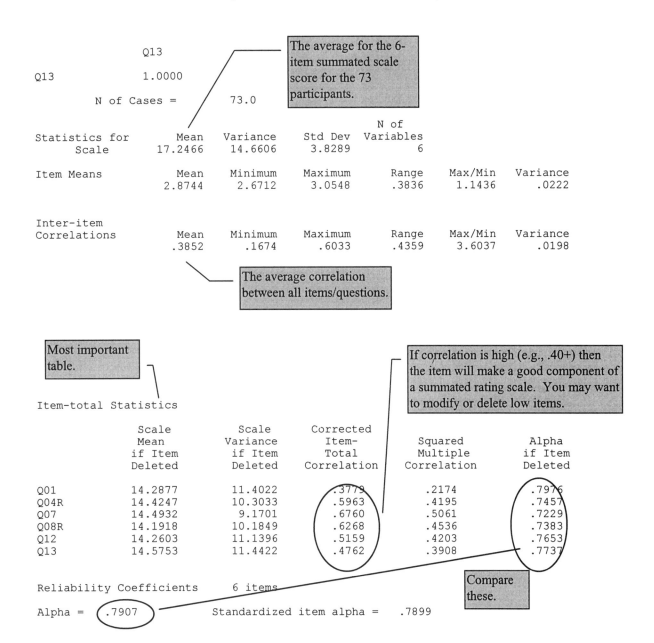

```
                  Q13

Q13              1.0000

        N of Cases =              73.0
```

The average for the 6-item summated scale score for the 73 participants.

```
                                                  N of
Statistics for      Mean    Variance    Std Dev  Variables
     Scale         17.2466   14.6606     3.8289      6

Item Means          Mean    Minimum    Maximum    Range    Max/Min    Variance
                   2.8744    2.6712     3.0548    .3836     1.1436      .0222


Inter-item
Correlations        Mean    Minimum    Maximum    Range    Max/Min    Variance
                   .3852     .1674      .6033    .4359     3.6037      .0198
```

The average correlation between all items/questions.

Most important table.

If correlation is high (e.g., .40+) then the item will make a good component of a summated rating scale. You may want to modify or delete low items.

```
Item-total Statistics

                 Scale         Scale      Corrected
                 Mean          Variance    Item-       Squared      Alpha
                 if Item       if Item     Total       Multiple     if Item
                 Deleted       Deleted    Correlation  Correlation  Deleted

Q01             14.2877       11.4022       .3779       .2174        .7976
Q04R            14.4247       10.3033       .5963       .4195        .7457
Q07             14.4932        9.1701       .6760       .5061        .7229
Q08R            14.1918       10.1849       .6268       .4536        .7383
Q12             14.2603       11.1396       .5159       .4203        .7653
Q13             14.5753       11.4422       .4762       .3908        .7737
```

Compare these.

```
Reliability Coefficients        6 items

Alpha =     .7907          Standardized item alpha =    .7899
```

Output 11.2: Reliability of the Math Attitude Scale for Competence

Syntax for the reliability for competence scale

```
RELIABILITY
  /VARIABLES=q03 q05r q09 q11r
  /FORMAT=LABELS
  /SCALE(ALPHA)=ALL/MODEL=ALPHA
  /STATISTICS=DESCRIPTIVE SCALE CORR
  /SUMMARY=TOTAL MEANS CORR .
```

****** Method 2 (covariance matrix) will be used for this analysis ******

R E L I A B I L I T Y   A N A L Y S I S   -   S C A L E   (A L P H A)

1.   Q03   question 3
2.   Q05R   Q05 reversed
3.   Q09   question 9
4.   Q11R   Q 11 reversed

		Mean	Std Dev	Cases
1.	Q03	2.8219	.9028	73.0
2.	Q05R	3.4110	.9404	73.0
3.	Q09	3.3151	.7615	73.0
4.	Q11R	3.6301	.7547	73.0

Correlation Matrix

	Q03	Q05R	Q09	Q11R
Q03	1.0000			
Q05R	.7418	1.0000		
Q09	.3252	.3403	1.0000	
Q11R	.5135	.6085	.3989	1.0000

N of Cases =   73.0

Statistics for Scale	Mean	Variance	Std Dev	N of Variables
	13.1781	7.0651	2.6580	4

Item Means	Mean	Minimum	Maximum	Range	Max/Min	Variance
	3.2945	2.8219	3.6301	.8082	1.2864	.1167

Inter-item Correlations	Mean	Minimum	Maximum	Range	Max/Min	Variance
	.4880	.3252	.7418	.4166	2.2812	.0247

Item-total Statistics

	Scale Mean if Item Deleted	Scale Variance if Item Deleted	Corrected Item-Total Correlation	Squared Multiple Correlation	Alpha if Item Deleted
Q03	10.3562	3.8436	.6798	.5599	.7063
Q05R	9.7671	3.5700	.7347	.6215	.6745
Q09	9.8630	5.0921	.4053	.1808	.8316
Q11R	9.5479	4.4734	.6334	.4167	.7357

Reliability Coefficients   4 items

Alpha =   .7957   Standardized item alpha =   .7922

132

Output 11.3: Reliability of the Math Attitude Scale for Pleasure

Syntax for the reliability of pleasure scale

```
RELIABILITY
  /VARIABLES=q02 q06r q10r
  /FORMAT=LABELS
  /SCALE(ALPHA)=ALL/MODEL=ALPHA
  /STATISTICS=DESCRIPTIVE SCALE CORR
  /SUMMARY=TOTAL MEANS CORR .
```

****** Method 2 (covariance matrix) will be used for this analysis ******

R E L I A B I L I T Y   A N A L Y S I S   -   S C A L E   (A L P H A)

1.	Q02	question 2
2.	Q06R	Q06 reversed
3.	Q10R	Q10 reversed

	Mean	Std Dev	Cases	
1.	Q02	3.5200	.9058	75.0
2.	Q06R	2.5733	.9750	75.0
3.	Q10R	3.5867	.7369	75.0

Correlation Matrix

	Q02	Q06R	Q10R
Q02	1.0000		
Q06R	.2852	1.0000	
Q10R	.3466	.2026	1.0000

N of Cases =   75.0

	Mean	Variance	Std Dev	N of Variables
Statistics for Scale	9.6800	3.5719	1.8899	3

	Mean	Minimum	Maximum	Range	Max/Min	Variance
Item Means	3.2267	2.5733	3.5867	1.0133	1.3938	.3212

	Mean	Minimum	Maximum	Range	Max/Min	Variance
Inter-item Correlations	.2781	.2026	.3466	.1440	1.7104	.0042

Item-total Statistics

	Scale Mean if Item Deleted	Scale Variance if Item Deleted	Corrected Item-Total Correlation	Squared Multiple Correlation	Alpha if Item Deleted
Q02	6.1600	1.7849	.3993	.1683	.3263
Q06R	7.1067	1.8263	.3017	.0936	.5067
Q10R	6.0933	2.2750	.3391	.1318	.4429

Reliability Coefficients   3 items

Alpha =   .5281   Standardized item alpha =   .5362

133

Output 11.4: Alpha Reliability of the Modified Math Attitude Scale for Motivation

Syntax for the modified motivation scale reliability

```
RELIABILITY
  /VARIABLES=q04r q07 q08r q12 q13
  /FORMAT=NOLABELS
  /SCALE(ALPHA)=ALL/MODEL=ALPHA
  /STATISTICS=SCALE
  /SUMMARY=TOTAL CORR .
```

 ****** Method 2 (covariance matrix) will be used for this analysis ******

      R E L I A B I L I T Y   A N A L Y S I S   -   S C A L E   (A L P H A)

         N of Cases =   74.0

                                              N of
Statistics for   Mean   Variance   Std Dev Variables
      Scale   14.3243   11.3454   3.3683   5

Inter-item
Correlations   Mean   Minimum   Maximum   Range   Max/Min   Variance
                 .4424   .3139   .6027   .2887   1.9198   .0140

Item-total Statistics

	Scale Mean if Item Deleted	Scale Variance if Item Deleted	Corrected Item-Total Correlation	Squared Multiple Correlation	Alpha if Item Deleted
Q04R	11.4865	7.4039	.6161	.4226	.7475
Q07	11.5676	6.8241	.6160	.4288	.7501
Q08R	11.2568	7.3715	.6349	.4571	.7415
Q12	11.3378	8.1446	.5411	.4163	.7714
Q13	11.6486	8.3954	.5025	.3905	.7822

Reliability Coefficients   5 items

Alpha =   .7979   Standardized item alpha =   .7987

Output 11.5: Alpha Reliability for Modified Math Attitude Scale for Competence

Syntax for the modified competence scale reliability

```
RELIABILITY
  /VARIABLES=q01 q03 q05r q11r
  /FORMAT=NOLABELS
  /SCALE(ALPHA)=ALL/MODEL=ALPHA
  /STATISTICS=SCALE
  /SUMMARY=TOTAL CORR .
```

```
****** Method 2 (covariance matrix) will be used for this analysis ******
  R E L I A B I L I T Y   A N A L Y S I S   -   S C A L E   (A L P H A)

     N of Cases =        73.0

                                              N of
Statistics for    Mean    Variance   Std Dev  Variables
`     Scale      12.7808   8.9791    2.9965      4

Inter-item
Correlations      Mean    Minimum   Maximum    Range    Max/Min   Variance
                  .5923    .4114     .7607     .3493     1.8491    .0147


Item-total Statistics

             Scale        Scale     Corrected
             Mean         Variance  Item-       Squared    Alpha
             if Item      if Item   Total       Multiple   if Item
             Deleted      Deleted   Correlation Correlation Deleted

Q01          9.8219       5.1206     .7058       .5886      .8136
Q03          9.9589       5.2066     .7178       .5266      .8082
Q05R         9.4110       4.5510     .8306       .7046      .7558
Q11R         9.1507       6.2964     .5579       .3472      .8694


Reliability Coefficients     4 items

Alpha =    .8557        Standardized item alpha =    .8532
```

Output 11.6: Reliability of the Visualization Score

Syntax for the correlation of visual and visual2

```
CORRELATIONS
  /VARIABLES=visual visual2
  /PRINT=TWOTAIL SIG
  /STATISTICS DESCRIPTIVES
  /MISSING=PAIRWISE .
```

Descriptive Statistics

	Mean	Std. Deviation	N
visualization score	5.2433	3.9120	75
Visualization retest	4.47	2.93	75

Correlations

		visualization score	Visualization retest
Pearson Correlation	visualization score	1.000	.886
	Visualization retest	.886	1.000
Sig. (2-tailed)	visualization score		.000
	Visualization retest	.000	
N	visualization score	75	75
	Visualization retest	75	75

Correlation between the first and second visualization test. It should be high, not just significant.

75 participants have both visualization scores.

Output 11.7: Checking Agreement/Reliability of Categorical Data With Kappa

Syntax for labeling mother's and father's education by student

```
FORMATS faedr2 (F8).
VARIABLE LABELS faedr2 "Father's ed by student".
VALUE LABELS faedr2
 1.00000000000000 "hs grad or less"
 2.00000000000000 "some college"
 3.00000000000000 "BS or more"
 .
FORMATS maedr2 (F8).
VARIABLE LABELS var00001 "Mother's ed by student".
VALUE LABELS maedr2
 1.00000000000000 "hs grad or less"
 2.00000000000000 "some college"
 3.00000000000000 "BS or more"
```

Syntax for checking agreement/reliability between faedr and faedr2

```
CROSSTABS
  /TABLES=faedr  BY faedr2
  /FORMAT= AVALUE TABLES
  /STATISTIC=KAPPA
  /CELLS= COUNT EXPECTED TOTAL .
```

Interpretation of Output 11.7

Because **kappa** is a measure of reliability, it usually should be .70 or greater. It is not enough to be significantly greater than zero. Note that in 14 out of 17 cases with complete data, the student listed the same father's education as in the school records, but there were discrepancies for three students. Note that in three cases, the student did not know his or her father's education.

Father's ed rev * Father's ed by student Crosstabulation

Disagreements.

			Father's ed by student			
			hs grad or less	some college	BS or more	Total
Father's ed rev	hs grad or less	Count	7	3	0	10
		Expected Count	4.1	2.9	2.9	10.0
		% of Total	41.2%	17.6%	.0%	58.8%
	some college	Count	0	2	0	2
		Expected Count	.8	.6	.6	2.0
		% of Total	.0%	11.8%	.0%	11.8%
	BS or more	Count	0	0	5	5
		Expected Count	2.1	1.5	1.5	5.0
		% of Total	.0%	.0%	29.4%	29.4%
Total		Count	7	5	5	17
		Expected Count	7.0	5.0	5.0	17.0
		% of Total	41.2%	29.4%	29.4%	100.0%

Agreements between school records and student's memory.

Case Processing Summary

	Cases					
	Valid		Missing		Total	
	N	Percent	N	Percent	N	Percent
Father's ed rev * Father's ed by student	17	22.7%	58	77.3%	75	100.0%

Symmetric Measures

		Value	Asymp. Std. Error[a]	Approx. T[b]	Approx. Sig.
Measure of Agreement	Kappa	.723	.137	4.376	.000
N of Valid Cases		17			

a. Not assuming the null hypothesis.

b. Using the asymptotic standard error assuming the null hypothesis.

As a measure of reliability, kappa should be high (usually > .70) not just statistically significant.

Output 11.8: Crosstabs and Cohen's Kappa

Syntax for Crosstabs and Kappa for maedr and maedr2

```
CROSSTABS
  /TABLES=maedr  BY maedr2
  /FORMAT= AVALUE TABLES
  /STATISTIC=KAPPA
  /CELLS= COUNT EXPECTED TOTAL .
```

Case Processing Summary

	Cases					
	Valid		Missing		Total	
	N	Percent	N	Percent	N	Percent
Mother's ed rev * Mother's ed by student	20	26.7%	55	73.3%	75	100.0%

Mother's ed rev * Mother's ed by student Crosstabulation

			Mother's ed by student			
			hs grad or less	some college	BS or more	Total
Mother's ed rev	hs grad or less	Count	14	1	0	15
		Expected Count	11.3	1.5	2.3	15.0
		% of Total	70.0%	5.0%	.0%	75.0%
	some college	Count	1	1	1	3
		Expected Count	2.3	.3	.5	3.0
		% of Total	5.0%	5.0%	5.0%	15.0%
	BS or more	Count	0	0	2	2
		Expected Count	1.5	.2	.3	2.0
		% of Total	.0%	.0%	10.0%	10.0%
Total		Count	15	2	3	20
		Expected Count	15.0	2.0	3.0	20.0
		% of Total	75.0%	10.0%	15.0%	100%

Symmetric Measures

		Value	Asymp. Std. Error[a]	Approx. T[b]	Approx. Sig.
Measure of Agreement	Kappa	.632	.177	3.790	.000
N of Valid Cases		20			

a. Not assuming the null hypothesis.

b. Using the asymptotic standard error assuming the null hypothesis.

CHAPTER 12

Multiple Regression

Multiple linear regression is one of several complex statistical methods based on the associational approach as discussed in chapter 1. Already, we have done assignments using two other complex associational methods, factor analysis and Cronbach's alpha, which, like multiple regression, are based on a correlation matrix of all the variables to be considered in a problem. In addition to multiple regression, two other complex associational analyses, logistic regression and discriminant analysis, will be computed in the next assignment. Like multiple regression, logistic and discriminant have the general purpose of predicting a dependent or criterion variable from *several* independent or predictor variables. As you can tell from examining Table 7.4, these three techniques, for predicting one outcome measure from several independent variables, vary in the scale and type of independent variable and/or type of outcome variable.

For multiple linear regression, the *dependent* or outcome variable should be an interval level variable which is normally distributed in the population from which it is drawn. The *independent* variables should be mostly interval level variables, but multiple regression can also have dichotomous independent variables, which are called dummy variables. Dummy variables are often nominal categories which have been given numerical codes, usually 1 and 0. The 0 stands for whatever the 1 is not, and is thus said to be "dumb" or silent. Thus, when we use gender, for instance, as a dummy variable in multiple regression we're really coding it as 1 = male and 0 = not male (i.e., female). This gets complex when there are more than two nominal categories. For example, if we were to use the ethnic group variable, we would have to code it into several dummy variables such as Euro-American and not Euro-American, African-American and not African-American, etc.

To reiterate, the purpose of multiple regression is to predict an interval scale dependent variable from a combination of several interval scale and/or dichotomous independent/predictor variables. In the following assignment, we will see if math achievement can be predicted better from a combination of several of our other variables such as the motivation attitude scores, grades in high school, and mother's and father's education. In Problems 1, 2, and 3, we will use the same combination of variables but run the multiple regression using three alternate methods provided by SPSS. In Problem 1, we will assume that all seven of the predictor variables are important and that we want to see what is the highest possible multiple correlation of these variables. For this purpose, we will use the method that SPSS calls **Enter** which tells the computer to consider all the variables at the same time.

In Problem 2, we will use a common method for computing multiple regression, **Stepwise**, which is, however, not popular with statisticians. In this case, the computer selects the variable that has the highest bivariate correlation with the outcome variable and enters it into the equation. Then it examines the semipartial correlations (which removes the correlation with the first predictor variable) and enters the predictor variable with the highest semipartial correlation. After each step variables already entered are examined to see if they still make a statistically significant contribution. If not, they are removed. Then the procedure continues until the remaining variables no longer make a significant additional contribution to the multiple correlation (R).

In Problem 3, we will use the hierarchical approach which enters variables in blocks or groups to see if the second group of variables adds anything to the prediction produced by the first block. In our example, we will enter gender first and then see if any of the other variables make an additional contribution. This method is intended to control for or eliminate the effects of gender on the prediction.

In Problem 4, we will combine/average two variables (mother's and father's education) that were quite highly correlated and were, thus, causing multicollinearity. This made our interpretation of Problems 1 and 2 more difficult.

We hope that by using these several methods you will be able to see that the method one uses to compute multiple regression influences the results. It may be necessary to try several different methods before being able to understand the best way to predict, for example, math achievement from these other seven variables in the hsbdata set.

Problems/Research Questions

1. How well can you predict math achievement from a combination of seven variables: motivation, competence, pleasure, grades in high school, father's and mother's education revised, and gender? In this problem the computer will enter/consider all the variables at the same time. Also, we will ask which of these seven predictors contribute significantly to the multiple correlation/regression.

2. Is there a combination of two or more of the above seven independent variables that predict math achievement better than any one alone? In this problem the computer will consider the independent contribution of the variables using the stepwise method.

3. If we control for gender differences in math achievement, do any of the other variables add anything significant to the prediction over and above what gender contributes?

4. Compute a new variable, parent's education, by combining/averaging mother's and father's (revised) education scores. Then rerun Problem 1 using the new parent's education variable (*paredr*) instead of *faedr* and *maedr*, and do not use the competence or pleasure scales.

Lab Assignment H

Logon and Get Data

*   Get your **hsbdataG** data file.

Problem 1: Using Multiple Linear Multiple Regression, Method = Enter

Let's predict *mathach* from the motivation, competence, and pleasure scales, grades in high school, father's education revised, mother's education revised, and gender.

- Click on the following: **Statistics => Regression => Linear**.
- Select *mathach* and click it over to the **Dependent** box (Dependent variable).
- Next select the variables *motivatn, competnc, pleasure, grades, faedr, maedr,* and *gend* and click them over to the **Independent(s)** box (Independent variables).
- Under **Method**, select **Enter**.
- Click on **Statistics,** click on **Estimates** (under **Regression coefficients**), and click on **Descriptives** and **Model fit.**
- Click on **Continue**.
- Click on **OK**.

Refer to Figs. 12.1 and 12.2 for assistance. Compare your output and syntax to Output 12.1.

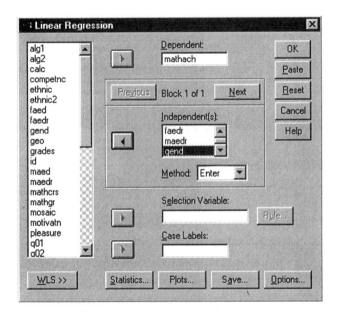

Fig. 12.1. Linear regression.

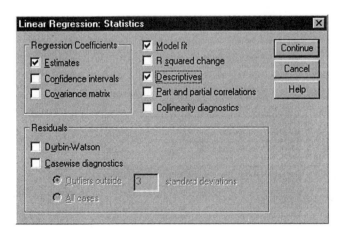

Fig. 12.2. Linear regression: Statistics.

Problem 2: Multiple Linear Regression, Method = Stepwise

Now try the same procedure yourself to predict math achievement scores from motivation, competence, pleasure, grades, father's education revised, mother's education revised, and gender. However, this time use the **Method = Stepwise** (not **Enter**) and click *off* **Descriptives** in the **Statistics** dialog box. Compare your output and syntax to Output 12.2.

Problem 3: Hierarchical Multiple Linear Regression Using Blocks

Now we will use the same variables to predict math achievement but do it in blocks.
- Click on the following: **Statistics => Regression => Linear**.
- Select *mathach* and click it over to the **Dependent** box (Dependent variable).
- Next, select *gend* and move it to the over to the **Independent(s)** box (Independent variables).
- Select **Enter** as your **method**.
- Click on **Next** beside **Block 1 of 1** (see Fig. 12.1). You will notice it changes to **Block 2 of 2**.
- Then move *motivatn, competnc, pleasure, grades, faedr,* and *maedr* to the **Independent(s)** box (Independent variables).
- Under **Method**, select **Enter**.
- The Statistics dialog box will be the same as in Problem 2. Compare your output and syntax to Output 12.3.

Problem 4: Compute Average Parent's Education and Rerun Regression

Now, on your own, compute a new variable, parent's education (*paedr*), by combining/averaging mother's and father's (revised) education scores. We will do this combination because it makes conceptual sense and because these two variables are quite highly related (r= .62). Motivation, competence, and pleasure are also moderately highly related (r= .52, .31, .46), but we decided not to combine them. Because this conceptual distinction was important for us and because motivation was more important to us than competence or pleasure, we decided to delete the later scales from the analysis. We wanted to see if motivation would contribute to the prediction of math achievement if its contribution was not canceled out by competence and/or pleasure.

Hint: Use **Transform => Compute** and name your **Target Variable** *paedr*. Also, use the **Mean** function; i.e., MEAN(*faedr, maedr*), to compute your average. Please refer to chapter 6 and the callout box near Fig. 6.9, on computing variables, if you need help. Now rerun Problem 1 using the new parent's education variable, *paedr* (instead of *faedr* and *maedr*), and *do not* use the competence or pleasure scales this time. Refer to Output 12.4 for comparison.

Print, Save, and Exit

- **Print** your lab assignment results if necessary.
- Save your SPSS log as **hsblogH** (Use **File => Save As**).
- **Save** your data as **hsbdataH** (Use **File => Save As**).
- **Exit** SPSS.

Interpretation Questions

1. In Output 12.2: a) How many steps were done in the stepwise multiple regression (Look under Model)? b) What variables entered the equation; i.e., what combination of the seven variables predict math achievement? c) What is the final multiple R? d) What is the adjusted R^2 and what does it mean? e) Compare the R, R^2, and adjusted R^2 in Output 12.1 and 12.2. Try to explain the differences.

2. Using Output 12.3, does entering gender first (controlling for gender) change the results from those in Output 12.1? Why or why not?

3. Compare Outputs 12.4 and 12.1. How are the results different? Why?

Outputs and Interpretations

```
GET
  FILE='A:\hsbdataG.sav'.
EXECUTE .
```

Output 12.1: Multiple Linear Regression, Method = Enter

Syntax for multiple linear regression, Method = Enter

```
REGRESSION
  /DESCRIPTIVES MEAN STDDEV CORR SIG N
  /MISSING LISTWISE
  /STATISTICS COEFF OUTS R ANOVA
  /CRITERIA=PIN(.05) POUT(.10)
  /NOORIGIN
  /DEPENDENT mathach
  /METHOD=ENTER motivatn competnc pleasure grades faedr maedr gend  .
```

Interpretation of Output 12.1 and 12.2

This output provides the usual descriptive statistics for all eight variables in the first table. Note that the N is 69 because six participants are missing a score on one or more variables. Multiple regression uses only the participants who have complete data. The next table is a correlation matrix. The first column shows the correlations of the other variables with math achievement. Note that motivation, competence, grades in high school, father's and mother's education, and gender are all significantly correlated with math achievement. Also notice that several of the predictor/independent variables are moderately correlated with each other; i.e., competence and motivation (.517) and mother's and father's education (.617).

The "model summary" table shows that the multiple correlation coefficient (R), using all the predictors simultaneously, is .67 and the **adjusted R^2** is .38, meaning that 38% of the variance in math achievement can be predicted from gender, competence, etc. combined. Note that the adjusted R^2 is lower than the unadjusted R^2. This is, in part, related to the number of variables in the equation. Even though only father's education and gender are significant the other five

143

variables will always add a little to the prediction of math achievement. An adjustment is necessary because so many independent variables were used.

The ANOVA table shows that $F = 6.93$ and is significant. This only indicates that one or more of the independent variables is a significant predictor of math achievement when used in this combination. This F is usually significant.

Probably, the most important table is the coefficients table. It indicates the **standardized beta coefficients**, which are interpreted like correlation coefficients or factor weights. The **Sig** opposite each independent variable indicates whether that variable makes a significant addition to the prediction of math achievement over and above the contribution of all other variables; i.e., does it add anything new? Thus, grades and gender, in this example, are the only variables that help the prediction when the other six variables are already considered. As we will see in Problems 2 and 3, this is somewhat misleading. Remember that the two parent education measures as well as competence and motivation were also significantly correlated with math achievement and each other. What has happened here is that neither father's education nor mother's education are significant when the other is already used as a predictor. Because they are correlated, the second one does not have much new to add. The same is true for motivation and competence. The high intercorrelation of independent/predictor variables is called *collinearity* and may cause problems in the interpretation of multiple regression. One way to handle this is to combine variables that are highly related if that makes conceptual sense. For example, you could make a new variable called average parents' education, as we will for Problem 4.

In Problem 2, we will let the computer select variables one at a time (**Stepwise**), which will avoid the problem of two related variables canceling out each other. But which one of two related variables is picked as the predictor could be due to small chance differences in the data. Note, (from the correlation table in Output 12.1) that motivation and competence are both significant and almost equally correlated (.256 and .260) with math achievement; yet, only motivation is significant in Problem 2. The same is true for father's education and mother's education.

Regression

Descriptive Statistics

	Mean	Std. Deviation	N
math achievement	12.7536	6.6629	69
Motivation scale	2.8913	.6268	69
Competence scale	3.3188	.6226	69
Pleasure scale	3.2464	.6357	69
grades in h.s.	5.71	1.57	69
Father's ed rev	1.72	.84	69
Mother's ed rev	1.46	.68	69
gender	1.54	.50	69

N is 69 because 6 participants have some missing data.

Correlations with math achievement.

Moderately high correlations among independent variables.

Correlations

		math achievement	Motivation scale	Competence scale	Pleasure scale	grades in h.s.	Father's ed rev	Mother's ed rev	gender
Pearson Correlation	math achievement	1.000	.256	.260	.091	.470	.453	.419	-.272
	Motivation scale	.256	1.000	.517	.308	.020	.036	.057	-.178
	Competence scale	.260	.517	1.000	.464	.216	.030	.228	-.037
	Pleasure scale	.091	.308	.464	1.000	-.094	-.009	.050	.041
	grades in h.s.	.470	.020	.216	-.094	1.000	.351	.308	.162
	Father's ed rev	.453	.036	.030	-.009	.351	1.000	.617	-.203
	Mother's ed rev	.419	.057	.228	.050	.308	.617	1.000	-.223
	gender	-.272	-.178	-.037	.041	.162	-.203	-.223	1.000
Sig. (1-tailed)	math achievement		.017	.015	.228	.000	.000	.000	.012
	Motivation scale	.017	.	.000	.005	.436	.386	.321	.072
	Competence scale	.015	.000	.	.000	.037	.404	.030	.380
	Pleasure scale	.228	.005	.000	.	.221	.471	.343	.370
	grades in h.s.	.000	.436	.037	.221	.	.002	.005	.091
	Father's ed rev	.000	.386	.404	.471	.002	.	.000	.047
	Mother's ed rev	.000	.321	.030	.343	.005	.000	.	.033
	gender	.012	.072	.380	.370	.091	.047	.033	.
N	math achievement	69	69	69	69	69	69	69	69
	Motivation scale	69	69	69	69	69	69	69	69
	Competence scale	69	69	69	69	69	69	69	69
	Pleasure scale	69	69	69	69	69	69	69	69
	grades in h.s.	69	69	69	69	69	69	69	69
	Father's ed rev	69	69	69	69	69	69	69	69
	Mother's ed rev	69	69	69	69	69	69	69	69
	gender	69	69	69	69	69	69	69	69

Significance level of correlations with math achievement.

Variables Entered/Removed [b]

Model	Variables Entered	Variables Removed	Method
1	gender, Competence scale, Father's ed rev, Pleasure scale, grades in h.s., Motivation scale, Mother's ed rev	.	Enter

a. All requested variables entered.

b. Dependent Variable: math achievement

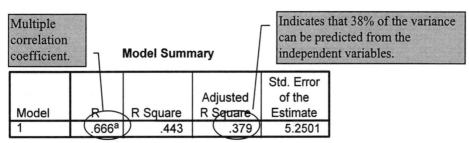

Model Summary

Model	R	R Square	Adjusted R Square	Std. Error of the Estimate
1	.666[a]	.443	.379	5.2501

a. Predictors: (Constant), gender, Competence scale, Father's ed rev, Pleasure scale, grades in h.s., Motivation scale, Mother's ed rev

Indicates that one or more of the independent variables is a statistically significant predictor.

ANOVA[b]

Model		Sum of Squares	df	Mean Square	F	Sig.
1	Regression	1337.491	7	191.070	6.932	.000[a]
	Residual	1681.347	61	27.563		
	Total	3018.838	68			

a. Predictors: (Constant), gender, Competence scale, Father's ed rev, Pleasure scale, grades in h.s., Motivation scale, Mother's ed rev

b. Dependent Variable: math achievement

Coefficients [a]

Model		Unstandardized Coefficients		Standardized Coefficients	t	Sig.
		B	Std. Error	Beta		
1	(Constant)	-4.293	5.152		-.833	.408
	Motivation scale	1.684	1.227	.158	1.373	.175
	Competence scale	.117	1.406	.011	.083	.934
	Pleasure scale	.874	1.177	.083	.742	.461
	grades in h.s.	1.762	.479	.416	3.680	.000
	Father's ed rev	1.477	1.027	.186	1.439	.155
	Mother's ed rev	1.027	1.268	.104	.810	.421
	gender	-3.359	1.394	-.253	-2.409	.019

a. Dependent Variable: math achievement

Only grades and gender combine to be significant predictors of math achievement.

146

Output 12.2: Multiple Linear Regression, Method = Stepwise

Syntax for multiple linear regression, Method = Stepwise

```
REGRESSION
  /MISSING LISTWISE
  /STATISTICS COEFF OUTS R ANOVA
  /CRITERIA=PIN(.05) POUT(.10)
  /NOORIGIN
  /DEPENDENT mathach
  /METHOD=STEPWISE motivatn competnc pleasure grades faedr maedr gend  .
```

Interpretation of Output 12.2

Each model in the **Model Summary** table represents a "step" in which a variable is added (or deleted) from the prediction equation if it makes a significant *additional* contribution to the prediction from the variables already entered. The R^2 for each step after the first indicates the prediction from a combination of variables. See the footnotes.

The **Excluded Variables** table provides the important statistics for each variable that has not yet entered the prediction equation. Thus, under **Model 1**, grades is omitted because it has entered the equation (see the **Coefficients** table). The variable with the highest partial correlation will enter on the next step/model if it meets the criterion for significance (sig. < .05). The last column in this table provides **Tolerances**. Low tolerance indicates that the variable is related to (not independent of) the variables already in the equation.

Regression

Variables Entered/Removed[a]

Model	Variables Entered	Variables Removed	Method
1	grades in h.s.	.	Stepwise (Criteria: Probability-of-F-to-enter <= .050, Probability-of-F-to-remove >= 100).
2	gender	.	Stepwise (Criteria: Probability-of-F-to-enter <= .050, Probability-of-F-to-remove >= 100).
3	Father's ed rev	.	Stepwise (Criteria: Probability-of-F-to-enter <= .050, Probability-of-F-to-remove >= 100).
4	Motivation scale	.	Stepwise (Criteria: Probability-of-F-to-enter <= .050, Probability-of-F-to-remove >= 100).

a. Dependent Variable: math achievement

Model Summary

Model	R	R Square	Adjusted R Square	Std. Error of the Estimate
1	.470[a]	.221	.209	5.9257
2	.588[b]	.345	.325	5.4727
3	.626[c]	.392	.364	5.3129
4	.654[d]	.428	.392	5.1934

a. Predictors: (Constant), grades in h.s.

b. Predictors: (Constant), grades in h.s., gender

c. Predictors: (Constant), grades in h.s., gender, Father's ed rev

d. Predictors: (Constant), grades in h.s., gender, Father's ed rev, Motivation scale

ANOVA[e]

Model		Sum of Squares	df	Mean Square	F	Sig.
1	Regression	666.172	1	666.172	18.971	.000[a]
	Residual	2352.666	67	35.114		
	Total	3018.838	68			
2	Regression	1042.085	2	521.042	17.397	.000[b]
	Residual	1976.753	66	29.951		
	Total	3018.838	68			
3	Regression	1184.110	3	394.703	13.983	.000[c]
	Residual	1834.728	65	28.227		
	Total	3018.838	68			
4	Regression	1292.679	4	323.170	11.982	.000[d]
	Residual	1726.159	64	26.971		
	Total	3018.838	68			

a. Predictors: (Constant), grades in h.s.

b. Predictors: (Constant), grades in h.s., gender

c. Predictors: (Constant), grades in h.s., gender, Father's ed rev

d. Predictors: (Constant), grades in h.s., gender, Father's ed rev, Motivation scale

e. Dependent Variable: math achievement

Significant predictor variables of math achievement using stepwise multiple regression.

Coefficients[a]

Model		Unstandardized Coefficients		Standardized Coefficients	t	Sig.
		B	Std. Error	Beta		
1	(Constant)	1.390	2.705		.514	.609
	grades in h.s.	1.990	.457	.470	4.356	.000
2	(Constant)	7.272	2.999		2.424	.018
	grades in h.s.	2.236	.428	.528	5.229	.000
	gender	-4.743	1.339	-.358	-3.543	.001
3	(Constant)	4.953	3.090		1.603	.114
	grades in h.s.	1.832	.452	.433	4.050	.000
	gender	-3.888	1.355	-.293	-2.870	.006
	Father's ed rev	1.919	.856	.241	2.243	.028
4	(Constant)	-1.524	4.421		-.345	.732
	grades in h.s.	1.784	.443	.421	4.026	.000
	gender	-3.395	1.347	-.256	-2.521	.014
	Father's ed rev	1.957	.837	.246	2.339	.022
	Motivation scale	2.052	1.023	.193	2.006	.049

a. Dependent Variable: math achievement

Excluded Variables [e]

Model		Beta In	t	Sig.	Partial Correlation	Collinearity Statistics Tolerance
1	Motivation scale	.246[a]	2.361	.021	.279	1.000
	Competence scale	.167[a]	1.523	.133	.184	.953
	Pleasure scale	.137[a]	1.268	.209	.154	.991
	Father's ed rev	.328[a]	3.018	.004	.348	.877
	Mother's ed rev	.303[a]	2.810	.007	.327	.905
	gender	-.358[a]	-3.543	.001	-.400	.974
2	Motivation scale	.188[b]	1.890	.063	.228	.966
	Competence scale	.140[b]	1.380	.172	.169	.948
	Pleasure scale	.158[b]	1.590	.117	.193	.988
	Father's ed rev	.241[b]	2.243	.028	.268	.807
	Mother's ed rev	.214[b]	1.995	.050	.240	.829
3	Motivation scale	.193[c]	2.006	.049	.243	.965
	Competence scale	.158[c]	1.603	.114	.196	.943
	Pleasure scale	.148[c]	1.538	.129	.189	.986
	Mother's ed rev	.121[c]	.961	.340	.119	.593
4	Competence scale	.077[d]	.669	.506	.084	.686
	Pleasure scale	.096[d]	.948	.347	.119	.879
	Mother's ed rev	.117[d]	.955	.343	.119	.593

These tolerances are low indicating that these variables are not likely to enter later due to multicollinearity.

Excluded variables have significance levels above .05.

a. Predictors in the Model: (Constant), grades in h.s.

b. Predictors in the Model: (Constant), grades in h.s., gender

c. Predictors in the Model: (Constant), grades in h.s., gender, Father's ed rev

d. Predictors in the Model: (Constant), grades in h.s., gender, Father's ed rev, Motivation scale

e. Dependent Variable: math achievement

Output 12.3: Hierarchical Multiple Linear Regression Using Blocks

Syntax for Hierarchical multiple linear regression using Blocks

```
REGRESSION
  /MISSING LISTWISE
  /STATISTICS COEFF OUTS R ANOVA
  /CRITERIA=PIN(.05) POUT(.10)
  /NOORIGIN
  /DEPENDENT mathach
  /METHOD=ENTER gend   /METHOD=ENTER motivatn competnc pleasure grades faedr
  maedr  .
```

Regression

Variables Entered/Removed [b]

Model	Variables Entered	Variables Removed	Method
1	gender[a]	.	Enter
2	Competence scale, Father's ed rev, Pleasure scale, grades in h.s., Motivation scale, Mother's ed rev	.	Enter

a. All requested variables entered.

b. Dependent Variable: math achievement

Model Summary

Model	R	R Square	Adjusted R Square	Std. Error of the Estimate
1	.272[a]	.074	.060	6.4596
2	.666[b]	.443	.379	5.2501

a. Predictors: (Constant), gender

b. Predictors: (Constant), gender, Competence scale, Father's ed rev, Pleasure scale, grades in h.s., Motivation scale, Mother's ed rev

Footnotes provide you with relevant information.

ANOVA [c]

Model		Sum of Squares	df	Mean Square	F	Sig.
1	Regression	223.191	1	223.191	5.349	.024[a]
	Residual	2795.647	67	41.726		
	Total	3018.838	68			
2	Regression	1337.491	7	191.070	6.932	.000[b]
	Residual	1681.347	61	27.563		
	Total	3018.838	68			

a. Predictors: (Constant), gender

b. Predictors: (Constant), gender, Competence scale, Father's ed rev, scale, grades in h.s., Motivation scale, Mother's ed rev

c. Dependent Variable: math achievement

At least one of these variables is a significant predictor.

Coefficients^a

Model		Unstandardized Coefficients		Standardized Coefficients		
		B	Std. Error	Beta	t	Sig.
1	(Constant)	18.294	2.519		7.264	.000
	gender	-3.607	1.559	-.272	-2.313	.024
2	(Constant)	-4.293	5.152		-.833	.408
	gender	-3.359	1.394	-.253	-2.409	.019
	Motivation scale	1.684	1.227	.158	1.373	.175
	Competence scale	.117	1.406	.011	.083	.934
	Pleasure scale	.874	1.177	.083	.742	.461
	grades in h.s.	1.762	.479	.416	3.680	.000
	Father's ed rev	1.477	1.027	.186	1.439	.155
	Mother's ed rev	1.027	1.268	.104	.810	.421

a. Dependent Variable: math achievement

Excluded Variables^b

Model		Beta In	t	Sig.	Partial Correlation	Collinearity Statistics Tolerance
1	Motivation scale	.214^a	1.822	.073	.219	.968
	Competence scale	.250^a	2.188	.032	.260	.999
	Pleasure scale	.103^a	.870	.387	.106	.998
	grades in h.s.	.528^a	5.229	.000	.541	.974
	Father's ed rev	.415^a	3.782	.000	.422	.959
	Mother's ed rev	.377^a	3.359	.001	.382	.950

a. Predictors in the Model: (Constant), gender

b. Dependent Variable: math achievement

Output 12.4: Another Multiple Linear Regression, Method = Enter

Syntax for multiple linear regression, Method = Enter, using Parent's Education Revised as a new variable and omitting motivation and pleasure

```
COMPUTE paedr = MEAN(faedr,maedr) .
VARIABLE LABELS paedr "Parent's ed revised" .
EXECUTE .
VALUE LABELS paedr
 1.00000000000000 "hs or less"
 2.00000000000000 "some college"
 3.00000000000000 "BS or more"
 .
REGRESSION
  /DESCRIPTIVES MEAN STDDEV CORR SIG N
  /MISSING LISTWISE
  /STATISTICS COEFF OUTS R ANOVA
  /CRITERIA=PIN(.05) POUT(.10)
  /NOORIGIN
  /DEPENDENT mathach
  /METHOD=ENTER motivatn grades paedr gend  .
```

Regression

Descriptive Statistics

	Mean	Std. Deviation	N
math achievement	12.6028	6.7568	73
Motivation scale	2.8744	.6382	73
grades in h.s.	5.68	1.59	73
Parent's ed revised	1.5890	.6939	73
gender	1.55	.50	73

Correlations

		math achievement	Motivation scale	grades in h.s.	Parent's ed revised	gender
Pearson Correlation	math achievement	1.000	.316	.504	.442	-.303
	Motivation scale	.316	1.000	.084	.065	-.209
	grades in h.s.	.504	.084	1.000	.309	.115
	Parent's ed revised	.442	.065	.309	1.000	-.202
	gender	-.303	-.209	.115	-.202	1.000
Sig. (1-tailed)	math achievement	.	.003	.000	.000	.005
	Motivation scale	.003	.	.241	.293	.038
	grades in h.s.	.000	.241	.	.004	.166
	Parent's ed revised	.000	.293	.004	.	.043
	gender	.005	.038	.166	.043	.
N	math achievement	73	73	73	73	73
	Motivation scale	73	73	73	73	73
	grades in h.s.	73	73	73	73	73
	Parent's ed revised	73	73	73	73	73
	gender	73	73	73	73	73

Variables Entered/Removed [b]

Model	Variables Entered	Variables Removed	Method
1	gender, grades in h.s., Motivation scale, Parent's ed revised[a]		Enter

a. All requested variables entered.

b. Dependent Variable: math achievement

Model Summary

Model	R	R Square	Adjusted R Square	Std. Error of the Estimate
1	.688[a]	.474	.443	5.0446

a. Predictors: (Constant), gender, grades in h.s., Motivation scale, Parent's ed revised

ANOVA[b]

Model		Sum of Squares	df	Mean Square	F	Sig.
1	Regression	1556.584	4	389.146	15.292	.000[a]
	Residual	1730.492	68	25.448		
	Total	3287.076	72			

a. Predictors: (Constant), gender, grades in h.s., Motivation scale, Parent's ed

b. Dependent Variable: math achievement

Coefficients[a]

Model		Unstandardized Coefficients		Standardized Coefficients	t	Sig.
		B	Std. Error	Beta		
1	(Constant)	-2.686	4.190		-.641	.524
	Motivation scale	2.212	.959	.209	2.308	.024
	grades in h.s.	1.881	.403	.442	4.664	.000
	Parent's ed revised	2.326	.931	.239	2.499	.015
	gender	-3.527	1.264	-.262	-2.790	.007

a. Dependent Variable: math achievement

CHAPTER 13

Logistic Regression and Discriminant Analysis

Logistic regression is helpful when you need to predict the presence or absence of a characteristic or outcome based on a set of predictor variables. It is similar to linear regression except that it is used when the dependent variable is dichotomous. Logistic regression also is useful when some or all of the independent variables are dichotomous.

Discriminant analysis, on the other hand, is useful when you have several continuous/interval scale independent variables and, as in logistic, an outcome/dependent variable that is categorical. The dependent variable can have more than two categories, but that makes the results and interpretation more complex. When you want to build a predictive model of group membership based on observed characteristics of each participant, discriminant analysis is ideal. SPSS will create a linear combination (or a set of linear combinations if there are more than two groups) of the predictor variables which provides the best discrimination between groups.

In Problems 1 and 2, we will use logistic regression to predict a dichotomous outcome (whether or not students took algebra 2), from several interval level and dichotomous predictors. In Problems 3 and 4, we will use discriminant analysis to do the same problems that we did with logistic regression in order to compare the two techniques.

Problems/Research Questions

1. Is there a combination of competence, father's and mother's education, motivation, pleasure, and gender that predicts whether students will take Algebra 2 better than any one of these variables alone?

2. We will rerun Problem 1, but this time ask the computer to consider the variables one at a time. This will be like the stepwise procedure used in multiple regression. In logistic regression it is called **Forward: LR**.

3. Is there a combination of *faedr, maedr, gend, motivatn, pleasure,* and *competnc* that predicts whether or not a student will take algebra 2 or not? This is the same question that we asked in Problem 1, but this time we will use discriminant analysis and the **Enter independents together** method.

4. Again, we will answer the same question, but use the **Stepwise** method for discriminant analysis. We will ask you to compare these four somewhat different methods (Problems 1-4) of answering the research question about predicting a dichotomous outcome--algebra 2, taken or not.

Lab Assignment I

Logon and Get Data

- Get your **hsbdataG** data file.

Problem 1: Logistic Regression, Method=Enter

Now let's try an approach known as logistic regression. It is used to predict a dichotomous (two category) dependent variable when the independent variables (called covariates here) are either dichotomous or interval.
- Use these commands: **Statistics => Regression => Logistics.**
- Move *alg2* into the **Dependent** variable box.
- Move *competnc, faedr, maedr, motivatn, pleasure,* and *gend* into the **Covariates** box.
- Make sure **Enter** is the selected **Method**.
- Click on **OK** (compare Fig. 13.1). Does your output look like Output 13.1?

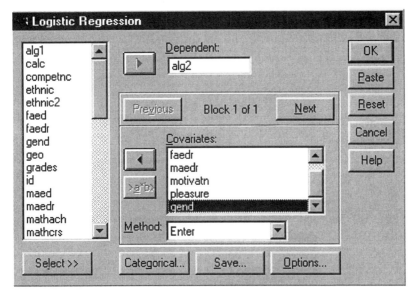

Fig. 13.1. Logistic regression.

Problem 2: Logistic Regression, Method=Forward: LR

Now try it yourself using the same dependent variable and covariates except select your **Method** as **Forward: LR**. Compare your output to Output 13.2.

Problem 3: Discriminant Analysis: Enter Independents Together

When you have a categorical outcome/grouping/dependent variable, you can use discriminant analysis instead of logistic regression. You should not use discriminant if you have any dichotomous independent variables, except when the dependent variable has a nearly 50-50 split (as in this case). Here we will use the same variables as in Problem 4. Follow these steps:

- Select Statistics =>**Classify => Discriminant**.
- Move *alg2* into the **Grouping Variable** box (see Fig. 13.2).

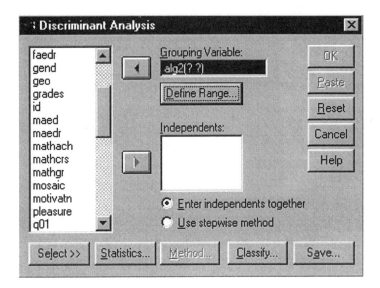

Fig. 13.2. Discriminant analysis.

- Click on **Define Range** and enter **0** for **Minimum** and **1** for **Maximum** (see Fig. 13.3).
- Click on **Continue**.

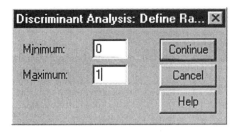

Fig. 13.3. Discriminant analysis: Define range.

- Now move *faedr, maedr, gend, motivatn, pleasure,* and *competnc* into the **Independents** box.
- Make sure **Enter independents together** is already selected.
- Click on **Statistics** and select **Means** and **Univariate ANOVAs** (see Fig. 13.4).
- Click on **Continue**.

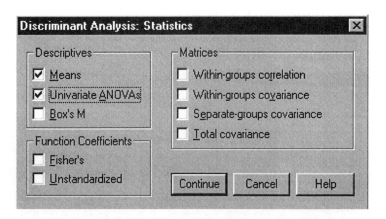

Fig. 13.4. Discriminant analysis: Statistics.

- Click on **Classify** and select **Summary Table** (see Fig. 13.5).
- Click on **Continue**.

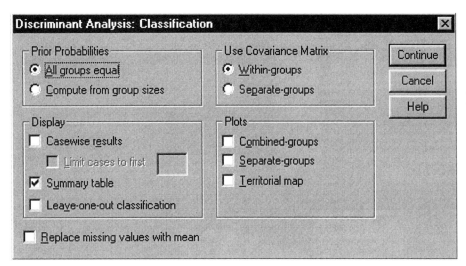

Fig. 13.5. Discriminant analysis: Classification.

- Finally click on **OK** and compare your output to Output 13.3.

Problem 4: Discriminant Analysis: Stepwise Method

Try the same set of variables again except select **Stepwise** as your method. Compare your output to Output 13.4.

Print, Save, and Exit

- **Print** your lab assignment results if necessary.
- Save your SPSS log as **hsblogI** (Use **File** => **Save As**).
- **Save** your data as **hsbdataI** (Use **File** => **Save As**).
- **Exit** SPSS.

Interpretation Questions

1. Using Output 13.2: a) Which variables combine to predict who took algebra 2? b) How accurate is the overall prediction? c) How well do the significant variables predict who *took* algebra 2? d) How about the prediction of who *didn't* take it? e) Why is the overall prediction lower than in Output 13.1?

2. In Output 13.4: a) which variables combine to predict who took algebra 2? b) How accurate is the prediction/classification overall and for who would not take algebra 2?

3. Compare Outputs 13.3 and 13.4, especially the **Classification Results** and the **Structure Matrix** table. How are they different and why?

Outputs and Interpretations

Output 13.1: Logistic Regression, Method = Enter

<u>Syntax for logistic regression, Method = Enter</u>

```
LOGISTIC REGRESSION VAR=alg2
  /METHOD=ENTER competnc faedr maedr motivatn pleasure gend
  /CRITERIA PIN(.05) POUT(.10) ITERATE(20) CUT(.5) .
```

Interpretation of Output 13.1

Logistic regression is useful when you want to be able to predict the presence or absence of a characteristic or effect based on values of a set of predictor variables. It is similar to a linear regression in many ways. However, it is suited to situations where the dependent variable is dichotomous. Independent variables can be interval level or dichotomous. Logistic regression does not rely on some of the assumptions on which multiple regression and discriminant analysis are based. As with other forms of regression, multicollinearity or high correlations among the predictors can lead to problems.

In this problem we have tried to predict whether or not students would take Algebra 2 from six other variables. Note from the classification table that overall 74% of the participants were predicted correctly. The independent/covariate variables were better at helping us predict who would *not* take algebra 2 (81% correct) than at who would take it (67% correct). Note, in the last table, that only father's education is significant. This is somewhat misleading and probably due to multicollinearity. (We can see from Output 13.2, under "Beginning Block Number 1" that mother's education is also significantly related to taking algebra 2, as is competence.) Remember from Chapter 12, Output 12.1 that *maedr* and *faedr* are correlated .62 and that *competnc* and *motivatn* are related .52. Thus, as in Output 12.1, they tend to cancel each other out.

```
     Total number of cases:       75 (Unweighted)
     Number of selected cases:   75
     Number of unselected cases: 0

     Number of selected cases:             75
     Number rejected because of missing data:  6
     Number of cases included in the analysis: 69

Dependent Variable Encoding:

Original      Internal
Value         Value
0             0
1             1
```

Dependent Variable..   ALG2   algebra 2 in h.s.

Beginning Block Number 0. Initial Log Likelihood Function

-2 Log Likelihood   95.523835

* Constant is included in the model.

Beginning Block Number 1. Method: Enter

Variable(s) Entered on Step Number
1.   COMPETNC   Competence scale
        FAEDR   Father's ed rev
        MAEDR   Mother's ed rev
        MOTIVATN   Motivation scale
        PLEASURE   Pleasure scale
        GEND   gender

Estimation terminated at iteration number 4 because
Log Likelihood decreased by less than .01 percent.

    -2 Log Likelihood   72.273
    Goodness of Fit   64.122
    Cox & Snell - R^2   .286
    Nagelkerke - R^2   .382

                    Chi-Square   df   Significance

    Model   23.251   6   .0007
    Block   23.251   6   .0007
    Step   23.251   6   .0007

Classification Table for ALG2 ——————— The Key Table

The Cut Value is .50
                         Predicted
                    not taken   taken   Percent Correct
                      n   I   t
Observed   +---------+---------+
   not taken   n   I   29   I   7   I   80.56%
                    +---------+---------+
   taken   t   I   11   I   22   I   66.67%
                    +---------+---------+
                              Overall   73.91%

```
-------------------- Variables in the Equation ----------------------
```

Variable	B	S.E.	Wald	df	Sig	R	Exp(B)
COMPETNC	1.2005	.6726	3.1859	1	.0743	.1114	3.3217
FAEDR	.9008	.4425	4.1441	1	.0418	.1498	2.4615
MAEDR	.6584	.5893	1.2482	1	.2639	.0000	1.9317
MOTIVATN	.2574	.5503	.2188	1	.6399	.0000	1.2936
PLEASURE	-.5643	.5200	1.1779	1	.2778	.0000	.5687
GEND	-.5676	.5986	.8993	1	.3430	.0000	.5669
Constant	-4.6203	2.5321	3.3297	1	.0680		

Output 13.2: Logistic Regression, Method = Forward: LR

Syntax for logistic regression, Method = Forward: LR

```
LOGISTIC REGRESSION VAR=alg2
  /METHOD=FSTEP(LR) competnc faedr maedr motivatn pleasure gend
  /CRITERIA PIN(.05) POUT(.10) ITERATE(20) CUT(.5) .
```

```
        Total number of cases:      75 (Unweighted)
        Number of selected cases:   75
        Number of unselected cases: 0

        Number of selected cases:                    75
        Number rejected because of missing data:     6
        Number of cases included in the analysis:    69
```

```
Dependent Variable Encoding:

Original      Internal
Value         Value
0             0
1             1
```

```
Dependent Variable..   ALG2        algebra 2 in h.s.
```

```
Beginning Block Number  0.  Initial Log Likelihood Function
-2 Log Likelihood    95.523835
```

```
* Constant is included in the model.
```

```
Estimation terminated at iteration number 2 because
parameter estimates changed by less than .001
```

```
Classification Table for ALG2                    ┌─────────────────────────────┐
The Cut Value is .50 ───────────────             │Preliminary Table in Stepwise Logistic│
                        Predicted                 │See the last Classification Table│
                   not taken    taken    Percent Correct └─────────────────────┘
                     n   I    t
Observed           +---------+---------+
   not taken    n  I   36    I    0    I  100.00%
                   +---------+---------+
   taken        t  I   33    I    0    I    .00%
                   +---------+---------+
                             Overall   52.17%


-------------------- Variables in the Equation ----------------------

Variable         B        S.E.     Wald     df      Sig      R      Exp(B)

Constant      -.0870     .2410    .1304     1      .7181
```

Beginning Block Number   1. Method: Forward Stepwise (LR)

```
--------------- Variables not in the Equation -----------------
Residual Chi Square      20.185 with      6 df      Sig =  .0026

Variable          Score      df      Sig         R

COMPETNC         4.9885      1      .0255      .1769    ┌──────────────────┐
FAEDR           12.2568      1      .0005      .3277    │Note that these three│
MAEDR           12.0906      1      .0005      .3250    │variables are each│
MOTIVATN         2.5059      1      .1134      .0728    │separately significantly│
PLEASURE          .0025      1      .9603      .0000    │related to algebra 1, before│
GEND             3.1898      1      .0741      .1116    │the first step.│
                                                        └──────────────────┘
```

Variable(s) Entered on Step Number
1..   FAEDR   Father's ed rev   → Step 1 enters *Faedr.*

```
Estimation terminated at iteration number 3 because
Log Likelihood decreased by less than .01 percent.
 -2 Log Likelihood        82.680
 Goodness of Fit          68.683
 Cox & Snell - R^2          .170
 Nagelkerke - R^2           .227

                Chi-Square   df Significance

   Model          12.844      1      .0003
   Block          12.844      1      .0003
   Step           12.844      1      .0003
```

```
Classification Table for ALG2
The Cut Value is .50
```

Prediction after Step 1, from *Faedr* only.

```
                         Predicted
                    not taken    taken        Percent Correct
                      n   I    t
Observed        +----------+----------+
   not taken  n I    25   I    11   I       69.44%
                +----------+----------+
   taken      t I    11   I    22   I       66.67%
                +----------+----------+
                              Overall     68.12%
```

```
-------------------- Variables in the Equation ----------------------

Variable          B       S.E.     Wald     df     Sig      R      Exp(B)

FAEDR          1.1216    .3398   10.8969    1    .0010   .3052   3.0698
Constant      -2.0054    .6263   10.2522    1    .0014
```

```
---------------- Model if Term Removed -----------------

Term       Log                                Significance
Removed    Likelihood   -2 Log LR    df       of Log LR

FAEDR        -47.762      12.844      1          .0003
```

```
--------------- Variables not in the Equation ----------------
Residual Chi Square       9.718 with        5 df    Sig = .0836

Variable        Score     df      Sig       R

COMPETNC       5.5686     1     .0183     .1933
MAEDR          3.7284     1     .0535     .1345
MOTIVATN       2.6021     1     .1067     .0794
PLEASURE        .0007     1     .9794     .0000
GEND           1.4800     1     .2238     .0000
```

Step 2 enters competence because it was still significant after Step 1.

```
Variable(s) Entered on Step Number
2..        COMPETNC  Competence scale
```

```
Estimation terminated at iteration number 4 because
Log Likelihood decreased by less than .01 percent.

   -2 Log Likelihood       76.533
   Goodness of Fit         69.424
   Cox & Snell - R^2         .241
   Nagelkerke - R^2          .321

                Chi-Square    df  Significance

   Model          18.991      2      .0001
   Block          18.991      2      .0001
   Step            6.148      1      .0132
```

```
Classification Table for ALG2                          Predictions after Step 2.
The Cut Value is .50
                              Predicted
                     not taken     taken        Percent Correct
                         n    I    t
                    +----------+----------+
Observed
   not taken    n   I    29   I    7    I      80.56%
                    +----------+----------+
   taken        t   I    13   I    20   I      60.61%
                    +----------+----------+
                                 Overall       71.01%
```

```
-------------------- Variables in the Equation ----------------------

Variable          B        S.E.      Wald      df      Sig        R      Exp(B)

COMPETNC       1.2176      .5406    5.0732      1     .0243     .1794    3.3789
FAEDR          1.2253      .3687   11.0445      1     .0009     .3077    3.4052
Constant      -6.2642     2.0898    8.9848      1     .0027
```

```
---------------- Model if Term Removed ------------------

Term        Log                              Significance
Removed     Likelihood    -2 Log LR    df    of Log LR

COMPETNC    -41.340          6.148      1       .0132
FAEDR       -45.061         13.589      1       .0002
```

```
--------------- Variables not in the Equation ----------------
Residual Chi Square       4.337 with        4 df      Sig =  .3623

Variable          Score      df      Sig        R

MAEDR           1.6916        1     .1934     .0000
MOTIVATN         .3380        1     .5610     .0000
PLEASURE        1.3877        1     .2388     .0000
GEND            1.4225        1     .2330     .0000
No more variables can be deleted or added.
```

Output 13.3: Discriminant Analysis, Enter Independents Together

Syntax for discriminant analysis, entering all independents together

```
DISCRIMINANT
  /GROUPS=alg2(0 1)
  /VARIABLES=faedr maedr gend motivatn pleasure competnc
  /ANALYSIS ALL
  /PRIORS  EQUAL
  /STATISTICS=MEAN STDDEV UNIVF TABLE
  /CLASSIFY=NONMISSING POOLED .
```

Interpretation of Output 13.3

Discriminant analysis is also appropriate when you want to predict which group participants will be in. The procedure produces a discriminant function (for more than two groups, a set of discriminant functions) based on linear combinations of the predictor variables that provide the best overall discrimination among the groups. Be advised that the grouping/dependent variable can have more than two values, but that greatly increases the complexity of the output. The codes for the grouping variable must be integers. You need to specify their minimum and maximum values as we did in Fig. 13.3. Cases with values outside these bounds are excluded from the analysis.

The Group Statistic table provides basic descriptive statistics for each of the independent/ predictor variables for each outcome group (didn't take algebra 2 and did take it) separately and for the whole sample. The next table shows which independent variables are significant predictors by themselves. That is it shows the variables on which there is a statistically significant difference between those who took algebra 2 and those who didn't. Again, *faedr, maedr*, and *competnc* are statistically significant.

Note, from the Discriminant Function Coefficients table that only father's education and competence are weighted heavily to maximize the discrimination between groups. However, mother's education, because it correlates highly with father's education, is correlated quite highly (.72) in the Structure Matrix table with the discriminant function.

The last table is similar to the classification table for logistic regression. It shows how well the combination of six independent variables classifies or predicts who will take algebra 2. Note that overall 72.5% of the sample was classified correctly. As with logistic regression, discriminant analysis did better at predicting who did not take algebra 2 (78% correct) than it did at predicting who would take it (67% correct).

Analysis Case Processing Summary

Unweighted Cases		N	Percent
Valid		69	92.0
Excluded	Missing or out-of-range group codes	0	.0
	At least one missing discriminating variable	6	8.0
	Both missing or out-of-range group codes and at least one missing discriminating variable	0	.0
	Total	6	8.0
Total		75	100.0

Group Statistics

M and SD for each independent variable, separately for the two outcome groups.

algebra 2 in h.s.		Mean	Std. Deviation	Valid N (listwise) Unweighted	Weighted
not taken	Father's ed rev	1.3889	.6449	36	36.000
	Mother's ed rev	1.1944	.4014	36	36.000
	gender	1.6389	.4871	36	36.000
	Motivation scale	2.7778	.6738	36	36.000
	Pleasure scale	3.2500	.6872	36	36.000
	Competence scale	3.1597	.6999	36	36.000
taken	Father's ed rev	2.0909	.8790	33	33.000
	Mother's ed rev	1.7576	.7918	33	33.000
	gender	1.4242	.5019	33	33.000
	Motivation scale	3.0152	.5549	33	33.000
	Pleasure scale	3.2424	.5850	33	33.000
	Competence scale	3.4924	.4780	33	33.000
Total	Father's ed rev	1.7246	.8381	69	69.000
	Mother's ed rev	1.4638	.6769	69	69.000
	gender	1.5362	.5023	69	69.000
	Motivation scale	2.8913	.6268	69	69.000
	Pleasure scale	3.2464	.6357	69	69.000
	Competence scale	3.3188	.6226	69	69.000

Tests of Equality of Group Means

	Wilks' Lambda	F	df1	df2	Sig.
Father's ed rev	.822	14.472	1	67	.000
Mother's ed rev	.825	14.234	1	67	.000
gender	.954	3.247	1	67	.076
Motivation scale	.964	2.525	1	67	.117
Pleasure scale	1.000	.002	1	67	.961
Competence scale	.928	5.221	1	67	.025

Variables with significant initial differences in predicting who took algebra 2.

Analysis 1
Summary of Canonical Discriminant Functions

Eigenvalues

Function	Eigenvalue	% of Variance	Cumulative %	Canonical Correlation
1	.414[a]	100.0	100.0	.541

a. First 1 canonical discriminant functions were used in the analysis.

Wilks' Lambda

Test of Function(s)	Wilks' Lambda	Chi-square	df	Sig.
1	.707	22.149	6	.001

Standardized Canonical Discriminant Function Coefficients

	Function 1
Father's ed rev	.577
Mother's ed rev	.330
gender	-.197
Motivation scale	.151
Pleasure scale	-.320
Competence scale	.530

These are weights for the linear combination of variables that maximally discriminates those who took algebra 2 from those who did not.

Structure Matrix

	Function 1
Father's ed rev	.723
Mother's ed rev	.717
Competence scale	.434
gender	-.342
Motivation scale	.302
Pleasure scale	-.009

Pooled within-groups correlations between discriminating variables and standardized canonical discriminant functions. Variables ordered by absolute size of correlation within function.

Functions at Group Centroids

algebra 2 in h.s.	Function 1
not taken	-.607
taken	.662

Unstandardized canonical discriminant functions evaluated at group means

Classification Statistics

Classification Processing Summary

Processed		75
Excluded	Missing or out-of-range group codes	0
	At least one missing discriminating variable	6
Used in Output		69

Prior Probabilities for Groups

algebra 2 in h.s.	Prior	Cases Used in Analysis	
		Unweighted	Weighted
not taken	.500	36	36.000
taken	.500	33	33.000
Total	1.000	69	69.000

Key table showing the accuracy of the prediction/classification.

Classification Results[a]

		algebra 2 in h.s.	Predicted Group Membership		Total
			not taken	taken	
Original	Count	not taken	28	8	36
		taken	11	22	33
	%	not taken	77.8	22.2	100.0
		taken	33.3	66.7	100.0

a. 72.5% of original grouped cases correctly classified.

Output 13.4: Discriminant Analysis, Stepwise Method

Syntax for discriminant analysis, stepwise method

```
DISCRIMINANT
  /GROUPS=alg2(0 1)
  /VARIABLES=faedr maedr gend motivatn pleasure competnc
  /ANALYSIS ALL
  /METHOD=WILKS
  /FIN= 3.84
  /FOUT= 2.71
  /PRIORS  EQUAL
  /HISTORY
  /STATISTICS=MEAN STDDEV UNIVF TABLE
  /CLASSIFY=NONMISSING POOLED .
```

Analysis Case Processing Summary

Unweighted Cases		N	Percent
Valid		69	92.0
Excluded	Missing or out-of-range group codes	0	.0
	At least one missing discriminating variable	6	8.0
	Both missing or out-of-range group codes and at least one missing discriminating variable	0	.0
	Total	6	8.0
Total		75	100.0

Group Statistics

algebra 2 in h.s.		Mean	Std. Deviation	Valid N (listwise) Unweighted	Weighted
not taken	Father's ed rev	1.3889	.6449	36	36.000
	Mother's ed rev	1.1944	.4014	36	36.000
	gender	1.6389	.4871	36	36.000
	Motivation scale	2.7778	.6738	36	36.000
	Pleasure scale	3.2500	.6872	36	36.000
	Competence scale	3.1597	.6999	36	36.000
taken	Father's ed rev	2.0909	.8790	33	33.000
	Mother's ed rev	1.7576	.7918	33	33.000
	gender	1.4242	.5019	33	33.000
	Motivation scale	3.0152	.5549	33	33.000
	Pleasure scale	3.2424	.5850	33	33.000
	Competence scale	3.4924	.4780	33	33.000
Total	Father's ed rev	1.7246	.8381	69	69.000
	Mother's ed rev	1.4638	.6769	69	69.000
	gender	1.5362	.5023	69	69.000
	Motivation scale	2.8913	.6268	69	69.000
	Pleasure scale	3.2464	.6357	69	69.000
	Competence scale	3.3188	.6226	69	69.000

Tests of Equality of Group Means

	Wilks' Lambda	F	df1	df2	Sig.
Father's ed rev	.822	14.472	1	67	.000
Mother's ed rev	.825	14.234	1	67	.000
gender	.954	3.247	1	67	.076
Motivation scale	.964	2.525	1	67	.117
Pleasure scale	1.000	.002	1	67	.961
Competence scale	.928	5.221	1	67	.025

Analysis 1
Stepwise Statistics

Variables Entered/Removed [a, b, c, d]

		Wilks' Lambda				Exact F			
Step	Entered	Statistic	df1	df2	df3	Statistic	df1	df2	Sig.
1	Father's ed rev	.822	1	1	67.000	14.472	1	67.000	.000
2	Competence scale	.757	2	1	67.000	10.616	2	66.000	.000

At each step, the variable that minimizes the overall Wilks' Lambda is entered.

a. Maximum number of steps is 12.

b. Minimum partial F to enter is 3.84.

c. Maximum partial F to remove is 2.71.

d. F level, tolerance, or VIN insufficient for further

Variables in the Analysis

Step		Tolerance	F to Remove	Wilks' Lambda
1	Father's ed rev	1.000	14.472	
2	Father's ed rev	.991	14.925	.928
	Competence scale	.991	5.736	.822

Variables Not in the Analysis

Step		Tolerance	Min. Tolerance	F to Enter	Wilks' Lambda
0	Father's ed rev	1.000	1.000	14.472	.822
	Mother's ed rev	1.000	1.000	14.234	.825
	gender	1.000	1.000	3.247	.954
	Motivation scale	1.000	1.000	2.525	.964
	Pleasure scale	1.000	1.000	.002	1.000
	Competence scale	1.000	1.000	5.221	.928
1	Mother's ed rev	.714	.714	3.425	.782
	gender	.984	.984	1.433	.805
	Motivation scale	.997	.997	2.575	.791
	Pleasure scale	1.000	1.000	.000	.822
	Competence scale	.991	.991	5.736	.757
2	Mother's ed rev	.680	.680	1.677	.738
	gender	.984	.975	1.349	.741
	Motivation scale	.757	.752	.220	.754
	Pleasure scale	.764	.757	1.658	.738

Wilks' Lambda

Step	Number of Variables	Lambda	df1	df2	df3	Exact F			
						Statistic	df1	df2	Sig.
1	1	.822	1	1	67	14.472	1	67.000	3.103E-04
2	2	.757	2	1	67	10.616	2	66.000	1.006E-04

Summary of Canonical Discriminant Functions

Eigenvalues

Function	Eigenvalue	% of Variance	Cumulative %	Canonical Correlation
1	.322[a]	100.0	100.0	.493

a. First 1 canonical discriminant functions were used in the analysis.

Wilks' Lambda

Test of Function(s)	Wilks' Lambda	Chi-square	df	Sig.
1	.757	18.408	2	.000

Standardized Canonical Discriminant Function Coefficients

	Function
	1
Father's ed rev	.874
Competence scale	.576

Structure Matrix

	Function
	1
Father's ed rev	.819
Mother's ed rev[a]	.544
Competence scale	.492
Pleasure scale[a]	.272
Motivation scale[a]	.240
gender[a]	-.099

Pooled within-groups correlations between discriminating variables and standardized canonical discriminant functions.
Variables ordered by absolute size of correlation within function.

a. This variable not used in the analysis.

Functions at Group Centroids

algebra 2 in h.s.	Function
	1
not taken	-.535
taken	.584

Unstandardized canonical discriminant functions evaluated at group means

Classification Statistics

Classification Processing Summary

Processed		75
Excluded	Missing or out-of-range group codes	0
	At least one missing discriminating variable	4
Used in Output		71

Prior Probabilities for Groups

algebra 2 in h.s.	Prior	Cases Used in Analysis	
		Unweighted	Weighted
not taken	.500	36	36.000
taken	.500	33	33.000
Total	1.000	69	69.000

                                                    Key Table

Classification Results[a]

		algebra 2 in h.s.	Predicted Group Membership		Total
			not taken	taken	
Original	Count	not taken	30	7	37
		taken	13	21	34
	%	not taken	81.1	18.9	100.0
		taken	38.2	61.8	100.0

a. 71.8% of original grouped cases correctly classified.

CHAPTER 14

Independent and Paired Samples *t* Tests and Equivalent Nonparametric Tests

In this assignment, we will examine five statistical tests (two parametric, two nonparametric ordinal, and chi-square for nominal data) that compare two groups of participants. With this assignment, we shift our focus from the associational approach that we have been using in the last six labs to the comparative approach and difference hypotheses/questions. Problems 1 through 4 below compare two independent groups (**between groups design**) such as boys and girls. Problems 5 and 6 use a **within subjects/repeated measures design** to see if the same participants differ significantly on two comparable measures such as their two visualization scores. Remember that chapter 7 discussed between groups and within subjects designs, which help determine the specific statistic to use.

The other determinant of which statistic to use has do with statistical assumptions. If the dependent variable is approximately normally distributed and measured on a scale that at least approximates interval data, one can use the parametric *t* test. If these assumptions are markedly violated, one should use a nonparametric test as shown in the following table:

Table 14.1. *Selection of an Appropriate Inferential Statistic for Basic, Two Variable Difference Questions or Hypotheses*

	Scale of Measurement of Dependent Variable	Compare	One Factor or Independent Variable With 2 Categories or Levels/Groups/Samples	
			Independent Samples or Groups (Between)	Repeated Measures or Related Samples (Within)
Parametric Statistics	Dependent Variable Approximates Interval or Ratio Data and Assumptions Not Markedly Violated	Means	INDEPENDENT SAMPLES *t* TEST (or ONE - WAY ANOVA)	PAIRED SAMPLES *t* TEST
Nonparametric Statistics	Dependent Variable Clearly Ordinal (or Ranked) Data of the ANOVA Assumptions Are Markedly Violated	Mean Ranks	MANN-WHITNEY	WILCOXON
	Dependent Variable is Nominal (categorical) Data	Counts	CHI-SQUARE	MC NEMAR

Table 14.1 is a piece of Table 7.1, which was a more comprehensive picture of basic difference inferential statistics. We have chosen to put the chi-square test (Problem 4) into this chapter and in Table 14.1 because one way to interpret chi square is as a test of whether there are differences between the groups formed by the independent variable (in Problem 4, gender) on the incidence of each category of the dependent variable.

Problems/ Research Questions

1. Do fathers with *some college education* have kids who do better on math achievement than the kids of fathers who have only a *high school education* or less?

2. Do boys and girls differ significantly on grades, math achievement, number of math courses taken, and math grades? You will assume that the scores for the three dependent variables are normally distributed and interval scale.

3. Next, assume that the above four dependent variables are ordinal data and/or not normally distributed. You will run the appropriate nonparametric statistic to see if boys and girls are different.

4. Do boys and girls differ on whether they receive high or low math grades?

5. Do fathers of this group of students have more education than the mothers? You also will compare the two visualization scores to see if they have significantly different means. Assume that these variables are normally distributed and interval data.

6. Finally, assume that the above variables are not normally distributed and/or are ordinal data. Do fathers have significantly higher educational levels than mothers, and do the visualization scores have significantly different mean ranks?

Lab Assignment J

Logon and Get Data

*   Retrieve **hsbdataI** from your data file (your latest data).

Check Transformed Variables

Go into your data file and check to see if father's education (*faedr*), mother's education (*maedr*) have values of 1, 2, or 3, and to see if *mathcrs* is listed (see Fig. 14.1). If not, refer to Assignment C to **Recode** those variables or check your other hsbdata files to see if you have them saved.

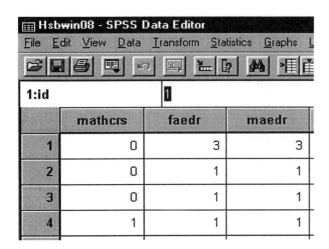

Fig. 14.1. Data file.

Problem 1: Independent Samples t Test, Between Groups Design

Let's determine if fathers with some college education have children who do better on math achievement than the children of fathers who have a high school education or less?

Follow these commands:

- Click on **Statistics => Compare means => Independent Samples T Test**.
- Move *mathach* to the **Test** (dependent) **Variable(s)** box and move *faedr* to the **Grouping** (independent) **Variable(s)** box (see Fig. 14.2).
- Next click on **Define Groups** and Type **1** in the **Group 1** box and **2** in the **Group 2** box (see Fig. 14.3).

Note: If we had compared students whose fathers had some college with those whose fathers had completed a B. S. or more, we would have typed 2 for Group 1 and 3 for Group 2.

- Click on **Continue** then on **OK**. Compare your syntax and output to Output 14.1.

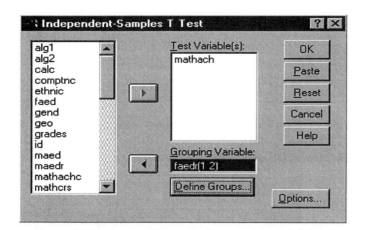

Fig. 14.2. Independent-samples *t* test.

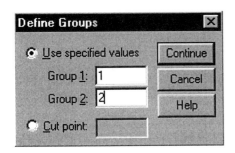

Fig. 14.3. Define groups.

Problem 2: Independent Samples t Test, Between Groups Design

Now try it yourself. Determine if boys and girls differ significantly on grades, math achievement, number of math classes taken, and math grades. You will assume that the scores for the four dependent variables are normally distributed and interval level. These assumptions are questionable for math grades because it is a dichotomous variable (high and low).

Compare your syntax and output to Output 14.2.

Problem 3: Nonparametric Equivalent of the t Test (Mann-Whitney)

What happens if the dependent variable data are not normally distributed or are not interval/ratio but, rather, ordinal? The answer is to run the appropriate nonparametric statistic.

Now let's try a nonparametric test for a between groups design with two levels of the independent variable. Let's see if boys and girls differ significantly on grades, math achievement, number of math classes taken, and math grades. Assume that the scores for the four dependent variables are ordinal scale.

- Click on **Statistics => Nonparametric Tests => 2 Independent Samples**.
- Move *grades, mathach, mathcrs,* and *mathgr* to the **Test** (dependent) **Variable List**.
- Next, click on *gend* and move it over to the **Grouping** (independent) **Variable** box.
- Click on **Define Groups** and enter 1 and 2 for groups 1 and 2, respectively because males are 1 and females are 2.
- Ensure that **Mann-Whitney U** is checked. Your window should look like Fig. 14.4.
- Click on **OK**.

Compare your syntax and output to Output 14.3 to check your work.

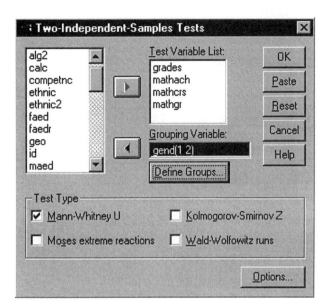

Fig. 14.4. Nonparametric tests for two independent samples.

Problem 4: Chi-Square

Let's see if boys and girls differ in terms of their math grades. Remember, this variable has two values: less A-B = 0 (low) and most A-B = 1 (high). If we assumed that *mathgr* is a nominal variable, then chi-square is the appropriate statistic (see Table 7.1). Follow these commands:

- Click on **Statistics => Summarize => Crosstabs**.
- Put *gend* in the **Columns** box using the arrow key and put *mathgr* in the **Rows** box (see Fig. 14.5).
- Next, click on **Statistics** and select **Chi-square**.
- Click on **Continue**.
- Once you return to the Crosstabs menu, click on **Cells**.
- Now, click on **Expected** and **Total**; ensure that **Observed** is also checked (see Fig. 14.6).
- Click on **Continue** then **OK**. Compare your syntax and output to Output 14.4.

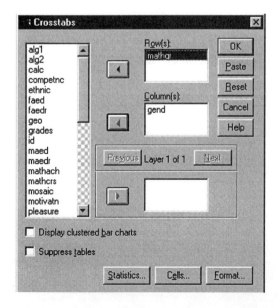

Fig. 14.5. Crosstabs.

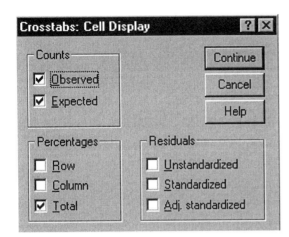

Fig. 14.6. Crosstabs: Cell display.

Problem 5: Paired Samples t Test, Within Subjects Design With Two Levels

Now we will determine if the fathers of these students have more education than their mothers. Remember that the fathers and mothers are paired; that is, each child has a pair of parents. In addition, we will see if the two visualization scores are significantly different. We would do a paired samples *t* test if the dependent variable data are approximately interval scale and normally distributed.

- Click on **Statistics => Compare means => Paired Sample T Test**.
- Click on both of the variables *faed* and *maed* (not *faedr* and *maedr*) and move them simultaneously to the **Paired Variable(s)** box (see Fig. 14.7).
- Repeat the same for *visual* and *visual2*.
- Click on **OK**.

Compare your syntax and output to Output 14.5.

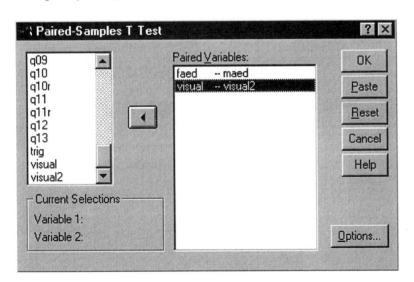

Fig. 14.7. Paired-samples *t* test.

Problem 6: Nonparametric Test for Two Related Samples (Wilcoxon)

Let's assume that education levels and visualization scores are not normally distributed and/or are ordinal data. Let's run an appropriate nonparametric test to see if fathers have significantly higher educational levels than mothers and to see if *visual* is significantly different from *visual2*.

Try this on your own. Hint: Use **nonparametric => 2 related samples**, and ensure that **Wilcoxon** is checked in the **Test Type** dialog box. Compare your syntax and output to Output 14.6.

Print, Save, and Exit

- **Print** your lab assignment results.
- **Save** your data file as **hsbdataJ** (**File** => **Save As**).
- **Save** the SPSS log files as **hsblogJ**.
- **Exit** SPSS.

Interpretation Questions

1. In Output 14.2: a) Are the *variances* equal or significantly different for the four dependent variables? b) List the appropriate *t*, *df*, and *p* (significance level) for each *t* test as you would in an article. c) Which *t* tests are statistically significant? d) Write sentences interpreting the gender difference between the means of *grades* and of *mathach*. e) Interpret the 95% confidence interval for these two variables.

2. In Output 14.3: a) Which Mann-Whitney tests are significant? b) Write a sentence about *mathcrs and mathgr*. c) Compare the statistical significance of the results in Output 14.2 and 14.3.

3. In Output 14.4: a) Is the (Pearson) chi-square statistically significant? Explain what it means. b) Are the expected values in at least 80% of the cells $\geq$ 5? How do you know? c) Compare the results of this output with the part of Output 14.3 that deals with math grades.

4. In Output 14.5: a) What does the paired samples correlation for mother's and father's education mean? b) Interpret/explain the results for both *t* tests.

5. In Output 14.6: a) Are the Wilcoxon tests significant? b) Compare the results to the paired *t* tests in Output 14.5.

Outputs and Interpretations

```
GET
  FILE='A:\hsbdataI.sav'.
EXECUTE .
```

Output 14.1: Independent Samples *t* Test--Between Groups Design

Syntax for t test comparing fathers' education groups on math achievement

```
T-TEST
  GROUPS=faedr(1 2)
  /MISSING=ANALYSIS
  /VARIABLES=mathach
  /CRITERIA=CIN(.95) .
```

Interpretation of Output 14.1

The first table shows descriptive statistics for the two groups (low and medium fathers' education) separately. Note, the means (10.09 and 14.40) seem to be different, but the standard deviations (which are the square root of the variances) are not grossly unequal.

The second table provides *two* statistical tests. The first is the Levene test for the *assumption* that the *variances* of the two groups are equal. If this *F* test is *not* significant (as in this case), the assumption is *not* violated and one uses the "equal variance assumed" line for the *t* test and related statistics. However, if Levene's *F* is statistically significant (sig ≤ .05), then variances are significantly different and the assumption of equal variances is violated. In that case the "equal variances not assumed" line is used. You should state the results as *t*(52)= -2.70, *p*= .009 (where the number in parentheses is the *df*) in a research report. The inspection of the two group means indicates that the average math achievement score for students whose fathers did not go to college is significantly lower than scores for those whose father's had some college (but did not get a Bachelor's). The difference between the means is -4.31 points on a 25 point test. The minus indicates that the second group (some college) had the higher average score. The 95% confidence interval tells us that 95 times out of 100 the true (population) difference would fall between 1.10 points and 7.51 points. If both the "upper" and "lower" bounds have the same sign (either + or -) we know that the difference is statistically significant.

Group Statistics

	Father's ed rev	N	Mean	Std. Deviation	Std. Error Mean
math achievement	hs grad or less	38	10.0877	5.6130	.9105
	some college	16	14.3958	4.6654	1.1664

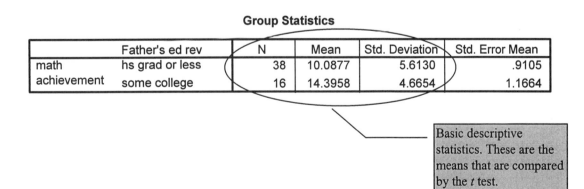

Basic descriptive statistics. These are the means that are compared by the *t* test.

Independent Samples Test

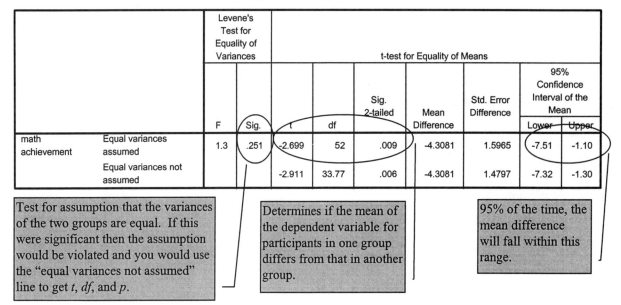

		Levene's Test for Equality of Variances		t-test for Equality of Means					95% Confidence Interval of the Mean	
		F	Sig.	t	df	Sig. 2-tailed	Mean Difference	Std. Error Difference	Lower	Upper
math achievement	Equal variances assumed	1.3	.251	-2.699	52	.009	-4.3081	1.5965	-7.51	-1.10
	Equal variances not assumed			-2.911	33.77	.006	-4.3081	1.4797	-7.32	-1.30

Test for assumption that the variances of the two groups are equal. If this were significant then the assumption would be violated and you would use the "equal variances not assumed" line to get *t*, *df*, and *p*.

Determines if the mean of the dependent variable for participants in one group differs from that in another group.

95% of the time, the mean difference will fall within this range.

Output 14.2: Independent Samples *t* tests on Four Dependent Variables

Syntax for comparing males and females on grades, math achievement, number of math classes taken, and math grades using *t* tests for a between groups design

```
T-TEST
  GROUPS=gend(1 2)
  /MISSING=ANALYSIS
  /VARIABLES=grades mathach mathcrs mathgr
  /CRITERIA=CIN(.95) .
```

Group Statistics

	gender	N	Mean	Std. Deviation	Std. Error Mean
grades in h.s.	male	34	5.50	1.64	.28
	female	41	5.83	1.51	.24
math achievement	male	34	14.7550	6.0315	1.0344
	female	41	10.7479	6.6961	1.0458
Math course taken	male	34	2.71	1.57	.27
	female	41	1.61	1.61	.25
math grades	male	34	.29	.46	7.93E-02
	female	41	.51	.51	7.90E-02

Independent Samples Test

		Levene's Test for Equality of Variances		t-test for Equality of Means						
		F	Sig.	t	df	Sig. (2-tailed)	Mean Difference	Std. Error Difference	95% Confidence Interval of the Mean	
									Lower	Upper
grades in h.s.	Equal variances assumed	.574	.451	-.903	73	.369	-.33	.36	-1.06	.40
	Equal variances not assumed			-.897	68.14	.373	-.33	.37	-1.06	.40
math achievement	Equal variances assumed	.537	.466	2.70	73	.009	4.0070	1.4855	1.0465	6.9676
	Equal variances not assumed			2.72	72.47	.008	4.0070	1.4709	1.0752	6.9389
Math course taken	Equal variances assumed	.008	.930	2.97	73	.004	1.10	.37	.36	1.83
	Equal variances not assumed			2.98	71.11	.004	1.10	.37	.36	1.83
math grades	Equal variances assumed	8.0	.006	-1.9	73	.057	-.22	.11	-.44	6.98E-03
	Equal variances not assumed			-1.9	72.28	.055	-.22	.11	-.44	5.12E-03

Output 14.3: Nonparametric Equivalent of the *t* Test (Mann-Whitney)

Syntax for the nonparametric equivalent of the independent samples *t* test comparing males and females on grades, math achievement, math courses taken, and math grades

```
NPAR TESTS
  /M-W= grades mathach mathcrs mathgr  BY gend(1 2)
  /MISSING ANALYSIS.
```

Interpretation of Output 14.3

The first table shows the mean or average ranks for males and females on each of the four dependent variables. The program ranks the 75 students from 75 (highest) to 1 (lowest) so that, in contrast to the typical ranking procedure, a high mean rank indicates the group scored higher. The second table provides the Mann-Whitney U and the approximate significance level or *p*. Note that the mean ranks of the genders differ significantly on math achievement but not on grades in high school.

Ranks

Mean ranks to be compared.

	gender	N	Mean Rank	Sum of Ranks
grades in h.s.	male	34	35.78	1216.50
	female	41	39.84	1633.50
	Total	75		
math achievement	male	34	45.10	1533.50
	female	41	32.11	1316.50
	Total	75		
Math course taken	male	34	46.01	1564.50
	female	41	31.35	1285.50
	Total	75		
math grades	male	34	33.53	1140.00
	female	41	41.71	1710.00
	Total	75		

Test Statistics [a]

	grades in h.s.	math achievement	Math course taken	math grades
Mann-Whitney U	621.500	455.500	424.500	545.000
Wilcoxon W	1216.500	1316.500	1285.500	1140.000
Z	-.818	-2.575	-2.950	-1.896
Asymp. Sig. (2-tailed)	.413	.010	.003	.058

a. Grouping Variable: gender

Output 14.4: Chi-Square

Syntax for comparing males and females on math grades (high vs. low)

```
CROSSTABS
  /TABLES=mathgr  BY gend
  /FORMAT= AVALUE TABLES
  /STATISTIC=CHISQ
  /CELLS= COUNT EXPECTED TOTAL .
```

Interpretation of Output 14.4

The **chi-square** statistic is used to determine if there is a relationship between two categorical variables. It tells you whether the relationship is statistically significant but does not indicate its *strength*, like a correlation does. In Output 14.4, use the **Pearson chi-square** ($p= .056$) or the **Fisher's exact test** ($p = .064$, two tailed) to interpret the results of the chi-square test. These results indicate that we cannot be confident that males and females are different on whether they get high math grades. Note that footnote b states that no cells have expected counts less than 5. That is good because that is one of the assumptions of chi-square. A good rule of thumb is that no more than 20% of the cells should have expected frequencies less than 5. For chi-square with 1 *df* (e.g., 2 x 2) none of the cells should have expected frequencies less than 5.

Case Processing Summary

	Cases					
	Valid		Missing		Total	
	N	Percent	N	Percent	N	Percent
math grades * gender	75	100.0%	0	.0%	75	100.0%

math grades * gender Crosstabulation

			gender		Total
			male	female	
math grades	less A-B	Count	24	20	44
		Expected Count	19.9	24.1	44.0
		% of Total	32.0%	26.7%	58.7%
	most A-B	Count	10	21	31
		Expected Count	14.1	16.9	31.0
		% of Total	13.3%	28.0%	41.3%
Total		Count	34	41	75
		Expected Count	34.0	41.0	75.0
		% of Total	45.3%	54.7%	100.0%

Chi-Square Tests

	Value	df	Asymp. Sig. (2-tailed)	Exact Sig. (2-tailed)	Exact Sig. (1-tailed)
Pearson Chi-Square	3.645[b]	1	.056		
Continuity Correction [a]	2.801	1	.094		
Likelihood Ratio	3.699	1	.054		
Fisher's Exact Test				.064	.046
Linear-by-Linear Association	3.597	1	.058		
N of Valid Cases	75				

a. Computed only for a 2x2 table

b. 0 cells (.0%) have expected count less than 5. The minimum expected count is 14.05.

Output 14.5: Paired Samples *t* Tests, Within Subjects Design With Two Levels

Syntax for comparing father's and mother's education, and for comparing visual and visual2 using paired samples *t* tests

```
T-TEST
  PAIRS= faed visual  WITH maed visual2 (PAIRED)
  /CRITERIA=CIN(.95)
  /MISSING=ANALYSIS.
```

Interpretation of Output 14.5 and 14.6

The first table shows the descriptive statistics used to compare the average mother's and father's education and to compare the average visualization score and retest. The second table provides correlations between the two paired scores. We have already seen (in the reliability assignment) that the visualization score and its retest are highly correlated ($r = .89$). The third table shows the two paired samples *t* tests. Note that the visualization score is .78 points higher than the retest score and that this is a significant difference: $t (74) = 3.55$, $p = .001$.

Output 14.6 shows the equivalent nonparametric (Wilcoxon) analyses. Note that the first table shows not only the mean ranks, but also the number of students who, for example, had mothers with less education than their fathers (27). The second table shows the significance level for the two tests.

Means to be compared.

Paired Samples Statistics

		Mean	N	Std. Deviation	Std. Error Mean
Pair 1	father's education	4.73	73	2.83	.33
	mother's education	4.14	73	2.26	.26
Pair 2	visualization score	5.2433	75	3.9120	.4517
	Visualization retest	4.47	75	2.93	.34

Paired Samples Correlations

		N	Correlation	Sig.
Pair 1	father's education & mother's education	73	.681	.000
Pair 2	visualization score & Visualization retest	75	.886	.000

Paired Samples Test

		Paired Differences							
					95% Confidence Interval of the Difference				Sig.
		Mean	Std. Deviation	Std. Error Mean	Lower	Upper	t	df	(2-tailed)
Pair 1	father's education - mother's education	.59	2.10	.25	9.90E-02	1.08	2.396	72	.019
Pair 2	visualization score - Visualization retest	.7767	1.8931	.2186	.3411	1.2122	3.553	74	.001

Output 14.6: Nonparametric Test for Two Related Samples - Wilcoxon

Syntax for the nonparametric test for two related samples - comparing father's and mother's education and comparing visual and visual2

```
NPAR TEST
  /WILCOXON=faed visual  WITH maed visual2 (PAIRED)
  /MISSING ANALYSIS.
```

Wilcoxon Signed Ranks Test

Ranks

		N	Mean Rank	Sum of Ranks
mother's education - father's education	Negative Ranks	27[a]	29.20	788.50
	Positive Ranks	21[b]	18.45	387.50
	Ties	25[c]		
	Total	73		
Visualization retest - visualization score	Negative Ranks	56[d]	35.91	2011.00
	Positive Ranks	14[e]	33.86	474.00
	Ties	5[f]		
	Total	75		

a. mother's education < father's education

b. mother's education > father's education

c. father's education = mother's education

d. Visualization retest < visualization score

e. Visualization retest > visualization score

f. visualization score = Visualization retest

Test Statistics[a]

	mother's education - father's education	Visualization retest - visualization score
Z	-2.085 [b]	-4.507 [b]
Asymp. Sig. (2-tailed)	.037	.000

a. Wilcoxon Signed Ranks Test

b. Based on positive ranks.

CHAPTER 15

One-Way ANOVA With Multiple Comparisons
for Between Groups Designs

In this lab, we will examine statistical techniques for comparing two or *more* independent groups on the central tendency of the dependent variable. The parametric statistic, called **one-way ANOVA** in SPSS, compares the *means* of the samples/groups in order to make inferences about the population means. As with the *t* test, ANOVA assumes that the dependent variable is approximately interval scale, normally distributed in the population, and the variances of the groups are equal. One-way ANOVA is also called single factor analysis of variance, because there is only one independent variable.

If the assumptions are markedly violated, we should use the nonparametric equivalent of the one-way ANOVA. This statistic, which is called the **Kruskal-Wallis** test, compares the mean *ranks* of the groups. We will use this nonparametric test in Problem 3.

In this assignment, we will introduce the concept of **post hoc multiple comparisons**, sometimes called follow-up tests. When you compare *three or more group means*, you will know that there will be a statistically significant difference somewhere if the **ANOVA F** (sometimes called the **overall** or **omnibus F**) is significant. However, we would usually like to know which specific means are different from which other ones. In order to know this, you can use *one* of several post hoc tests that are built into the SPSS one-way ANOVA program. The **LSD** post hoc test is quite liberal and the **Scheffe** test is quite conservative so many statisticians recommend a middle of the road test such as the **Tukey** honestly significant differences (HSD) test.

Ordinarily, you *do post hoc tests only if the overall F is significant*. For this reason, we have separated Problems 1 and 2, which could have been done in one step. In Problem 4, we have disregarded the above rules and done two post hoc tests, even though the overall F was not significant. We did this to show you what can happen if you ignore the rule. Fig. 15.1 shows the steps one should use in deciding whether to use post hoc multiple comparison tests.

Unfortunately, there is no post hoc test built into SPSS for the Kruskal-Wallis test. You could do the Tukey test with a calculator. Or, several Mann-Whitney U tests could be done with SPSS to compare the several combinations of mean ranks. Of course, you would only do either of these follow-up tests if the overall Kruskal-Wallis test was significant. Using the Mann-Whitney as a follow-up test is analogous to using LSD and, thus, is quite liberal (i.e., it is easier to find a statistically significant result). For this reason, you might want to use the .01 significance level or another adjustment such as the Bonferroni (which divides .05 by the number of comparisons) to reduce the likelihood of identifying a difference by chance.

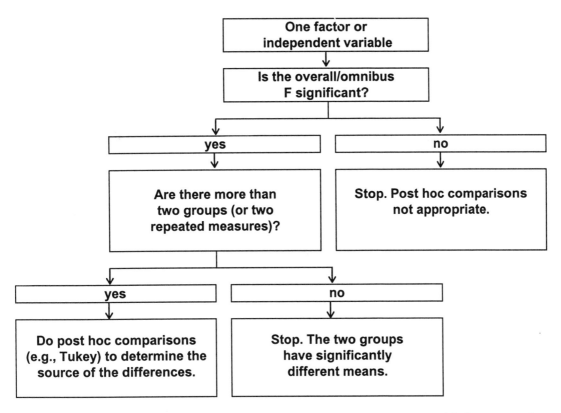

Fig. 15.1. Schematic representation of when to use post hoc multiple comparisons with a one-way ANOVA.

Problems/Research Questions

1. Are there difference's between the *three* fathers' education (revised) groups on grades, math achievement, and visualization scores?

2. If the overall *F* is significant, which pairs of means are significantly different? We will use the **Tukey** HSD if the Levene test finds that the variances are not significantly different or the **Dunnett's C** if the variances are different.

3. Now compare the three fathers' education groups on math achievement and mosaic scores using an appropriate nonparametric test. Remember that mosaic was not normally distributed. In the case of math achievement, the variances of the three fathers' education groups were significantly different.

4. Are there differences between Euro-American, African-American, Hispanic-American, and Asian-American students on the average of math achievement test scores?

5. Then, to demonstrate the differences between the tests, you will do post hoc comparisons of the various combinations of the means using both the **LSD** and **Scheffe** tests.

Lab Assignment K

Logon and Get Data

- Retrieve **hsbdataJ**.

Problem 1: One-Way ANOVA

We will use the **One-Way ANOVA** procedure since we have one independent variable with three values or levels to analyze. So, let's do these commands:

- **Statistics => Compare Means => One-Way ANOVA.**
- Move *grades*, *mathach,* and *visual* into the **Dependent List** box.
- Click on *faedr* and move it to the **Factor** box (independent variable).
- Finally, click on **Options** and choose **Descriptives** and **Homogeneity-of-variance**. See Fig. 15.2 through 15.3 for assistance.
- Click on **Continue** then **OK**. Compare your syntax and output to Output 15.1.

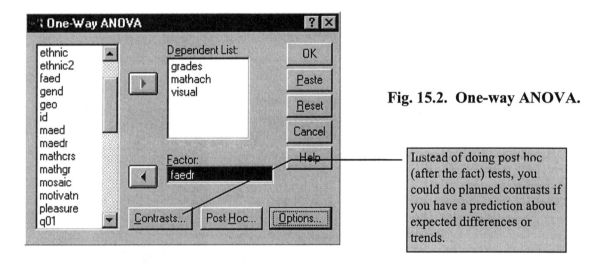

Fig. 15.2. One-way ANOVA.

Instead of doing post hoc (after the fact) tests, you could do planned contrasts if you have a prediction about expected differences or trends.

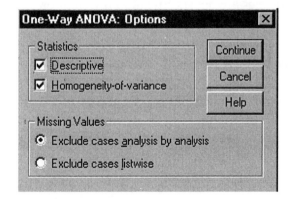

Fig. 15.3. One-way ANOVA: Options.

Problem 2: Tukey and Dunnett's C Multiple Comparison Tests

After you have examined Output 15.1 to see if the assumption of equality of variances was met and if the overall or omnibus F was significant, you will do appropriate post hoc multiple comparisons. To do these, get the **One-Way ANOVA** dialog box again by doing the following:

- Select **Statistics** => **Compare Means** => **One-Way ANOVA**.
- Move *visual* and *mathach* out of the **Dependent List** by highlighting each one and clicking on the arrow pointing left. (The reasons were that the overall F for *visual* was not significant and Levene's test was significant for *mathach*. See interpretation for Output 15.1.)
- Keep *grades* in the **Dependent List** because it had a significant F and homogeneous ("equal") variances.
- Insure *faedr* is in the **Factor** box.
- Next, click on **Options** and *remove* the **Descriptive** and **Homogeneity of variance** checks because we do not need to do them again.
- Then click on **Continue**.
- In the main dialogue box (Fig. 15.2), press **Post Hoc** to get Fig. 15.4.
- Check on **Tukey** because equal variances can be assumed for *grades*.
- Click on **Continue** and then **OK** to run this post hoc test. Compare your syntax and output to Output 15.2a.

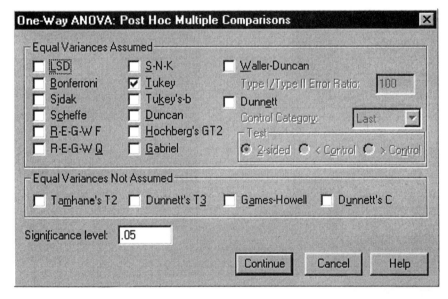

Fig. 15.4. One-way ANOVA: Post hoc multiple comparisons.

After you do the Tukey test, let's go back and do Dunnett's C. Follow these steps:

- Select **Statistics** => **Compare Means** => **One-Way ANOVA**.
- Move *grades* out of the **Dependent List** by highlighting it and clicking on the arrow pointing left.
- Move *mathach* into the **Dependent List**.
- Insure *faedr* is still in the **Factor** box.
- In the main dialogue box (Fig. 15.2), press **Post Hoc** to get Fig. 15.4.
- Check on **Dunnett's C** because equal variances can not be assumed for *mathach*.
- Remove the check mark from **Tukey**.

- Click on **Continue** and then **OK** to run this post hoc test. Compare your syntax and output to Output 15.2b.

Problem 3: Nonparametric Test (Kruskal-Wallis)

What do you do if your data are ordinal or other assumptions are violated? The answer is nonparametric statistics. Let's make the comparisons similar to Problem 1, assuming that the data are ordinal or other assumptions of ANOVA such as equality of group variances or normality are violated. Remember that the variances for the three fathers' education groups were significantly different on *mathach*, and that *mosaic* was not normally distributed.

Follow these commands:
- **Statistics => Nonparametric Test => K Independent Samples**.
- Move the dependent variables of *mathach* and *mosaic* to the **Test Variable List**.
- Move the independent variable *faedr* to the **Grouping Variable** box (see Fig. 15.5).
- Click on **Define Range** and insert **1** and **3** into the **minimum** and **maximum** boxes (Fig. 15.6) because father's education revised has values of 1, 2, and 3.
- Click on **Continue**.
- Also, ensure that **Kruskal-Wallis H** (under **Test Type**) in the main dialogue box is on.
- Then, click on **OK**. Do your results look like Output 15.3?

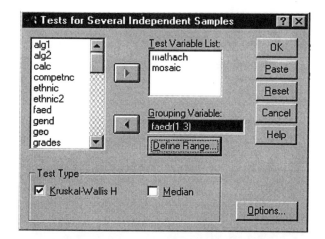

Fig. 15.5. Tests for several independent samples.

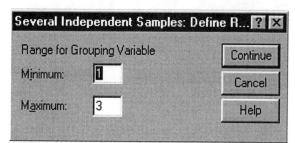

Fig. 15.6. Define range.

Problem 4: One-Way ANOVA

Try a one-way ANOVA yourself. Compare Euro-American, African-American, Hispanic-American, and Asian-American students (ethnic is the variable) on math achievement (*mathach*). Refer to Problems 1 and 2 for help. ***Important***: Begin by clicking **Reset** once you start your ANOVA.

- Helpful Hints: **Statistic => Compare Means => One-Way ANOVA.**
- Move *mathach* to the **Dependent List** and *ethnic* to the **Factor** box.
- Under **Options** choose **Descriptives** and **Homogeneity-of-variance.**

Problem 5: Comparing LSD and Scheffe Post Hoc Tests

Usually, we would *not* do a post hoc test if the overall F was not significant. However, we want to show you what can happen if you do a liberal post hoc test with a nonsignificant overall F. So, do follow-up comparisons of all the various combinations of the means using both the **LSD** and **Scheffe** tests, which are liberal and conservative post hoc tests, respectively. Compare your output to Output 15.5 when you finish. Note that usually *you* should choose only *one* post hoc test. We have asked you to choose these two tests in order to compare the results and make a point. Follow these steps:
- **Statistics => Compare Means => One-Way ANOVA.**
- Make sure *mathach* is in the **Dependent List** and *ethnic* is in the **Factor** box.
- Under **Options**, click *off* **Descriptives** and **Homogeneity of variance.**
- Click on **Continue.**
- Under **Post Hoc**, choose **LSD** and **Scheffe.**
- Click on **Continue** then **OK.**

Print, Save, and Exit

- **Print** your outputs, if necessary.
- **Save** your data as **hsbdataK** (Use **File => Save As**).
- **Save** the SPSS log files as **hsblogK.**
- **Exit** SPSS.

Interpretation Questions

1. In Output 15.1: a) Was the assumption of homogeneity (i.e., equality) of variances justified for the three dependent variables, *grades, mathach*, and *visual*? b) List the *F, df,* and *p* values for each dependent variable as you would in an article. c) Describe the results in nontechnical terms for visualization and grades. Use the group means in your description.

2. In Outputs 15.2a and 15.2b: a) What pairs of means were significantly different? b) Why did we use different post hoc tests?

3. In Output 15.3: a) Are the Kruskal-Wallis tests significant? b) Describe the results for mosaic. c) Compare Output 15.1 and 15.3 for math achievement.

4. In Output 15.4: a) Are there significant differences between the ethnic groups? b) Should you do post hoc tests?

5. In Output 15.5, compare the results of the LSD and Scheffe tests.

Outputs and Interpretations

```
GET
FILE='A:\hsbdataJ.sav'
EXECUTE.
```

Output 15.1: One-Way ANOVA

Syntax for one-way ANOVA-grades, mathach, and visual by faedr

```
ONEWAY
  grades mathach visual BY faedr
  /STATISTICS DESCRIPTIVES HOMOGENEITY
  /MISSING ANALYSIS .
```

Interpretation of Output 15.1

The first table provides familiar descriptive statistics for the three fathers' education groups on each of the three dependent variables that we requested (*grades, mathach,* and *visual)* for this analysis. Note that although those three dependent variables appear together in the tables, we have really computed three separate one-way ANOVAs.

The second table in Output 15.1 provides the Levene test to check the assumption that the variances of the three father's education groups are equal; i.e., not significantly different. Notice that for grades and visualization the tests are not significant. Thus, the assumption is not violated. However, for math achievement; the Levene test is significant (barely) and, thus, the assumption of equal variances is violated. In this case, we could use the equivalent nonparametric test (Kruskal-Wallis). Or, if the overall *F* is significant (as you can see it was in the ANOVA table), you could use a post hoc test designed for situations in which the variances are unequal. We will do the latter in Problem 2 and the former in Problem 3 for math achievement.

The ANOVA table in Output 15.1 is the key table because it shows whether the overall *F*s for these three ANOVAs were significant. Note that the three father's education groups differ significantly on grades and math achievement but not visualization. When reporting these findings one should write, for example, $F(2, 70)=4.09, p=.021$, for grades. The 2, 70 are the degrees of freedom (*df*). *F tables* also usually include the mean squares, which indicates the amount of variance for that "effect" divided by the degrees of freedom for that "effect." It is a good idea to report the means so that one can see which groups were high and low. Remember, however, that if you have three or more groups you will not know which specific pairs of means are significantly different, unless you do a post hoc test.

Descriptives

			N	Mean	Std. Deviation	Std. Error	95% Confidence Interval for Mean		Minimum	Maximum
							Lower Bound	Upper Bound		
grades in h.s.	Father's ed rev	hs grad or less	38	5.34	1.48	.24	4.86	5.83	3	8
		some college	16	5.56	1.79	.45	4.61	6.52	2	8
		BS or more	19	6.53	1.22	.28	5.94	7.11	4	8
		Total	73	5.70	1.55	.18	5.34	6.06	2	8
math achievement	Father's ed rev	hs grad or less	38	10.09	5.6130	.9105	8.2428	11.93	1.00	22.67
		some college	16	14.40	4.6654	1.17	11.910	16.88	5.00	23.67
		BS or more	19	16.35	7.4092	1.70	12.780	19.92	1.00	23.67
		Total	73	12.66	6.4966	.7604	11.146	14.18	1.00	23.67
visualization score	Father's ed rev	hs grad or less	38	4.6711	3.9606	.6425	3.3692	5.9729	-.25	14.75
		some college	16	6.0156	4.5602	1.14	3.5857	8.4456	-.25	14.75
		BS or more	19	5.4605	2.7904	.6402	4.1156	6.8055	-.25	9.75
		Total	73	5.1712	3.8279	.4480	4.2781	6.0643	-.25	14.75

Test of Homogeneity of Variances

	Levene Statistic	df1	df2	Sig.
grades in h.s.	1.546	2	70	.220
math achievement	3.157	2	70	.049
visualization score	1.926	2	70	.153

The Levene test is significant for math achievement so the variances are significantly different.

ANOVA

		Sum of Squares	df	Mean Square	F	Sig.
grades in h.s.	Between Groups	18.143	2	9.071	4.091	.021
	Within Groups	155.227	70	2.218		
	Total	173.370	72			
math achievement	Between Groups	558.481	2	279.240	7.881	.001
	Within Groups	2480.324	70	35.433		
	Total	3038.804	72			
visualization score	Between Groups	22.505	2	11.252	.763	.470
	Within Groups	1032.480	70	14.750		
	Total	1054.985	72			

Grades in high school and math achievement are significant while visualization is not.

Output 15.2a: Tukey Multiple Comparison Test

Syntax for Tukey multiple comparison tests for grades

```
ONEWAY
  grades BY faedr
  /MISSING ANALYSIS
  /POSTHOC = TUKEY ALPHA(.05).
```

Interpretation of Output 15.2a and 15.2b

The first table repeats the ANOVA for grades.. The next table shows the **Tukey HSD** test for *grades*. Note that each comparison is presented twice. Do not interpret lines that have the same mean differences. For grades and the Tukey test, there is only a small mean difference (-.22) between the mean grades of students whose fathers were high school grads or less (mean = 5.34 from Output 15.1) and those fathers who had some college (5.56). The difference is not significant (p = .873) using the Tukey test. Similarly, we can tell that there was a significant difference between the grades of students with low and high fathers' education (p = .017), but the medium versus high education difference was not significant (p = .144).

Output 15.2b shows the Dunnett C test for math achievement. There is an error in the **sig** column as a result of an SPSS 7.5 bug so examine the confidence limits which indicate whether the groups are significantly different. If the lower and upper bounds have the same sign, the means are statistically significantly different. Thus, both students whose fathers had some college and those whose fathers had a B.S. degree were significantly different on math achievement from those whose fathers had a high school degree or less.

ANOVA

		Sum of Squares	df	Mean Square	F	Sig.
grades in h.s.	Between Groups	18.143	2	9.071	4.091	.021
	Within Groups	155.227	70	2.218		
	Total	173.370	72			

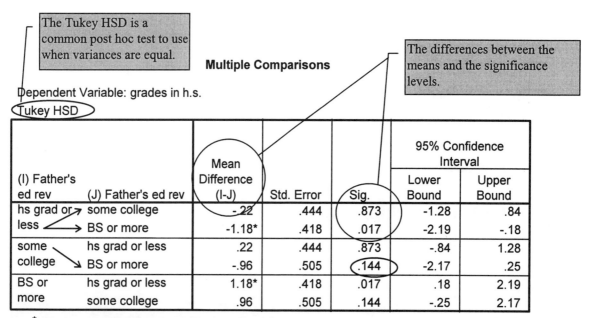

The Tukey HSD is a common post hoc test to use when variances are equal.

Multiple Comparisons

The differences between the means and the significance levels.

Dependent Variable: grades in h.s.
Tukey HSD

(I) Father's ed rev	(J) Father's ed rev	Mean Difference (I-J)	Std. Error	Sig.	95% Confidence Interval Lower Bound	95% Confidence Interval Upper Bound
hs grad or less	some college	-.22	.444	.873	-1.28	.84
	BS or more	-1.18*	.418	.017	-2.19	-.18
some college	hs grad or less	.22	.444	.873	-.84	1.28
	BS or more	-.96	.505	.144	-2.17	.25
BS or more	hs grad or less	1.18*	.418	.017	.18	2.19
	some college	.96	.505	.144	-.25	2.17

*. The mean difference is significant at the .05 level.

204

grades in h.s.

Tukey HSD[a,b]

Father's ed rev	N	Subset for alpha = .05	
		1	2
hs grad or less	38	5.34	
some college	16	5.56	5.56
BS or more	19		6.53
Sig.		.880	.096

Another way of computing and displaying the post hoc test. Groups listed in the same subset are not significantly different.

Means for groups in homogeneous subsets are displayed.

   a. Uses Harmonic Mean Sample Size = 21.209

   b. The group sizes are unequal. The harmonic mean of the group sizes is used. Type I error levels are not guaranteed.

Output 15.2b: Dunnett's C Multiple Comparison Test

Syntax for Dunnett's C multiple comparison tests for mathach when variances are unequal
```
mathach BY faedr
/MISSING ANALYSIS
/POSTHOC = C ALPHA(.05).
```

ANOVA

		Sum of Squares	df	Mean Square	F	Sig.
math achievement	Between Groups	558.481	2	279.240	7.881	.001
	Within Groups	2480.324	70	35.433		
	Total	3038.804	72			

Post Hoc Tests

Multiple Comparisons

Dependent Variable: math achievement

Dunnett C

Use Dunnett C when the Levene test indicates that the variances are significantly different.

(I) Father's ed rev	(J) Father's ed rev	Mean Difference (I-J)	Std. Error	Sig. see note below	95% Confidence Interval Lower Bound	95% Confidence Interval Upper Bound
hs grad or less	some college	-4.3081*	1.774	.000	-8.0642	-.5520
	BS or more	-6.2632*	1.673	.000	-11.1370	-1.3895
some college	hs grad or less	4.3081*	1.774	.000	.5520	8.0642
	BS or more	-1.9551	2.020	.000	-7.2463	3.3360
BS or more	hs grad or less	6.2632*	1.673	.000	1.3895	11.1370
	some college	1.9551	2.020	.000	-3.3360	7.2463

*. The mean difference is significant at the .05 level.   Note: SPSS 7.5 has a bug in it that prints .000 as the sig. for all Dunnett C tests. Ignore that column.

Output 15.3: Nonparametric Tests - Kruskal-Wallis

Syntax for nonparametric equivalent of one-way ANOVA - comparing father's education groups on mathach and mosaic

```
NPAR TESTS
  /K-W=mathach mosaic    BY faedr(1 3)
  /MISSING ANALYSIS.
```

Interpretation of Output 15.3

As in the case of the Mann-Whitney test (Assignment I), the first table provides mean ranks for the two dependent variables, math achievement and mosaic. In this case, the Kruskal-Wallis test will compare the mean ranks for the three father's education groups. The second table shows when there is an overall difference between the three groups. Unfortunately, there is not a post hoc test built into the K-W test, as there is for the one-way ANOVA. For example, you cannot tell which of the pairs of father's education means are different on math achievement. One method to check this would be to run three Mann-Whitney tests comparing each pair of father's education mean ranks. Note, you would only do the post hoc M-W tests if the K-W test was statistically significant. It would be prudent to adjust the significance level by dividing .05 by 3 so that you would require that **Sig.**=.017 to be statistically significant.

Kruskal-Wallis Test

Ranks

	Father's ed rev	N	Mean Rank
math achievement	hs grad or less	38	28.43
	some college	16	43.78
	BS or more	19	48.42
	Total	73	
mosaic, pattern test	hs grad or less	38	35.91
	some college	16	38.03
	BS or more	19	38.32
	Total	73	

Test Statistics[a,b]

	math achievement	mosaic, pattern test
Chi-Square	13.384	.212
df	2	2
Asymp. Sig.	.001	.899

a. Kruskal-Wallis Test

b. Grouping Variable: Father's ed rev

Output 15.4: One-Way ANOVA

Syntax for ANOVA - mathach by ethnic

```
ONEWAY
  mathach BY ethnic
  /STATISTICS DESCRIPTIVES HOMOGENEITY
  /MISSING ANALYSIS
```

Descriptives

			N	Mean	Std. Deviation	Std. Error	95% Confidence Interval for Mean		Minimum	Maximum
							Lower Bound	Upper Bound		
math achievement	ethnicity	Euro-Amer	41	12.98	6.9194	1.0806	10.7998	15.1678	1.00	23.67
		African-Amer	15	9.733	6.2694	1.6187	6.2614	13.2051	-1.67	19.67
		Hispanic-Amer	10	12.13	7.1720	2.2680	7.0028	17.2638	1.00	23.67
		Asian-Amer	7	17.19	3.6457	1.3780	13.8187	20.5622	13.00	21.00
		Total	73	12.60	6.7568	.7908	11.0263	14.1792	-1.67	23.67

Test of Homogeneity of Variances

	Levene Statistic	df1	df2	Sig.
math achievement	1.372	3	69	.259

ANOVA

		Sum of Squares	df	Mean Square	F	Sig.
math achievement	Between Groups	278.994	3	92.998	2.133	.104
	Within Groups	3008.082	69	43.595		
	Total	3287.076	72			

Output 15.5: Comparing LSD and Scheffe Post Hoc Tests

Syntax for comparing LSD and Scheffe post hoc tests

```
ONEWAY
  mathach BY ethnic
  /MISSING ANALYSIS
  /POSTHOC = SCHEFFE LSD ALPHA(.05).
```

ANOVA

		Sum of Squares	df	Mean Square	F	Sig.
math achievement	Between Groups	278.994	3	92.998	2.13	.104
	Within Groups	3008.082	69	43.595		
	Total	3287.076	72			

Post Hoc Tests

Multiple Comparisons

The nonredundant significance levels are circled.

Dependent Variable: math achievement

	(I) ethnicity	(J) ethnicity	Mean Difference (I-J)	Std. Error	Sig.	95% Confidence Interval Lower Bound	Upper Bound
Scheffe	Euro-Amer	African-Amer	3.2505	1.992	.452	-2.4592	8.9602
		Hispanic-Amer	.8505	2.329	.987	-5.8229	7.5240
		Asian-Amer	-4.2066	2.700	.493	-11.9448	3.5315
	African-Amer	Euro-Amer	-3.2505	1.992	.452	-8.9602	2.4592
		Hispanic-Amer	-2.4000	2.696	.851	-10.1247	5.3247
		Asian-Amer	-7.4572	3.022	.118	-16.1183	1.2040
	Hispanic-Amer	Euro-Amer	-.8505	2.329	.987	-7.5240	5.8229
		African-Amer	2.4000	2.696	.851	-5.3247	10.1247
		Asian-Amer	-5.0571	3.254	.495	-14.3818	4.2675
	Asian-Amer	Euro-Amer	4.2066	2.700	.493	-3.5315	11.9448
		African-Amer	7.4572	3.022	.118	-1.2040	16.1183
		Hispanic-Amer	5.0571	3.254	.495	-4.2675	14.3818
LSD	Euro-Amer	African-Amer	3.2505	1.992	.107	-.7242	7.2253
		Hispanic-Amer	.8505	2.329	.716	-3.7951	5.4961
		Asian-Amer	-4.2066	2.700	.124	-9.5934	1.1802
	African-Amer	Euro-Amer	-3.2505	1.992	.107	-7.2253	.7242
		Hispanic-Amer	-2.4000	2.696	.376	-7.7775	2.9774
		Asian-Amer	-7.4572*	3.022	.016	-13.4865	-1.4278
	Hispanic-Amer	Euro-Amer	-.8505	2.329	.716	-5.4961	3.7951
		African-Amer	2.4000	2.696	.376	-2.9774	7.7775
		Asian-Amer	-5.0571	3.254	.125	-11.5484	1.4341
	Asian-Amer	Euro-Amer	4.2066	2.700	.124	-1.1802	9.5934
		African-Amer	7.4572*	3.022	.016	1.4278	13.4865
		Hispanic-Amer	5.0571	3.254	.125	-1.4341	11.5484

*. The mean difference is significant at the .05 level.

Asterisk indicates this is significant.

Homogeneous Subsets

math achievement

	ethnicity	N	Subset for alpha = .05 1
Scheffe[a]	African-Amer	15	9.7333
	Hispanic-Amer	10	12.1333
	Euro-Amer	41	12.9838
	Asian-Amer	7	17.1904
	Sig.		.063

Means for groups in homogeneous subsets are displayed.

a. Uses Harmonic Mean Sample Size = 11.979

198

CHAPTER 16

Factorial ANOVA, Including Interactions, and ANCOVA

In Assignments J and K, we compared two or more groups based on the levels of *one* independent variable or factor. These were called single factor between groups designs. In this lab, we will compare groups based on *two* independent variables. The appropriate statistic for Problems 1 and 2 is called a two factor or 2-way ANOVA. This statistic is used when there are two different groups in a between groups design. There are two SPSS programs to do factorial analysis of variance, **Simple Factorial** and **General Factorial**; both are found on the **General Linear Model** (GLM) menu. For Problems 1 and 2, we will use the General Factorial program because it provides useful addition information.[1]

The appropriate statistic for Problems 3 and 4 is called analysis of covariance or ANCOVA. It is used to adjust or control for differences between the groups based on another, typically interval level variable, called the covariate. For example, we found in Assignment I that boys and girls differ on math achievement. However, this could be due to the fact that boys take more math courses in high school. ANCOVA allows us to adjust the math achievement scores based on the relationship between number of math courses taken and math achievement. We can determine if boys and girls still have different math achievement scores after making the adjustment.

SPSS does not offer an ordinal data nonparametric equivalent for factorial ANOVA or ANCOVA so you will not have an alternate approach for these problems if the dependent variable is not normally distributed and/or is not interval scale. Because most statisticians agree that these assumptions can be violated quite a bit without invalidating an analysis of variance (and the typical violations are dealt with by the way SPSS does this procedure), we will not worry about not having a nonparametric alternative. Note that the loglinear analysis can be used to produce results similar to those of factorial ANOVA if one has nominal data for all variables.

Problems/Research Questions

1. Do math grades and gender each seem to have an effect on math achievement, and if there is an interaction between *mathgr* and *gend,* i.e., does the level of *mathgr* or *gend* affect the "influence" of the other independent variable on the dependent variable?

2. Do father's education (revised) and math grades seem to have an effect on math achievement, and do *faedr* and *mathgr* interact?

---

[1] If you do not have access to the advanced SPSS package, you can use the Simple Factorial ANOVA program with the **unique** method.

3. If the overall *F* for *faedr* is statistically significant, which pairs of means are significantly different?

4. Do boys have higher math achievement than girls if we control for differences in the number of math courses taken?

5. Do boys have higher math achievement if we control for differences in mosaic scores?

Lab Assignment L

Logon and Get Data

*   Retrieve **hsbdataK**.

Problem 1: General Factorial (2-Way) ANOVA

Let's find out if math grades (*mathgr*) and gender seem to have an effect on math achievement. Follow these commands:
*   **Statistics => General Linear Model => General Factorial**.
*   Move *mathach* to the **Dependent** (variable) box.
*   Move the first independent variable (*mathgr*) to the **Fixed Factor(s)** box.
*   Also, move the second independent variable *gend* (gender) to the **Fixed Factor(s)** box.
*   Click on **Continue**.

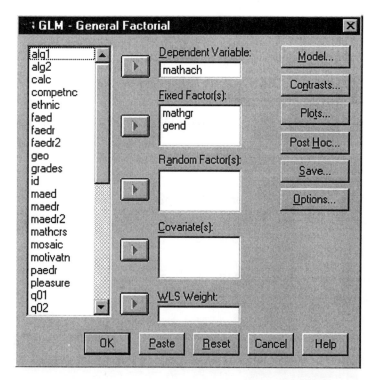

Fig. 16.1. GLM - General factorial ANOVA.

Now that we know the variables we will be dealing with, let's determine our options.
- Click on **Plots** and move *mathgr* to the **horizontal axis** and *gend* to **Separate Lines** box.
- Then press **Add**. See Fig. 16.2. Press **Continue.**

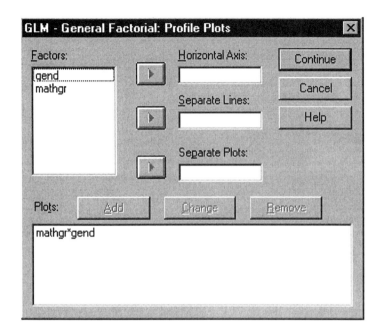

Fig. 16.2 General factorial:
Profile plots.

- Select **Options** and click **Descriptive statistics, Estimates of effect size,** and **Homogeneity tests**. See Fig. 16.3 for help.
- Click on **Continue**.
- Click on **OK**. Compare your syntax and output to Output 16.1.

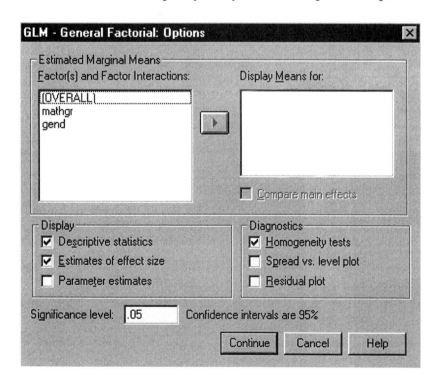

Fig. 16.3. General
factorial: Options.

Problem 2: Another Factorial ANOVA Using the GLM Program

Now try it yourself. Use *mathach* as the **Dependent** variable and *mathgr* and *faedr* as the **Fixed Factor(s)** (independent variables). Use the same options as for Problem 1. Hint: The plot will be easier to read if you put *faedr* with its three values on the **horizontal axis**. Compare your syntax and output to Output 16.2.

Problem 3: Post Hoc Test for Father's Education Revised

Let's go back and do something similar. However, this time we are going to cut out some of the options. This time remove the **Profile Plots** (highlight *mathgr*faedr* and then click on **Remove**) and click off each of the **Options** you selected for Problems 1 and 2. Now we want to see which pairs of the three father's education groups are significantly different from each other. Follow these steps:
- Click on **Post Hoc.**
- Move *faedr* to **Post Hoc Tests** for box (do not move *mathgr* because there are only two values and, therefore, post hoc tests are not needed). See Fig. 16.4.
- Select **Dunnett's C** under **Equal Variances Not Assumed** because the **Levene's** test from Output 16.2 indicated that the variances are significantly different. Thus, the assumption of equal variances is violated.
- Click on **Continue** and then **OK**.

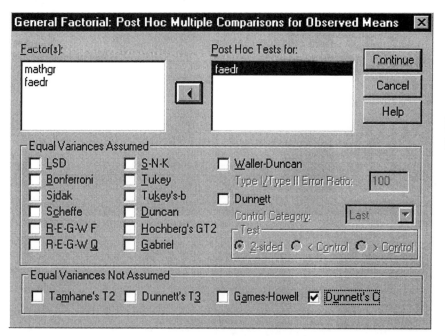

Fig. 16.4. General factorial: Post hoc.

Problem 4: Analysis of Covariance (ANCOVA)

In Problem 1 we found that boys have significantly higher *mathach* scores. Now, to see if the male's higher math achievement scores are due to differences in the number of math courses taken by the male and female students, we will use *mathcrs* as a covariate and do ANCOVA.

Instead of using the General Factorial, we will use the Simple Factorial to do ANCOVA:

- **Statistics => General Linear Model => Simple Factorial**.
- Next, move *mathach* to the **Dependent** box and *gend* to the **Factor(s)** box (see Fig. 16.5).
- Now, click on **Define Range** for *gender* and type **1** and **2**.
- Click on **Continue**.
- Move *mathcrs* to the **Covariates** box. You will get a window that looks like Fig. 16.5.

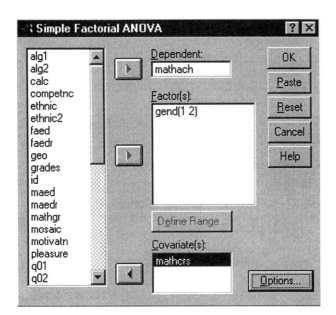

Fig. 16.5. Simple factorial ANOVA.

- Click on **Options**.
- Select **Experimental, Means and counts, MCA**, and (under **Enter Covariates**) **Before effects**. See Fig. 16.6 for help.

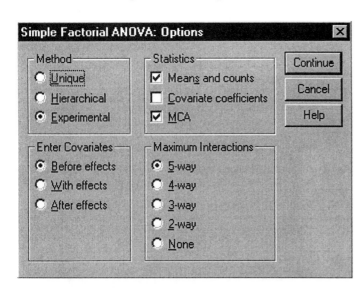

Fig. 16.6. Simple factorial ANOVA: Options.

- Click on **Continue** and then **OK**. Your syntax and output should look like Output 16.4.

Problem 5: Analysis of Covariance (ANCOVA)

Now, try an ANCOVA on your own. Using the same dependent variable (*mathach*) and the same factor/independent variable (*gend*), see if adjusting for *mosaic* as a covariate eliminates the gender differences in math achievement. Use the same options as before and compare your output to Output 16.5.

Print, Save, and Exit

- **Print** your output (**File => Print**).
- Save your data as **hsbdataL** (Use **File => Save As**).
- **Save** the SPSS log files as **hsblogL**.
- **Exit** SPSS (**File => Exit SPSS**).

Interpretation Questions

1. In Output 16.2: a) Is the interaction significant? b) Examine the profile plots of the cell means that illustrates the interaction. Describe it in words.

2. In Output 16.2: a) Is the main effect of father's education significant? Interpret the eta squared. b) How about the "effect" of math grades? c) Why did we put the word effect in quotes? d) How might focusing on the main effects be misleading? e) Why did we do Output 16.3?

3. In Output 16.3, which father's education groups are significantly different from each other?

4. In Output 16.5: a) Are the adjusted main effects of gender significant? b) What are the adjusted math achievement means for males and females? c) Is the effect of the covariate (mosaic) significant?

Outputs and Interpretations

```
GET
  FILE='A:\hsbdataK.sav'.
EXECUTE .
```

Output 16.1: GLM General Factorial (2-Way) ANOVA - Mathach by Mathgr and Gender

Syntax for GLM General factorial (2-way) ANOVA - mathach by mathgr and gender

```
GLM
  mathach  BY mathgr gend
  /METHOD = SSTYPE(3)
  /INTERCEPT = INCLUDE
  /PLOT = PROFILE( mathgr*gend )
  /PRINT = DESCRIPTIVE ETASQ HOMOGENEITY
  /CRITERIA = ALPHA(.05)
  /DESIGN .
```

Interpretation of Output 16.1

Fig. 16.7 is a decision tree that indicates the steps that one should use to interpret the output from a factorial ANOVA. Note that you start by examining the interaction effect. Note also that the word "effect" can be misleading because this study was not a randomized experiment. Thus, we cannot have confidence that the differences in the dependent variable were *caused* by the independent variable.

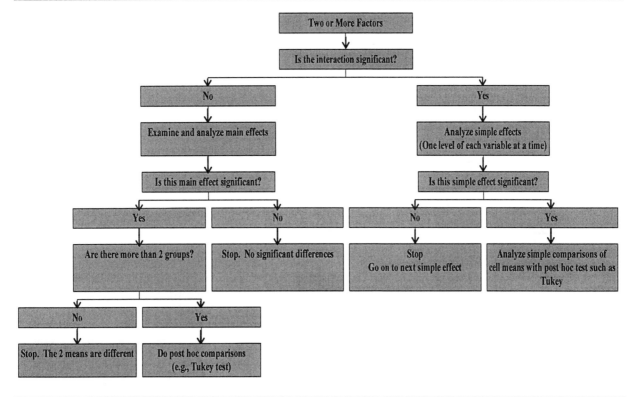

Fig. 16.7. Schematic representation of the steps in interpreting a factorial analysis of variance with no planned comparisons (Adapted/expanded from Keppel and Zedeck, 1989).

The first table in Output 16.1 shows that all 75 participants are "included" in the analysis because they all had data on these three variables. The second table shows the cell means; they are very important for interpreting the ANOVA table and explaining the results of the test for the interaction. You could use the simple factorial program's **Unique** method rather than the **GLM General Factorial** program we used in this assignment. The **GLM General Factorial** program has several advantages: It allows you to print the means and counts, provides measures of effect size (eta squared) and power, and plots the interaction, which is helpful in interpreting it. None of these are available with the simple factorial program.

The ANOVA table, called **Tests of Between Subjects Effects**, is the key table. Usually you will skip over the corrected model and intercept lines. Note that the main effect of math grades is statistically significant, $F(1,71) = 14.769$, $p < .001$. This means that students with less than an A-B math average scored lower ($M = 10.81$ vs. 15.05) on math achievement than those with high math grades, and this difference is statistically significant. Gender is also significant ($p < .001$), but the interaction (*mathgr*gend*) is not significant ($p = .563$). Thus, the "effect" of math grades on math achievement is about the same for both genders. If the interaction were significant, we would say that the "effect" of math grades depended on which gender you were considering. For example, it might be large for boys and small for girls. If you find a significant interaction you should examine the **profile plots** of cell means to visualize the differential effects. When the lines on the profile plot are parallel there is not a significant interaction. If the interaction is significant, you should also analyze the differences between cell means (the simple effects) as indicated in Fig. 16.7.

Note the callout boxes about R squared and eta squared.

Between-Subjects Factors

		Value Label	N
math grades	0	less A-B	44
	1	most A-B	31
gender	1	male	34
	2	female	41

Descriptive Statistics

	math grades	gender	Mean	Std. Deviation	N
math achievement	less A-B	male	12.8751	5.7314	24
		female	8.3333	5.3256	20
		Total	10.8106	5.9444	44
	most A-B	male	19.2667	4.1718	10
		female	13.0476	7.1658	21
		Total	15.0538	6.9417	31
	Total	male	14.7550	6.0315	34
		female	10.7479	6.6961	41
		Total	12.5645	6.6703	75

The means are important for interpreting ANOVAs and explaining results.

Levene's Test of Equality of Error Variances[a]

	F	df1	df2	Sig.
math achievement	1.691	3	71	.177

Tests the null hypothesis that the error variance of the dependent variable is equal across

a. Design: MATHGR+GEND+MATHGR * GEND

These *F*s and significance levels tell you important information about differences between means and the interaction.

Tests of Between-Subjects Effects

Dependent Variable: math achievement

Source	Type III Sum of Squares	df	Mean Square	F	Sig.	Eta Squared	Noncent. Parameter	Observed Power[a]
Corrected Model	814.481[b]	3	271.494	7.779	.000	.247	23.337	.985
Intercept	11971.773	1	11971.773	343.017	.000	.829	343.017	1.000
MATHGR	515.463	1	515.463	14.769	.000	172	14.769	.966
GEND	483.929	1	483.929	13.866	.000	.163	13.866	.957
MATHGR * GEND	11.756	1	11.756	.337	.563	.005	.337	.088
Error	2478.000	71	34.901					
Total	15132.393	75						
Corrected Total	3292.481	74						

a. Computed using alpha = .05

b. R Squared = .247 (Adjusted R Squared = 216)

Percent of variance in math achievement predictable from both independent variables.

Eta squared is an index of the effect size. Thus, only about 17% of the variance in math achievement can be predicted from math grades. This is a relatively low effect size.

Profile Plots

Estimated Marginal Means of

Math Achievement

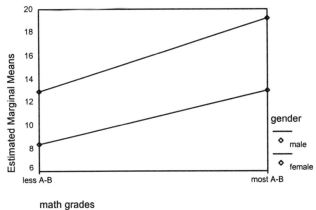

Output 16.2: Simple Factorial (2-Way) ANOVA - Mathach by Mathgr and Faedr

Syntax for The GLM General factorial ANOVA - mathach by mathgr and faedr

```
GLM
  mathach  BY mathgr faedr
  /METHOD = SSTYPE(3)
  /INTERCEPT = INCLUDE
  /PLOT = PROFILE( faedr*mathgr )
  /PRINT = DESCRIPTIVE ETASQ HOMOGENEITY
  /CRITERIA = ALPHA(.05)
  /DESIGN .
```

Between-Subjects Factors

		Value Label	N
math grades	0	less A-B	43
	1	most A-B	30
Father's ed rev	1	hs grad or less	38
	2	some college	16
	3	BS or more	19

Descriptive Statistics

	math grades	Father's ed rev	Mean	Std. Deviation	N
math achievement	less A-B	hs grad or less	9.8261	5.0371	23
		some college	12.8149	5.0555	9
		BS or more	12.3636	7.1841	11
		Total	11.1008	5.6907	43
	most A-B	hs grad or less	10.4889	6.5657	15
		some college	16.4284	3.4306	7
		BS or more	21.8335	2.8452	8
		Total	14.9000	7.0064	30
	Total	hs grad or less	10.0877	5.6130	38
		some college	14.3958	4.6654	16
		BS or more	16.3509	7.4092	19
		Total	12.6621	6.4966	73

Levene's Test of Equality of Error Variances[a]

	F	df1	df2	Sig.
math achievement	2.548	5	67	.036

Tests the null hypothesis that the error variance of the dependent variable is equal across groups.

a. Design: Intercept+MATHGR+FAEDR+MATHGR * FAEDR

Tests of Between-Subjects Effects

Dependent Variable: math achievement

Source	Type III Sum of Squares	df	Mean Square	F	Sig.	Eta Squared	Noncent. Parameter	Observed Power[a]
Corrected Model	1029.236[b]	5	205.847	6.863	.000	.339	34.315	.997
Intercept	12094.308	1	12094.308	403.23	.000	.858	403.230	1.000
MATHGR	325.776	1	325.776	10.862	.002	.139	10.862	.901
FAEDR	646.015	2	323.007	10.769	.000	.243	21.538	.987
MATHGR * FAEDR	237.891	2	118.946	3.966	.024	.106	7.931	.693
Error	2009.569	67	29.994					
Total	14742.823	73						
Corrected Total	3038.804	72						

a. Computed using alpha = .05

b. R Squared = .339 (Adjusted R Squared = .289)

Profile Plots
Estimated Marginal Means of math achievement

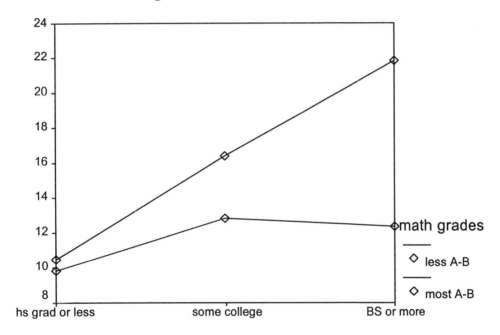

Father's ed rev

Output 16.3: Post Hoc Test for Father's Education

Syntax for general factorial ANOVA - mathach by mathgr and faedr with post hoc for faedr

```
GLM
  mathach  BY mathgr faedr
  /METHOD = SSTYPE(3)
  /INTERCEPT = INCLUDE
  /POSTHOC = faedr ( C )
  /CRITERIA = ALPHA(.05)
  /DESIGN .
```

General Linear Model

Between-Subjects Factors

		Value Label	N
math grades	0	less A-B	43
	1	most A-B	30
Father's ed rev	1	hs grad or less	38
	2	some college	16
	3	BS or more	19

These tables are repeats of ones in Output 16.2. Skip them.

Tests of Between-Subjects Effects

Dependent Variable: math achievement

Source	Type III Sum of Squares	df	Mean Square	F	Sig.	Noncent. Parameter	Observed Power[a]
Corrected Model	1029.236[b]	5	205.847	6.863	.000	34.315	.997
Intercept	12094.308	1	12094.308	403.23	.000	403.230	1.000
MATHGR	325.776	1	325.776	10.862	.002	10.862	.901
FAEDR	646.015	2	323.007	10.769	.000	21.538	.987
MATHGR * FAEDR	237.891	2	118.946	3.966	.024	7.931	.693
Error	2009.569	67	29.994				
Total	14742.823	73					
Corrected Total	3038.804	72					

a. Computed using alpha = .05

b. R Squared = .339 (Adjusted R Squared = .289)

Post Hoc Tests
Father's ed rev

Multiple Comparisons

Dependent Variable: math achievement

Dunnett C

(I) Father's ed rev	(J) Father's ed rev	Mean Difference (I-J)	Std. Error	95% Confidence Interval	
				Lower Bound	Upper Bound
hs grad or less	some college	-4.3081*	1.632	-8.0642	-.5520
	BS or more	-6.2632*	1.539	-11.1370	-1.3895
some college	hs grad or less	4.3081*	1.632	.5520	8.0642
	BS or more	-1.9551	1.858	-7.2463	3.3360
BS or more	hs grad or less	6.2632*	1.539	1.3895	11.1370
	some college	1.9551	1.858	-3.3360	7.2463

Based on observed means. The error term is Error.

*. The mean difference is significant at the .05 level.

Output 16.4: Analysis of Covariance (ANCOVA)

Syntax for analysis of covariance (ANCOVA) - mathach by gend with mathcrs

```
ANOVA
  VARIABLES=mathach
  BY gend(1 2)
  WITH  mathcrs
  /COVARIATES FIRST
  /MAXORDERS ALL
  /STATISTICS MCA MEAN
  /METHOD EXPERIM .
```

An extension of ANOVA that provides a way of statistically eliminating the effects of variables you are concerned about but that may not be of interest in this study. These variables are called covariates or control variables.

Interpretation of Output 16.4

The ANOVA table is interpreted in much the same way in earlier outputs. The covariate is found to have a highly significant "effect" on math achievement, as should be the case. However, the "effect" of gender is no longer significant (now $F = (1,72) = .36, p = .55$), as it was in Output 16.1. You can see from the MCA table that the statistically adjusted math achievement means for boys and girls are almost equal.

Case Processing Summary[a]

Cases					
Included		Excluded		Total	
N	Percent	N	Percent	N	Percent
75	100.0%	0	.0%	75	100.0%

a. math achievement by gender with Math course taken

Cell Means[b]

	math achievement	
gender	Mean	N
male	14.7550	34
female	10.7479	41
Total	12.5645[a]	75

Note that the mean score of males was significantly higher than females on math.

a. Grand Mean

b. math achievement by gender with Math course taken

ANOVA[a,b]

			Experimental Method				
			Sum of Squares	df	Mean Square	F	Sig.
math achievement	Covariates	Math course taken	2076.327	1	2076.327	123.534	.000
	Main Effects	gender	6.001	1	6.001	.357	.552
	Model		2082.329	2	1041.164	61.946	.000
	Residual		1210.152	72	16.808		
	Total		3292.481	74	44.493		

a. math achievement by gender with Math course taken

b. Covariates entered first

Now the covariate is highly significant but the gender difference is not.

MCA[a]

				Predicted Mean		Deviation	
			N	Unadjusted	Adjusted for Factors and Covariates	Unadjusted	Adjusted for Factors and Covariates
math achievement	gender	male	34	14.7550	12.8933	2.1905	.3289
		female	41	10.7479	12.2917	-1.8165	-.2727

a. math achievement by gender with Math course taken

Note these are nearly equal.

Factor Summary[a]

		Eta	Beta Adjusted for Factors and Covariates
math achievement	gender	.301	.045

> Remember that eta *Squared* is an index of the size of the "effect."

a. math achievement by gender with Math course taken

Model Goodness of Fit

	Factors and Covariates	
	R	R Squared
math achievement by gender with Math course taken	.795	.632

> Percent of variance in math achievement predictable from both gender and math courses taken. This is another measure of the size of the effect.

Output 16.5: Analysis of Covariance (ANCOVA)

Syntax for analysis of covariance (ANCOVA) - mathach by gend with mosaic

```
ANOVA
  VARIABLES=mathach
  BY gend(1 2)
  WITH  mosaic
  /COVARIATES FIRST
  /MAXORDERS ALL
  /STATISTICS MCA MEAN
  /METHOD EXPERIM .
```

Case Processing Summary [a]

Cases					
Included		Excluded		Total	
N	Percent	N	Percent	N	Percent
75	100.0%	0	.0%	75	100.0%

a. math achievement by gender with mosaic, pattern test

Cell Means [b]

gender	math achievement	
	Mean	N
male	14.7550	34
female	10.7479	41
Total	12.5645[a]	75

a. Grand Mean

b. math achievement by gender with mosaic, pattern test

ANOVA[a,b]

			Experimental Method				
			Sum of Squares	df	Mean Square	F	Sig.
math achievement	Covariates	mosaic, pattern test	149.407	1	149.407	3.788	.056
	Main Effects	gender	303.315	1	303.315	7.690	.007
	Model		452.722	2	226.361	5.739	.005
	Residual		2839.759	72	39.441		
	Total		3292.481	74	44.493		

a. math achievement by gender with mosaic, pattern test

b. Covariates entered first

MCA[a]

				Predicted Mean		Deviation	
			N	Unadjusted	Adjusted for Factors and Covariates	Unadjusted	Adjusted for Factors and Covariates
math achievement	gender	male	34	14.7550	14.7730	2.1905	2.2085
		female	41	10.7479	10.7330	-1.8165	-1.8314

a. math achievement by gender with mosaic, pattern test

Factor Summary[a]

			Beta
		Eta	Adjusted for Factors and Covariates
math achievement	gender	.301	.304

a. math achievement by gender with mosaic, pattern test

Model Goodness of Fit

	Factors and Covariates	
	R	R Squared
math achievement by gender with mosaic, pattern test	.371	.138

CHAPTER 17

Repeated Measures and Mixed ANOVAs

In this assignment, we will compare four products each evaluated by 12 consumers/judges, six male and six female. The analysis requires statistical techniques for **within subjects** and **mixed designs**, addressing difference hypotheses.

After entering some repeated measures data in Problem 1, you will analyze it in Problem 2 using SPSS's General Linear Model program (called GLM) to do a **repeated measures ANOVA**. In Problem 4, you will use the same program to do a **mixed ANOVA**, one that has a repeated measures independent variable *and* a between groups independent variable. In Problem 3, you will use the nonparametric equivalent of the repeated measures ANOVA, which is called the **Friedman test**. SPSS does not have a nonparametric equivalent to the mixed ANOVA.

Chapter 7 provides several tables to help you decide what statistic to use with various types of difference statistics problems. Fig. 7.1 and 7.3 include the statistics used in Assignments J-N.

Problems/Research Questions

1. Each subject has evaluated each of four products (or it could be types of program) on 1-7 Likert scales. You will enter this new data into the SPSS data editor.

2. Are there differences between the average ratings for the four products, assuming the product ratings are interval data and meet other assumptions?

3. Assuming that the product scores are ordinal data, or that normality and other assumptions are markedly violated, are there differences between the mean *ranks* of the product ratings?

4. Finally, are there gender as well as product differences, and is there an interaction between gender and product?

Lab Assignment M

Logon and Get Data

Open SPSS. You should see a blank data file. Do *not* retrieve **hsbdata** for this assignment.

Problem 1: Entering Data

Enter the following data as you see it below: Refer to Assignment A if you do not remember how to enter data. Begin at row one, column one and enter numeric data. You can choose to do one column at a time or the entire set.

Subj	P1	P2	P3	P4	Gender
01	7	7	6	6	1
02	7	6	6	5	1
03	6	5	5	4	1
04	6	4	4	3	1
05	5	3	3	2	1
06	4	2	2	1	1
07	6	5	5	4	2
08	5	4	5	4	2
09	4	3	4	3	2
10	3	2	3	2	2
11	2	1	2	1	2
12	1	1	1	1	2

> Note you are entering data for a small number of subjects. In most studies the *N* would be larger.

- Once you enter the data, click on **var0001**.
- Next, click on **Data => Define Variable.** You should see Fig. 17.1.
  In the **Variable Name** box, type **p1** and then click on **Type** to get Fig. 17.2.
  In the **Width** box, type 2 and in the (number of) **Decimal Places** box, type **0**.
- Click on **Continue**.

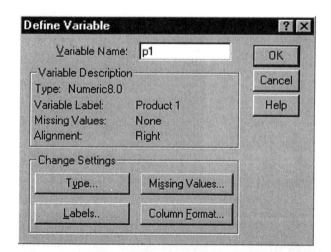

Fig. 17.1. Define variable.

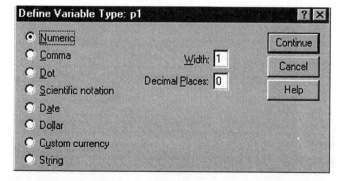

Fig. 17.2. Define variable type.

216

Now let's give the variable a label and provide it with some relevant information.

- Click on **Labels**. Type the full name of the variable, **Product 1**.
- Click on **Value** and type **1**.
- Click on **Value Labels** and type **Very Low**.
- Click on **Add**.
- Again, click on **Value** and type **7**.
- Click on **Value Labels** and type **Very High** (see Fig. 17.3), click on **Add**.
- Finally, click on **Continue** then **OK**.

Repeat the same steps for **p2, p3, and p4** labeling these variables **Product 2, Product 3**, and **Product 4** and label the values as **1 = Very Low** and **7 = Very High** in the **Values** and **Value Labels** boxes. For **Gender**, the **Value /Value Labels** should be **1 = male** and **2 = female**.

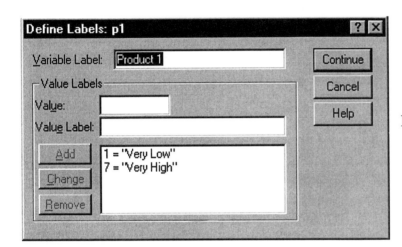

Fig. 17.3. Define labels.

After entering, defining, and labeling your data, go ahead and save it. Click on **File => Save As**. Insure you save it to your disk (A) and call it **"product"**, *not hsbdata.*

Problem 2: Repeated Measures ANOVA

Let's test for whether there are differences between the average ratings of the four products. We are assuming the product ratings are interval data. Follow these commands: **Statistics => General Linear Model => GLM - Repeated Measures** (see Fig. 17.4). *Delete* the **factor 1** from the **Within-Subject Factor Name** box and *replace* it with the name **product**. Type **4** in the **Number of Levels** box since there are four products established in the data file. Click on **Add**, then click on **Define**, which changes the screen to a new menu box (see Fig. 17.5).

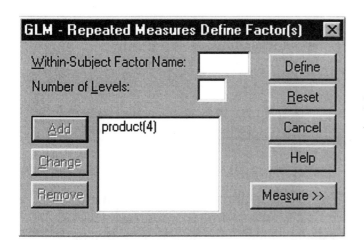

Fig. 17.4. Repeated measures ANOVA define factor(s).

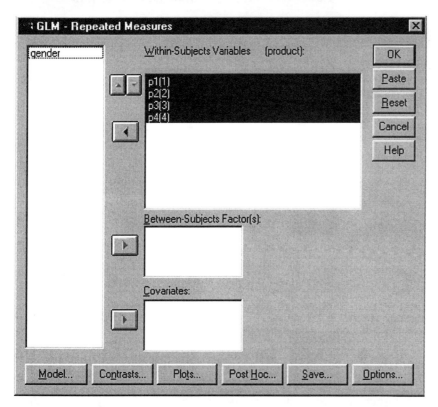

Fig. 17.5. Repeated measures ANOVA.

- Now move **p1, p2, p3,** and **p4** over to the **Within-Subjects Variables** box.
- Click on **Contrasts,** then **Polynomial**.
- Click on **Continue**, then on **OK**.

Compare your syntax and output to Output 17.2.

Problem 3: Nonparametric Test With Several Related Samples (Friedman)

What do you do if the product ratings are *rankings* or *ordinal* data or the ANOVA assumptions are markedly violated? The answer is nonparametric statistics.

Let's use *p1 to p4* again using the following commands:

- **Statistics => Nonparametric tests => K Related Samples** and move *p1 to p4* to the **Test Variables** box (see Fig. 17.6).
- Make sure the **Friedman** test type is checked and then click on **Statistics.**
- Now click on **Descriptive** statistics (see Fig. 17.7).
- Click on **Continue,** then **OK.** Look at your output and compare it to Output 17.3.

Unfortunately, the Friedman test does not have a post hoc test built into SPSS.

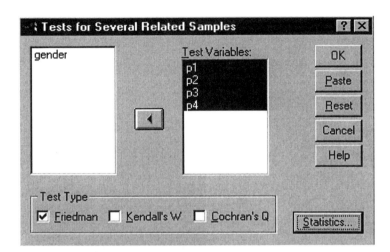

Fig. 17.6. Friedman nonparametric test for several related samples.

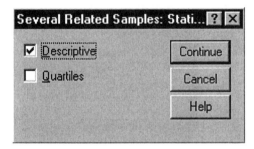

Fig. 17.7. Descriptive for nonparametric tests for several related samples.

Problem 4: Mixed ANOVA

Now try one on your own. Repeat Problem 2 except add *gender* to see if there are any gender differences as well as product differences and if there is an interaction between *gender* and *product*. Is gender a between groups/subjects or within subjects variable? The answer is important in how you do and interpret the analysis.

Hints:
- Click on **Statistics => General Linear Model => GLM - Repeated Measures**.
- In the **GLM - Repeated Measures Define Factor(s)** dialog menu, you should see, *product* (4) in the big box. If so, click on **Define.**
- Then move *gender* to the **Between Subjects Factor(s)** box.
- Click **Contrasts**, then click *off* polynomial if it is on.
- Click on **OK.**

Compare your syntax and output with Output 17.4.

Print, Save, and Exit

- **Print** your output.
- Save your data as **product,** *not hsbdata* (Use **File** => **Save As** => **product**).
- Save your SPSS log as **Prodlog1** (Use **File** => **Save As** => **Prodlog1**).
- **Exit** SPSS.

Interpretation Questions

1. In Output 17.3: a) Explain the results in nontechnical terms. b) What do we need to do for a complete interpretation of the results?

2. In Output 17.4: a) Is the Mauchly sphericity test significant and the assumption violated? If so, what do you do? b) How would you interpret the *F* for *product* (within subjects)? Compare it to the same *F* in Output 17.2. c) Is the interaction between product and gender significant? How would you describe it in non-technical terms? d) Is there a significant difference between the genders? Is a post hoc multiple comparison test needed? Explain.

Outputs and Interpretations

Output 17.1: Entering Data

Syntax for defining variables

```
NEW FILE
RENAME VARIABLES (var00001=p1).
FORMATS p1 (F1).
VARIABLE LABELS p1 "Product 1".
VALUE LABELS p1
 1.00 "Very Low"
 7.00 "Very High".

RENAME VARIABLES (var00002=p2).
FORMATS p2 (F1).
VARIABLE LABELS p2 "Product 2".
VALUE LABELS p2
 1.00 "Very Low"
 7.00 "Very High".

RENAME VARIABLES (var00003=p3).
FORMATS p3 (F1).
VARIABLE LABELS p3 "Product 3".
VALUE LABELS p3
 1.00"Very Low"
 7.00 "Very High".

RENAME VARIABLES (var00004=p4).
FORMATS p4 (F1).
VARIABLE LABELS p4 "Product 4".
VALUE LABELS p4
 1.00 "Very Low"
 7.00 "Very High".
```

```
RENAME VARIABLES (var00001=Gender).
FORMATS Gender (F1).
VARIABLE LABELS Gender "Gender".
VALUE LABELS Gender
 1.00 "Male"
 2.0 "Female".
 2.1
```

Output 17.2: Repeated Measures ANOVA Using the General Linear Model Program

```
GLM
  p1 p2 p3 p4
  /WSFACTOR = product 4 Polynomial
  /METHOD = SSTYPE(3)
  /CRITERIA = ALPHA(.05)
  /WSDESIGN
  /DESIGN .
General Linear Model
```

The GLM Repeated Measures procedure provides a variety of analysis of variance procedures when the same measurement is made several times on each subject or the same measurement is made on several related subjects. If between subjects factors are specified, they divide the population into groups. There are no between subject or group factors in this problem. Using this general linear model procedure, you can test null hypotheses about the effects of both the between groups factors and the within subjects factors. You can investigate interactions between factors as well as the effects of individual factors on one or more dependent variable.

Interpretation of Output 17.2

The first table identifies the four levels of the within subjects repeated measures independent variable, *product*. For each level (P1 to P4), there is a rating from 1-7, which is the dependent variable.

The second table presents four similar **Multivariate Tests** of the within subjects effect (i.e., whether the four products are rated equally). **Wilks' Lambda** is a commonly used multivariate test. Notice that in this case, the Fs, df, and significance are all the same: $F(3, 9) = 19.07, p < .001$. The significant F means that there is a difference somewhere in how the products are rated.

The third table shows that the **Mauchly Test of Sphericity** is significant so these data violate this assumption of the univariate approach to repeated measures analysis of variance. Thus, we should either use the multivariate approach or the appropriate nonparametric test (Friedman) or correct the univariate approach with the **Greenhouse-Geisser** or other similar correction. These corrections reduce the degrees of freedom by multiplying them by **Epsilon**. In this case, 3 x .544 = 1.63 and 33 x .544 = 17.95. Even with this adjustment, the **Within-Subjects Effects** (of product) is significant, $F(1.63, 17.95) = 23.63, p < .001$, as were the multivariate tests. This means that the ratings of the four products are significantly different. However, this overall (product) F does not tell you which pairs of products have significantly different means. SPSS has several tests of within subject contrasts. We have chosen to use the polynomial contrast on the assumption that the products are ordered, say from the most expensive as P1 to the least as P4. The **Tests of Within-Subjects Contrasts** table shows whether the four product means are significantly like a straight line (linear effect), a one curve line (quadratic), and a two bend line (cubic). You can see (Product_1)that there is a highly significant linear trend and a significant cubic trend (Product_3). If you plot the means (shown in Output 17.3), these trends should be there is a linear decline in ratings from Product 1 (4.67) to Product 4 (3.00). However, Product 2 has a somewhat lower mean (3.52) than Product 3 (3.83) producing the cubic trend.

For Problem 4 and Output 17.4, if we had three groups, instead of just males and females, for our between groups/subjects variable and if the ANOVA had been significant, we would have used a post hoc test. SPSS provides the same wide variety of post hoc multiple comparisons, including the Tukey and Dunnett's C, that were available for the one-way ANOVA. However, in Output 17.2, we ignore the "tests of between subject effects" because we do not have a between subject/groups variable.

Within-Subjects Factors

Measure: MEASURE_1

PRODUCT	Dependent Variable
1	P1
2	P2
3	P3
4	P4

This shows four similar multivariate tests of the within subjects effect. These are actually a form of MANOVA, which will be discussed in the next chapter. They could be used when the sphericity assumption is violated instead of correcting the degrees of freedom. Note, that, in this case, all four tests have the same Fs, dfs, and are significant.

Multivariate Tests[c]

Effect		Value	F	Hypothesis df	Error df	Sig.	Noncent. Parameter	Observed Power[a]
PRODUCT	Pillai's Trace	.864	19.065[b]	3.000	9.000	.000	57.194	1.000
	Wilks' Lambda	.136	19.065[b]	3.000	9.000	.000	57.194	1.000
	Hotelling's Trace	6.355	19.065[b]	3.000	9.000	.000	57.194	1.000
	Roy's Largest Root	6.355	19.065[b]	3.000	9.000	.000	57.194	1.000

a. Computed using alpha = .05

b. Exact statistic

c. Design: Intercept
   Within Subjects Design: PRODUCT

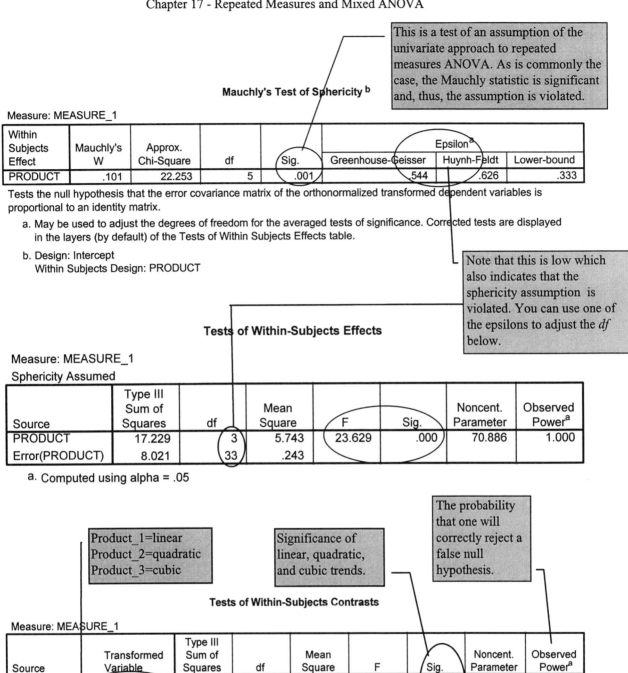

Mauchly's Test of Sphericity [b]

> This is a test of an assumption of the univariate approach to repeated measures ANOVA. As is commonly the case, the Mauchly statistic is significant and, thus, the assumption is violated.

Measure: MEASURE_1

Within Subjects Effect	Mauchly's W	Approx. Chi-Square	df	Sig.	Epsilon [a]		
					Greenhouse-Geisser	Huynh-Feldt	Lower-bound
PRODUCT	.101	22.253	5	.001	.544	.626	.333

Tests the null hypothesis that the error covariance matrix of the orthonormalized transformed dependent variables is proportional to an identity matrix.

a. May be used to adjust the degrees of freedom for the averaged tests of significance. Corrected tests are displayed in the layers (by default) of the Tests of Within Subjects Effects table.

b. Design: Intercept
   Within Subjects Design: PRODUCT

> Note that this is low which also indicates that the sphericity assumption is violated. You can use one of the epsilons to adjust the *df* below.

Tests of Within-Subjects Effects

Measure: MEASURE_1

Sphericity Assumed

Source	Type III Sum of Squares	df	Mean Square	F	Sig.	Noncent. Parameter	Observed Power [a]
PRODUCT	17.229	3	5.743	23.629	.000	70.886	1.000
Error(PRODUCT)	8.021	33	.243				

a. Computed using alpha = .05

> Product_1=linear
> Product_2=quadratic
> Product_3=cubic

> Significance of linear, quadratic, and cubic trends.

> The probability that one will correctly reject a false null hypothesis.

Tests of Within-Subjects Contrasts

Measure: MEASURE_1

Source	Transformed Variable	Type III Sum of Squares	df	Mean Square	F	Sig.	Noncent. Parameter	Observed Power [a]
PRODUCT	PRODUCT_1	13.537	1	13.537	26.532	.000	26.532	.997
	PRODUCT_2	.187	1	.187	3.667	.082	3.667	.416
	PRODUCT_3	3.504	1	3.504	20.883	.001	20.883	.985
Error(PRODUCT)	PRODUCT_1	5.612	11	.510				
	PRODUCT_2	.562	11	5.114E-02				
	PRODUCT_3	1.846	11	.168				

a. Computed using alpha = .05

223

Tests of Between-Subjects Effects

Ignore this. There were no between groups/subjects variables in this problem.

Measure: MEASURE_1

Transformed Variable: Average

Source	Type III Sum of Squares	df	Mean Square	F	Sig.	Noncent. Parameter	Observed Power[a]
Intercept	682.521	1	682.521	56.352	.000	56.352	1.000
Error	133.229	11	12.112				

a. Computed using alpha = .05

Output 17.3: Nonparametric Tests With Four Related Samples

NPAR
 /FRIEDMAN = p1 p2 p3 p4
 /STATISTICS DESCRIPTIVES
 /MISSING LISTWISE.

Descriptive Statistics

	N	Mean	Std. Deviation	Minimum	Maximum
Product 1	12	4.67	1.92	1	7
Product 2	12	3.58	1.93	1	7
Product 3	12	3.83	1.64	1	6
Product 4	12	3.00	1.65	1	6

Friedman Test

Tests the null hypothesis that the four related variables come from the same population. For each rater/case, the four variables are ranked from 1 to 4. The test statistic is based on these ranks.

Ranks

	Mean Rank
Product 1	3.67
Product 2	2.25
Product 3	2.75
Product 4	1.33

Test Statistics[a]

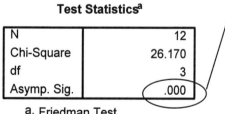

N	12
Chi-Square	26.170
df	3
Asymp. Sig.	.000

Significance of the overall difference between the mean ranks.

a. Friedman Test

Output 17.4: Mixed ANOVA: Product by Gender

GLM
 p1 p2 p3 p4 BY gender
 /WSFACTOR = product 4
 /METHOD = SSTYPE(3)
 /CRITERIA = ALPHA(.05)
 /WSDESIGN
 /DESIGN .
General Linear Model

Known as a mixed design because it involves both between subjects/groups and within subjects analyses.

Within-Subjects Factors

Measure: MEASURE_1

PRODUCT	Dependent Variable
1	P1
2	P2
3	P3
4	P4

Between-Subjects Factors

		Value Label	N
Gender	1	Male	6
	2	Female	6

Multivariate Tests[c]

Effect		Value	F	Hypothesis df	Error df	Sig.	Noncent. Parameter	Observed Power[a]
PRODUCT	Pillai's Trace	.897	23.152[b]	3.000	8.000	.000	69.455	1.000
	Wilks' Lambda	.103	23.152[b]	3.000	8.000	.000	69.455	1.000
	Hotelling's Trace	8.682	23.152[b]	3.000	8.000	.000	69.455	1.000
	Roy's Largest Root	8.682	23.152[b]	3.000	8.000	.000	69.455	1.000
PRODUCT * GENDER	Pillai's Trace	.763	8.606[b]	3.000	8.000	.007	25.818	.925
	Wilks' Lambda	.237	8.606[b]	3.000	8.000	.007	25.818	.925
	Hotelling's Trace	3.227	8.606[b]	3.000	8.000	.007	25.818	.925
	Roy's Largest Root	3.227	8.606[b]	3.000	8.000	.007	25.818	.925

a. Computed using alpha = .05

b. Exact statistic

c. Design: Intercept+GENDER
   Within Subjects Design: PRODUCT

Mauchly's Test of Sphericity [b]

Measure: MEASURE_1

Within Subjects Effect	Mauchly's W	Approx. Chi-Square	df	Sig.	Epsilon[a]		
					Greenhouse-Geisser	Huynh-Feldt	Lower-bound
PRODUCT	.176	15.138	5	.010	.547	.705	.333

Tests the null hypothesis that the error covariance matrix of the orthonormalized transformed dependent variables i proportional to an identity matrix.

a. May be used to adjust the degrees of freedom for the averaged tests of significance. Corrected tests are displa in the layers (by default) of the Tests of Within Subjects Effects table.

b. Design: Intercept+GENDER
   Within Subjects Design: PRODUCT

Tests of Within-Subjects Effects ——— Univariate within subjects and interaction effects.

Measure: MEASURE_1

Sphericity Assumed

Source	Type III Sum of Squares	df	Mean Square	F	Sig.	Noncent. Parameter	Observed Power[a]
PRODUCT	17.229	3	5.743	41.768	.000	125.303	1.000
PRODUCT * GENDER	3.896	3	1.299	9.444	.000	28.333	.993
Error(PRODUCT)	4.125	30	.137				

a. Computed using alpha = .05

Tests of Between-Subjects Effects

Measure: MEASURE_1

Transformed Variable: Average

Source	Type III Sum of Squares	df	Mean Square	F	Sig.	Noncent. Parameter	Observed Power[a]
Intercept	682.521	1	682.521	65.183	.000	65.183	1.000
GENDER	28.521	1	28.521	2.724	.130	2.724	.321
Error	104.708	10	10.471				

a. Computed using alpha = .05

Test of whether males and females rate the products differently.

CHAPTER 18

Multivariate Analysis of Variance (MANOVA)

In this chapter we introduce multivariate analysis of variance (**MANOVA**), which is a complex statistic similar to ANOVA but with multiple dependent variables analyzed together. The dependent variables should be related conceptually, and should be correlated with one another at a low to moderate level. If they are too highly correlated one runs the risk of multicollinearity. If they are uncorrelated there is usually no reason to analyze them together. MANOVA provides you with a multivariate F based on a linear combination of dependent variables, as well as univariate Fs, for each separate dependent variable.

First, you will do a MANOVA that is similar to the one-way ANOVA that you did in Problem 1 of chapter 15. However, instead of doing *three* one-way ANOVAs, in this chapter you will do the problem as one MANOVA. The second problem is also a one-way or single factor MANOVA with math grades as the independent variable/fixed factor and three test scores as dependent variables. The third problem is a two-way or two-factor MANOVA because there are two independent variables (*mathgr* and *gend*) and three test scores as dependent variables.

Problems/Research Questions

1. Are there differences between the three father's education groups on a linear combination of grades, math achievement, and visualization? If so, are there differences between groups on any of these variables? Which ones?

2. Are there differences between male and female students on a linear combination of grades, achievement, and number of math courses taken? If so, are there differences between males and females on any of these variables? Which ones?

3. Do math grades and gender each seem to have an effect on three dependent variables (math achievement, mosaic, and visualization)? Is there an interaction of grades and gender? Is there a linear combination of the three dependent variables that is statistically significant?

Lab Assignment N

Logon and Get Data

- Retrieve **hsbdataL**. Note: You are to get the **hsbdataL** file, *not the product* file from the last lab assignment.

Problem 1: GLM Single-Factor Multivariate Analysis of Variance

Sometimes you have more than one dependent variable that you want to analyze simultaneously. The GLM Multivariate procedure allows you to analyze multiple dependent variables with one or more independent variables or covariates. To do this multivariate analysis, follow these steps:

- Select **Statistics => General Linear Model => GLM Multivariate**.
- Move *grades*, *mathach*, and *visual* into the **Dependent Variables** box.
- Move *faedr* into the **Fixed Factor(s)** box (see Fig. 18.1).

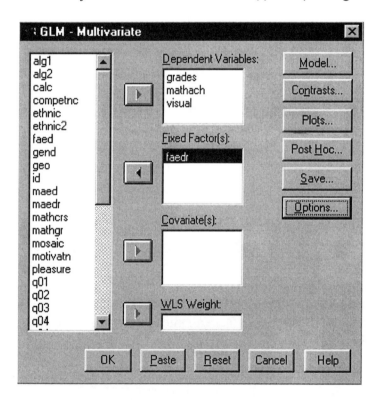

Fig. 18.1. GLM multivariate ANOVA.

- Click on **Options**.
- Check **Descriptive statistics** and **Estimates of effect size** (see Fig. 18.2).
- Click on **Continue.**

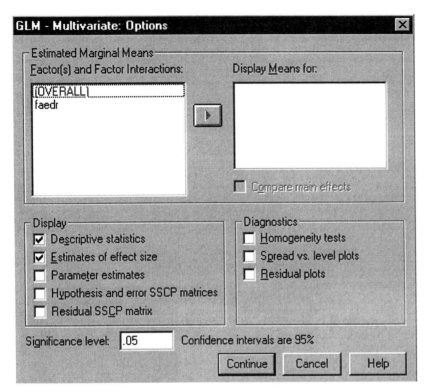

Fig. 18.2. GLM multivariate options.

- Click on **OK**. Compare your output to Output 18.1.

Problem 2: GLM Single-Factor Multivariate Analysis of Variance

Now try a multivariate analysis on your own. Try *grades, mathach,* and *mathcrs* as your dependent variables and *gender* as your independent variable. Use the same **Options** as you did in Problem 1. Compare your output to Output 18.2. Do they look the same?

Problem 3: GLM Two-Factor Multivariate Analysis of Variance

Now let's try another, more complex, multivariate analysis. Follow these steps:
- Select **Statistics => General Linear Model => GLM Multivariate**.
- Move *mathach, visual,* and *mosaic* into the **Dependent Variables** box (see Fig. 18.1 if you need help).
- Move both *mathgr* and *gend* into the **Fixed Factor(s)** box.
- Click on **Options**.
- Check **Descriptive statistics, Estimates of effect size** (see Fig. 18.2).
- Click on **Continue**.
- Click on **OK**. Compare your output to Output 18.3.

Print, Save, and Exit

- **Print** your outputs, if necessary.
- **Save** your data as **hsbdataN** (Use **File => Save As**).

- **Save** the SPSS log files as **hsblogN**.
- **Exit** SPSS.

Interpretation Questions

1. In Output 18.2: a) Are the multivariate tests statistically significant? What does this mean? b) For which individual/univariate dependent variables are the genders significantly different? c) How are the results similar and different from Output 14.2?

2. In Output 18.3: a) Are the multivariate tests statistically significant? b) Which individual dependent variables are significant? c) How are the results similar and different from Output 16.1?

Outputs and Interpretations

Output 18.1: One-Way Multivariate Analysis of Variance

Syntax for Multivariate Analysis for three dependent variables and one independent variable

```
GLM
  grades mathach visual  BY faedr
  /METHOD = SSTYPE(3)
  /INTERCEPT = INCLUDE
  /PRINT = DESCRIPTIVE ETASQ
  /CRITERIA = ALPHA(.05)
  /DESIGN .
General Linear Model
```

Interpretation of Output 18.1

The GLM Multivariate procedure provides an analysis for multiple dependent variables by one or more fixed factor/independent variables and/or covariates.

Note that many of the results refer to the univariate ANOVA (e.g., descriptive statistics and the test of between subjects effects) and thus are the same as those you encountered in Output 15.1. In addition, MANOVA provides four similar multivariate tests of whether the three father's education groups differ on a linear combination of the dependent variables, grades, math achievement, and visualization. Wilks' Lambda provides a commonly used multivariate F (in this case 3.04, $df= 6$, 136, $p=.008$), which is significant in spite of the fact that the visualization score is not. Note that the Fs and sigs for the univariate tests (in the **Tests of Between Subject Effects** table) are the same as in the similar problem in Output 15.1, which was done with a univariate one-way ANOVA. Because the grades and math achievement dependent variables are statistically significant and there are three levels or values of father's education, we need to do post hoc multiple comparisons to see which pairs of means are different. This was done in Output 15.2a and 15.2b.

Note that both multivariate and univariate (between subjects) tests provide measures of effect size (eta squared) and power.

Between-Subjects Factors

		Value Label	N
Father's ed rev	1	hs grad or less	38
	2	some college	16
	3	BS or more	19

Descriptive Statistics

	Father's ed rev	Mean	Std. Deviation	N
grades in h.s.	hs grad or less	5.34	1.48	38
	some college	5.56	1.79	16
	BS or more	6.53	1.22	19
	Total	5.70	1.55	73
math achievement	hs grad or less	10.0877	5.6130	38
	some college	14.3958	4.6654	16
	BS or more	16.3509	7.4092	19
	Total	12.6621	6.4966	73
visualization score	hs grad or less	4.6711	3.9606	38
	some college	6.0156	4.5602	16
	BS or more	5.4605	2.7904	19
	Total	5.1712	3.8279	73

Multivariate Tests [d]

Effect		Value	F	Hypothesis df	Error df	Sig.	Eta Squared	Noncent. Parameter	Observed Power[a]
Intercept	Pillai's Trace	.938	341.884[b]	3.000	68.000	.000	.938	1025.652	1.000
	Wilks' Lambda	.062	341.884[b]	3.000	68.000	.000	.938	1025.652	1.000
	Hotelling's Trace	15.083	341.884[b]	3.000	68.000	.000	.938	1025.652	1.000
	Roy's Largest Root	15.083	341.884[b]	3.000	68.000	.000	.938	1025.652	1.000
FAEDR	Pillai's Trace	.229	2.970	6.000	138.000	.009	.114	17.823	.892
	Wilks' Lambda	.777	3.040[b]	6.000	136.000	.008	.118	18.238	.900
	Hotelling's Trace	.278	3.106	6.000	134.000	.007	.122	18.637	.907
	Roy's Largest Root	.245	5.645[c]	3.000	69.000	.002	.197	16.936	.934

a. Computed using alpha = .05

b. Exact statistic

c. The statistic is an upper bound on F that yields a lower bound on the significance level.

d. Design: Intercept+FAEDR

These are the univariate analyses of variance or ANOVAs.

Tests of Between-Subjects Effects

Source	Dependent Variable	Type III Sum of Squares	df	Mean Square	F	Sig.	Eta Squared	Noncent. Parameter	Observed Power[a]
Corrected Model	grades in h.s.	18.143[b]	2	9.071	4.091	.021	.105	8.182	.708
	math achievement	558.481[c]	2	279.240	7.881	.001	.184	15.762	.945
	visualization score	22.505[d]	2	11.252	.763	.470	.021	1.526	.175
Intercept	grades in h.s.	2148.057	1	2148.057	968.67	.000	.933	968.672	1.000
	math achievement	11788.512	1	11788.512	332.70	.000	.826	332.697	1.000
	visualization score	1843.316	1	1843.316	124.97	.000	.641	124.973	1.000
FAEDR	grades in h.s.	18.143	2	9.071	4.091	.021	.105	8.182	.708
	math achievement	558.481	2	279.240	7.881	.001	.184	15.762	.945
	visualization score	22.505	2	11.252	.763	.470	.021	1.526	.175
Error	grades in h.s.	155.227	70	2.218					
	math achievement	2480.324	70	35.433					
	visualization score	1032.480	70	14.750					
Total	grades in h.s.	2544.000	73						
	math achievement	14742.823	73						
	visualization score	3007.125	73						
Corrected Total	grades in h.s.	173.370	72						
	math achievement	3038.804	72						
	visualization score	1054.985	72						

a. Computed using alpha = .05

b. R Squared = .105 (Adjusted R Squared = .079)

c. R Squared = .184 (Adjusted R Squared = .160)

d. R Squared = .021 (Adjusted R Squared = -.007)

Output 18.2: One-Way Multivariate Analysis of Variance

Syntax for Multivariate analysis with three dependent variables and one independent variable

```
GLM
 grades mathach mathcrs  BY gend
 /METHOD = SSTYPE(3)
 /INTERCEPT = INCLUDE
 /PRINT = DESCRIPTIVE ETASQ
 /CRITERIA = ALPHA(.05)
 /DESIGN .
General Linear Model
```

Between-Subjects Factors

		Value Label	N
gender	1	male	34
	2	female	41

Descriptive Statistics

	gender	Mean	Std. Deviation	N
grades in h.s.	male	5.50	1.64	34
	female	5.83	1.51	41
	Total	5.68	1.57	75
math achievement	male	14.7550	6.0315	34
	female	10.7479	6.6961	41
	Total	12.5645	6.6703	75
Math course taken	male	2.71	1.57	34
	female	1.61	1.61	41
	Total	2.11	1.67	75

Multivariate Tests[c]

Effect		Value	F	Hypothesis df	Error df	Sig.	Eta Squared	Noncent. Parameter	Observed Power[a]
Intercept	Pillai's Trace	.943	388.548[b]	3.000	71.0	.000	.943	1165.645	1.000
	Wilks' Lambda	.057	388.548[b]	3.000	71.0	.000	.943	1165.645	1.000
	Hotelling's Trace	16.418	388.548[b]	3.000	71.0	.000	.943	1165.645	1.000
	Roy's Largest Root	16.418	388.548[b]	3.000	71.0	.000	.943	1165.645	1.000
GEND	Pillai's Trace	.253	8.029[b]	3.000	71.0	.000	.253	24.086	.988
	Wilks' Lambda	.747	8.029[b]	3.000	71.0	.000	.253	24.086	.988
	Hotelling's Trace	.339	8.029[b]	3.000	71.0	.000	.253	24.086	.988
	Roy's Largest Root	.339	8.029[b]	3.000	71.0	.000	.253	24.086	.988

a. Computed using alpha = .05

b. Exact statistic

c. Design: Intercept+GEND

Tests of Between-Subjects Effects

Source	Dependent Variable	Type III Sum of Squares	df	Mean Square	F	Sig.	Eta Squared	Noncent. Parameter	Observed Power[a]
Corrected Model	grades in h.s.	2.015[b]	1	2.015	.816	.369	.011	.816	.145
	math achievement	298.435[c]	1	298.435	7.276	.009	.091	7.276	.759
	Math course taken	22.332[d]	1	22.332	8.821	.004	.108	8.821	.834
Intercept	grades in h.s.	2385.642	1	2385.642	965.874	.000	.930	965.874	1.000
	math achievement	12088.727	1	12088.727	294.744	.000	.801	294.744	1.000
	Math course taken	346.172	1	346.172	136.734	.000	.652	136.734	1.000
GEND	grades in h.s.	2.015	1	2.015	.816	.369	.011	.816	.145
	math achievement	298.435	1	298.435	7.276	.009	.091	7.276	.759
	Math course taken	22.332	1	22.332	8.821	.004	.108	8.821	.834
Error	grades in h.s.	180.305	73	2.470					
	math achievement	2994.046	73	41.014					
	Math course taken	184.815	73	2.532					
Total	grades in h.s.	2602.000	75						
	math achievement	15132.393	75						
	Math course taken	540.000	75						
Corrected Total	grades in h.s.	182.320	74						
	math achievement	3292.481	74						
	Math course taken	207.147	74						

a. Computed using alpha = .05

b. R Squared = .011 (Adjusted R Squared = -.002)

c. R Squared = .091 (Adjusted R Squared = .078)

d. R Squared = .108 (Adjusted R Squared = .096)

Output 18.3: Two-Way Multivariate Analysis of Variance

<u>Syntax for Multivariate analysis with three dependent variables and two independent variables</u>

GLM
  mathach visual mosaic BY mathgr gend
  /METHOD = SSTYPE(3)
  /INTERCEPT = INCLUDE
  /PRINT = DESCRIPTIVE ETASQ
  /CRITERIA = ALPHA(.05)
  /DESIGN .
General Linear Model

Interpretation of Output 18.3
Many of the tables are similar to those in Output 18.1. The main difference is that both the **Multivariate Tests** table and the univariate **Tests of Between Subjects Effects** table have an *F* test for the interaction of math grades and gender (*mathgr * gend*). The interpretation of this interaction is similar to that in Output 16.1.

Between-Subjects Factors

		Value Label	N
math grades	0	less A-B	44
	1	most A-B	31
gender	1	male	34
	2	female	41

Descriptive Statistics

	math grades	gender	Mean	Std. Deviation	N
math achievement	less A-B	male	12.8751	5.7314	24
		female	8.3333	5.3256	20
		Total	10.8106	5.9444	44
	most A-B	male	19.2667	4.1718	10
		female	13.0476	7.1658	21
		Total	15.0538	6.9417	31
	Total	male	14.7550	6.0315	34
		female	10.7479	6.6961	41
		Total	12.5645	6.6703	75
visualization score	less A-B	male	5.7188	4.5285	24
		female	3.2750	2.7421	20
		Total	4.6080	3.9757	44
	most A-B	male	8.1250	4.0419	10
		female	5.2024	3.2012	21
		Total	6.1452	3.6962	31
	Total	male	6.4265	4.4707	34
		female	4.2622	3.1059	41
		Total	5.2433	3.9120	75
mosaic, pattern test	less A-B	male	26.896	8.754	24
		female	28.925	10.486	20
		Total	27.818	9.519	44
	most A-B	male	28.250	4.467	10
		female	26.167	11.532	21
		Total	26.839	9.779	31
	Total	male	27.294	7.697	34
		female	27.512	10.985	41
		Total	27.413	9.574	75

Multivariate Tests[c]

Effect		Value	F	Hypothesis df	Error df	Sig.	Eta Squared	Noncent. Parameter	Observed Power[a]
Intercept	Pillai's Trace	.915	247.327[b]	3.000	69.0	.000	.915	741.980	1.000
	Wilks' Lambda	.085	247.327[b]	3.000	69.0	.000	.915	741.980	1.000
	Hotelling's Trace	10.753	247.327[b]	3.000	69.0	.000	.915	741.980	1.000
	Roy's Largest Root	10.753	247.327[b]	3.000	69.0	.000	.915	741.980	1.000
MATHGR	Pillai's Trace	.205	5.938[b]	3.000	69.0	.001	.205	17.814	.946
	Wilks' Lambda	.795	5.938[b]	3.000	69.0	.001	.205	17.814	.946
	Hotelling's Trace	.258	5.938[b]	3.000	69.0	.001	.205	17.814	.946
	Roy's Largest Root	.258	5.938[b]	3.000	69.0	.001	.205	17.814	.946
GEND	Pillai's Trace	.208	6.046[b]	3.000	69.0	.001	.208	18.138	.950
	Wilks' Lambda	.792	6.046[b]	3.000	69.0	.001	.208	18.138	.950
	Hotelling's Trace	.263	6.046[b]	3.000	69.0	.001	.208	18.138	.950
	Roy's Largest Root	.263	6.046[b]	3.000	69.0	.001	.208	18.138	.950
MATHGR * GEND	Pillai's Trace	.012	.290[b]	3.000	69.0	.832	.012	.870	.103
	Wilks' Lambda	.988	.290[b]	3.000	69.0	.832	.012	.870	.103
	Hotelling's Trace	.013	.290[b]	3.000	69.0	.832	.012	.870	.103
	Roy's Largest Root	.013	.290[b]	3.000	69.0	.832	.012	.870	.103

a. Computed using alpha = .05

b. Exact statistic

c. Design: Intercept+MATHGR+GEND+MATHGR * GEND

Tests of Between-Subjects Effects

Source	Dependent Variable	Type III Sum of Squares	df	Mean Square	F	Sig.	Eta Squared	Noncent. Parameter	Observed Power[a]
Corrected Model	math achievement	814.481[b]	3	271.494	7.779	.000	.247	23.337	.985
	visualization score	165.986[c]	3	55.329	4.064	.010	.147	12.193	.824
	mosaic, pattern test	91.768[d]	3	30.589	.325	.808	.014	.974	.110
Intercept	math achievement	11971.773	1	11972	343.02	.000	.829	343.017	1.000
	visualization score	2082.167	1	2082.2	152.96	.000	.683	152.956	1.000
	mosaic, pattern test	50785.758	1	50786	538.91	.000	.884	538.908	1.000
MATHGR	math achievement	515.463	1	515.463	14.769	.000	.172	14.769	.966
	visualization score	78.485	1	78.485	5.766	.019	.075	5.766	.659
	mosaic, pattern test	8.240	1	8.240	.087	.768	.001	.087	.060
GEND	math achievement	483.929	1	483.929	13.866	.000	.163	13.866	.957
	visualization score	120.350	1	120.350	8.841	.004	.111	8.841	.835
	mosaic, pattern test	1.226E-02	1	1.E-02	.000	.991	.000	.000	.050
MATHGR * GEND	math achievement	11.756	1	11.756	.337	.563	.005	.337	.088
	visualization score	.958	1	.958	.070	.792	.001	.070	.058
	mosaic, pattern test	70.680	1	70.680	.750	.389	.010	.750	.137
Error	math achievement	2478.000	71	34.901					
	visualization score	966.510	71	13.613					
	mosaic, pattern test	6690.919	71	94.238					
Total	math achievement	15132.393	75						
	visualization score	3194.438	75						
	mosaic, pattern test	63144.500	75						
Corrected Total	math achievement	3292.481	74						
	visualization score	1132.497	74						
	mosaic, pattern test	6782.687	74						

a. Computed using alpha = .05

b. R Squared = .247 (Adjusted R Squared = .216)

c. R Squared = .147 (Adjusted R Squared = .111)

d. R Squared = .014 (Adjusted R Squared = -.028)

APPENDIX A

Writing Research Problems and Questions

Frameworks for Stating Research Problems

Although a common definition of a research problem is that it is a statement that asks what relationship exists between two or more variables, most research problems are much more complex than this definition implies. The research problem should be a fairly broad statement that covers the several more specific research questions to be investigated, perhaps by using broader terms that stand for several variables. One way to state the problem, that can help you figure out what the independent and dependent variables are, is as follows (underlines indicate that you fill in the appropriate name for the variable or group of variables):

Format

The research problem is to investigate the presumed effect of (put independent variable 1 or group of variables here) (and independent variable 2, if any, here) (and independent variable 3, if any) on (dependent variable 1, here) (and dependent variable 2, if any) in (population).

Except in a totally descriptive study, there must always be at least one independent and one dependent variable. However, there can be two or more of each, and there often are. In the statement of the problem, in contrast to the research question/hypotheses, it is desirable to use broad descriptors for groups of similar variables. For example demographics covers four variables: gender, mother's and father's education, and ethnicity. Spatial performance includes a mosaic/pattern score and a visualization score. Likewise, grades and math attitudes refer to more than one variable. In other studies, concepts such as self-esteem or teaching style have several aspects so usually result in more than one variable.

The examples presented below use the HSB (high school and beyond) data set, which is described in the next section. The first example is in the above format. The second and third are suggested variations.

Examples

1. The research problem is to investigate the *presumed* effect of demographic variables, grades, and math attitudes on quantitative/spatial achievement in high school students.

This format can be used with any approach but is most appropriate for studies that use the *experimental and quasi-experimental approaches*. If you do not have an active/manipulated variable and, thus, will use the *comparative or associational* approach, it may be better to phrase the sample problem as follows:

2. The problem is to investigate the relationships of demographics, grades, and math attitudes with quantitative and spatial achievement in high school students.

If you have *more than two or three independent variables*, as we do in this study, it may be best to say:

3. The problem is to investigate whether demographics, math courses, grades, spatial scores, and math attitudes are predictors of math achievement. More generally, we could say the problem is to investigate the factors that predict or seem to influence math achievement.

This latter format is used when the approach is a complex (many independent variables) associational one.

Framework for Stating Research Questions/Hypotheses

Although it is fine to phrase a research problem (as in the format and first example above) as a "study of the presumed effect of...," we think it is best to phrase your research questions or hypotheses so that they do not appear to imply cause and effect; i.e., as *difference* or *associational* questions/hypotheses or as *descriptive* questions. The former are answered with inferential statistics and the latter with descriptive statistics.

Descriptive Questions

Basic descriptive questions. These questions are about some aspect of one variable at a time. Descriptive questions ask about the central tendency, frequency distribution/percentage in each category, variability, or shape of the distribution. Some descriptive questions are intended to test assumptions. Some questions simply describe the sample demographics. Some HSB **examples** are as follows:

1. What percentage of participants arc of each gender?

2. What is the mean, mode, and median of the math achievement scores?

3. Is math achievement distributed approximately normally?

Complex descriptive questions. These questions deal with two or more variables at a time, but do not involve inferential statistics. Cross-tabulations of two categorical variables, box plots, factor analysis, and measures of reliability (e.g., Cronbach's alpha) are examples.

An HSB **example** is:

1. What is the reliability of the visualization score?

Difference Questions/Hypotheses

Basic difference questions. The **format** is as follows:

Is there a difference between the average (put the **dependent** variable here) scores of the (put **value 1** of the independent variable here, then **value 2,** and **value 3** etc., if any here).

An HSB **example** is as follows:

1. Is there a difference between the average math achievement scores of the students whose fathers have high, medium and low education?

Complex difference and interaction questions. When you have two categorical independent variables considered together, you will have *three* research questions or hypotheses. There are advantages of considering two or three independent variables at a time. See chapter 16 for how to interpret the *interaction* question. Sample **formats** are as follows:

1. Is there a difference between the average (put **dependent** variable 1 here) scores of the (insert **value 1** of **independent variable 1**), (**value 2** of independent variable 1) and (**value 3**, if there is one, of independent variable 1, etc.)?

2. Is there a difference between the average (**dependent** variable 1) scores of the (insert **value 1** of independent **variable 2**), (**value 2** of independent variable 2), (**value 3**, if one, of independent variable 2, etc.)?

3. Is there an interaction of (independent **variable 1**) and (independent **variable 2**) on (**dependent** variable 1)?

Repeat these three questions if there is more than one dependent variable.

An HSB **example** is as follows:

1. Is there a difference between the average math achievement scores of students having high versus low math grades?

2. Is there a difference between the average math achievement scores of male and female students?"

3. Is there an interaction between math grades and gender on math achievement?

Note that the first question states the *values* or categories of the first independent variable; i.e., it states the groups that are to be compared (high vs. low math grade students). The second question does the same for the second independent variable; i.e., states the **values** (male and female) to be compared. However, in the third (interaction) question, it is asked whether the first

variable itself (math grades) interacts with the second variable (gender). No mention is made, at this point, of the values/levels/groups.

Associational/Relationship Questions/Hypotheses

Basic associational questions. When both the independent and dependent variables are ordered and essentially continuous (e.g., have five or more ordered categories) the approach and research question are considered to be associational. The **format** is as follows:

Is there an association between (**independent variable 1**) and (**dependent variable 1**)?

If there is more than one independent variable and/or dependent variable, which is common, and each pair of variables is associated separately, you can have a series of questions asking whether there is an association between each independent variable and each dependent variable. If it is arbitrary which variables are independent/antecedent/predictors and which are dependent/outcome variables, one might ask whether every variable is related to every other variable. This would produce a **correlation matrix**. (See chapter 9.)

An HSB **example** for a single association/relationship is as follows:

1. Is there an association between grades in high school and math achievement?

An HSB **example** that would produce a correlation matrix is as follows:

2. Are there associations among the three math attitude scale scores?

Note that what is said to be associated in these questions is the variable itself; no mention is made of the values here. In the interpretation of Output 9.1, we indicated that a nontechnical *interpretation* of a significant correlation/association may involve mentioning the values in general terms; e.g., high, medium, and low.

Complex associational questions. In the associational approach, when two or more **independent** variables are considered together, rather than separately, as in the basic format above, you get a new kind of question. The **format** can be phrased something like:

 Is there a combination of factors (list the several specific independent variables here) that predicts (put dependent variable here) better than any one alone and, if so, what is the best combination?

An HSB **example** is as follows:

1. Is there a combination of number of math courses, gender, father's education, math grades, and motivation for math that predicts math achievement better than any one alone and, if so, what is the best combination?

APPENDIX B

Select Cases: Analyzing Parts of a Sample

The **select cases** command is used when one wants to pick (filter) certain cases for analysis, leaving the rest out. In the examples shown in this assignment, we will use the filter to select only those with high (or low) math grades. You can also select a random sample, certain cases/subject numbers, or use a formula (see Fig. B.1 and B.2).

Problem 1: Descriptives for Those With High Math Grades

Now let us find the mean, standard deviation, minimum, and maximum for just those persons with high math grades.
- In your menu bar click on **data** then **Select Cases.** Your screen should look like Fig. B.1.
- Click on **If condition is satisfied;** then click on **If...**

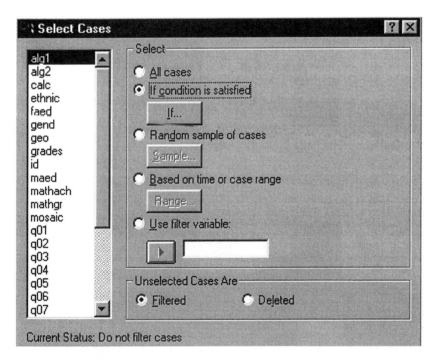

Fig. B.1. Select cases dialog box.

You should be at a window like Fig. B.2.
- Highlight *mathgr* and then click on the **arrow** button, then on "=", and then on "**1.**" You should have *mathgr* = 1 like in Fig. B.2.
- Click on **Continue.** Then back at the main **Select Cases** dialog box, click **OK.**
- **Don't forget to click on OK or the selection will not be complete.**

Look at your data editor and see if Filter_$ is the last variable. Compare the syntax in Output B.1 to yours to see if you are on the right track.

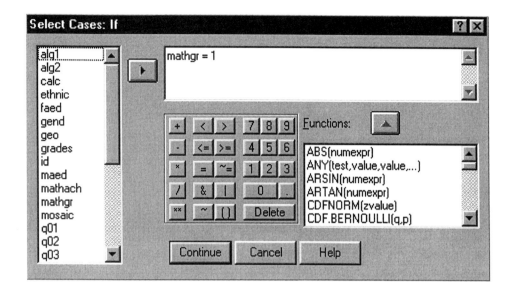

Fig. B.2.
Select cases.

Now repeat the steps you used in Assignment A to find the mean, standard deviation, minimum and maximum for each variable using **Descriptive** statistics (Fig. 4.7, 4.8, and 4.9 if you need help). This time, however, move the **Filter_$** over to the **Variables box** as well. The **Filter_$** is the selection you just made of only those subjects with high math grades. Does your output and syntax look like Output B.1?

Problem 2: Select Cases and Descriptives for Those With Low Math Grades

Now try it once more but just describe those with low math grades (*mathgr* = 0). **One caution-- don't forget to *reset* by clicking on Select All cases in Fig. B.1 before changing it back to "If condition is satisfied"** so that you can start with all cases again. Using **Descriptive** statistics find the mean, standard deviation, minimum, and maximum for each variable.

Follow the steps you used in Problem 1 above. What does your output look like now?

When you finish don't forget to reset the select cases as above!! If you don't, next time you will be using only those participants with low math grades.

Check your syntax and output with Output B.2.

Important: Before going any further go to your data editor and locate the **Filter_$** column. You should delete this now or your future outputs could have problems.

- Click once on the gray **Filter_$.** You will probably notice that all the numbers below it are highlighted.
- Now hit the **delete** key. **Filter_$** should disappear.

Outputs and Interpretation

```
GET
  FILE='A:\HSBWIN01.SAV'.
EXECUTE .
```

Output B.1: Descriptives Filtered for High Math Grades

SYNTAX FOR MATHGR = 1

```
USE ALL.
COMPUTE FILTER_$=(MATHGR = 1).
VARIABLE LABEL FILTER_$ 'MATHGR = 1 (FILTER)'.
VALUE LABELS FILTER_$ 0 'NOT SELECTED' 1 'SELECTED'.
FORMAT FILTER_$ (F1.0).
FILTER BY FILTER_$.
EXECUTE .
```

SYNTAX FOR THE MEAN, STANDARD DEVIATION, MINIMUM, AND MAXIMUM FOR ALL VARIABLES FILTERED WITH MATHGR = 1

```
DESCRIPTIVES
  VARIABLES=FILTER_$ ALG1 ALG2 CALC ETHNIC FAED GEND GEO GRADES ID MAED
  MATHACH MATHGR MOSAIC Q01 Q02 Q03 Q04 Q05 Q06 Q07 Q08 Q09 Q10 Q11 Q12 Q13
  TRIG VISUAL
  /STATISTICS=MEAN STDDEV MIN MAX .
```

Interpretation of Output B.1

Notice that there are **28** participants with valid or complete data. Note also, that on the math grades line, both minimum and maximum are 1. That is how it should be because you asked the computer to only select/filter for high math grades. You could also compare the means of this high math grades group with the means of the low math grades group (Output B.2) on any variable.

Descriptive Statistics

	N	Minimum	Maximum	Mean	Std. Deviation
mathgr = 1 (FILTER)	31	1	1	1.00	.00
algebra 1 in h.s.	31	0	1	.84	.37
algebra 2 in h.s.	31	0	1	.61	.50
calculus in h.s.	31	0	1	.23	.43
ethnicity	30	1	4	1.77	.90
father's education	30	2	10	4.70	2.82
gender	31	1	2	1.68	.48
geometry in h.s.	31	0	1	.58	.50
grades in h.s.	31	5	8	6.84	1.00
identification	31	3	75	39.84	19.73
mother's education	31	2	9	3.94	2.37
math achievement	31	1.00	23.67	15.0538	6.9417
math grades	31	1	1	1.00	.00
mosaic, pattern test	31	-4.0	56.0	26.839	9.779
question 1	31	1	4	2.97	.80
question 2	31	1	4	3.42	.99
question 3	30	1	4	2.97	.89
question 4	31	1	4	2.10	.83
question 5	31	1	4	1.48	.81
question 6	31	1	4	2.45	.99
question 7	31	1	4	2.71	.94
question 8	31	1	4	2.06	.93
question 9	31	1	4	3.32	.75
question 10	31	1	4	1.39	.72
question 11	31	1	4	1.29	.64
question 12	31	1	4	2.97	.87
question 13	31	1	4	2.52	.77
trigonometry in h.s.	31	0	1	.45	.51
visualization score	31	1.00	14.75	6.1452	3.6962
Valid N (listwise)	28				

Output B.2: Descriptives Filtered for Low Math Grades

SYNTAX FOR MATHGR = 0

```
USE ALL.
COMPUTE FILTER_$=(MATHGR = 0).
VARIABLE LABEL FILTER_$ 'MATHGR = 0 (FILTER)'.
VALUE LABELS FILTER_$ 0 'NOT SELECTED' 1 'SELECTED'.
FORMAT FILTER_$ (F1.0).
FILTER BY FILTER_$.
EXECUTE .
```

SYNTAX FOR THE MEAN, STANDARD DEVIATION, MINIMUM, AND MAXIMUM FOR ALL VARIABLES FILTERED WITH MATHGR = 0

```
DESCRIPTIVES
  VARIABLES=FILTER_$ ALG1 ALG2 CALC ETHNIC FAED GEND GEO GRADES ID MAED
  MATHACH MATHGR MOSAIC Q01 Q02 Q03 Q04 Q05 Q06 Q07 Q08 Q09 Q10 Q11 Q12 Q13
  TRIG VISUAL
  /STATISTICS=MEAN STDDEV MIN MAX .
```

Descriptive Statistics

	N	Minimum	Maximum	Mean	Std. Deviation
mathgr = 0 (FILTER)	44	1	1	1.00	.00
algebra 1 in h.s.	44	0	1	.75	.44
algebra 2 in h.s.	44	0	1	.36	.49
calculus in h.s.	44	0	1	2.27E-02	.15
ethnicity	43	1	4	1.77	1.11
father's education	43	2	10	4.74	2.87
gender	44	1	2	1.45	.50
geometry in h.s.	44	0	1	.41	.50
grades in h.s.	44	2	7	4.86	1.37
identification	44	1	74	36.70	23.27
mother's education	44	2	10	4.23	2.17
math achievement	44	-1.67	23.67	10.8106	5.9444
math grades	44	0	0	.00	.00
mosaic, pattern test	44	7.5	56.0	27.818	9.519
question 1	43	1	4	2.95	1.02
question 2	44	1	4	3.59	.84
question 3	44	1	4	2.73	.90
question 4	43	1	4	2.21	.99
question 5	44	1	4	1.70	1.07
question 6	44	1	4	2.41	.97
question 7	44	1	4	2.80	1.13
question 8	44	1	4	1.86	.90
question 9	43	1	4	3.33	.78
question 10	44	1	4	1.43	.76
question 11	44	1	4	1.41	.82
question 12	44	1	4	3.02	.79
question 13	44	1	4	2.77	.80
trigonometry in h.s.	44	0	1	.14	.35
visualization score	44	-.25	14.75	4.6080	3.9757
Valid N (listwise)	39				

APPENDIX C

Working with SPSS Syntax (Log) Files
Mei-Huei Tsay

It is possible to modify syntax files to run slightly different statistics and/or complex, customized statistics. Sometimes output files are too large to save on a disk or take up too much space on your hard drive. Therefore, it is a good idea to understand how to use the syntax or log files that contain SPSS commands. You can use the SPSS logs from your output file to run these commands.

It is possible to open a syntax window and type in commands, but sometimes it is easier to build your syntax file by using one of the following methods:

- Paste syntax commands from dialog boxes.
- Copy syntax from the output log.
- Copy syntax from the journal file.

Creating Syntax Commands From Dialog Boxes: Using Paste Instead of OK

The easiest way to generate a syntax command file is to make selections in dialogue boxes and paste the syntax of the selections into a syntax window. By pasting the syntax in the syntax window, you can generate a job file which allows you to repeat the analysis, edit it, save the syntax in a syntax file, and copy/cut it into an output log.

To paste syntax commands from a dialog box:

- Retrieve the data file.
- Open the dialog box and make desired selections. For example: **Statistics => Summarize => Frequencies**.
- After making all the desired selections, click **Paste** instead of **OK** (see Fig. C.1). The syntax command is pasted to the syntax window. If you don't have an open syntax window, SPSS will open a new syntax window and paste the syntax there (see Fig. C.2).

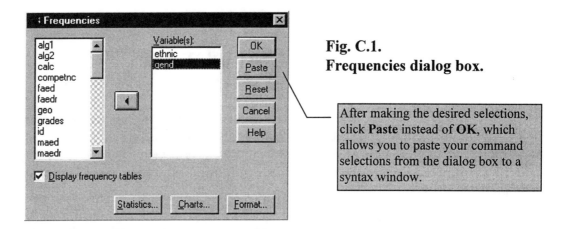

Fig. C.1.
Frequencies dialog box.

After making the desired selections, click **Paste** instead of **OK**, which allows you to paste your command selections from the dialog box to a syntax window.

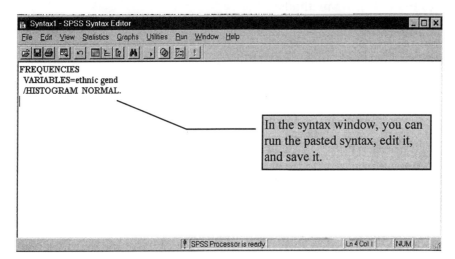

Fig. C.2.
The syntax window.

In the syntax window, you can run the pasted syntax, edit it, and save it.

- To run/use a syntax file, when there is only one syntax file in the window, just simply click on **Run** in the menu bar.
- If there are many syntax files in the window, *highlight* the desired syntax first, then click **Run** then **Selection**. The output will show on the output window.
- If you need to repeat all the analyses in the syntax window, you can click on **Run** and then **All**.

Using Syntax From the SPSS Log

This is useful when you don't have much room to spare on your computer or disk. You can save only the SPSS logs and delete all the output tables, charts, and other heavy files.

You can build a syntax file by copying syntax commands from the SPSS output log in the Output Navigator.
- First of all, you must select **Display commands in the log** in the SPSS Options dialog box before running the analysis, as we did in Assignment A (chapter 4).

- To do this, from the menus click on **Edit** => **Options** => **Navigator** => **Display commands in the log**. Each command you did will then be recorded in the SPSS log as in Fig. C.3.

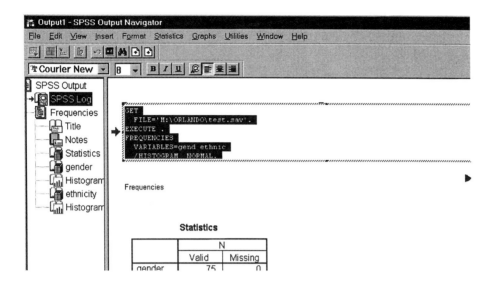

Fig. C.3. Syntax commands in the SPSS log.

- To copy the syntax from the Output Navigator, first *double click* on the syntax file table to activate it (which allows you to edit the table), then **highlight** the desired syntax file (see Fig. C.3); from **Edit**, click on **Copy**.
- Second, open a previously saved syntax file or create a new one.
- To create a new syntax file, from the menus choose **File** => **New** => **Syntax**; then in the syntax window, choose **Edit** then **Paste**. You can run or change the pasted syntax as we did above.

Using Syntax From the Journal File

This is a more complicated way of doing things, but it is worth mentioning here.

By default, SPSS records all commands executed during a session in a journal file named *spss.jnl* (set with **Options** on the **Edit** menu). You can edit the journal file and save it as a syntax file that you can use to repeat the previous analysis.

To open the journal file,
- from the menus choose **File** => **Open**; under the **Files of Type**,
- choose **All files** (*.*);
- then choose *spss.jnl* from the file name box or enter **.jnl* in the **File Name box,**
- then click **Open** (see Fig. C.4).

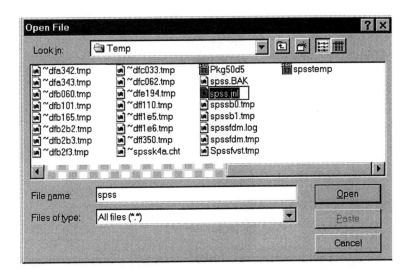

Fig. C.4. Open spss.jnl.

The journal file is a text file that can be edited like any other text file. But notice, because error and warning messages are also recorded in the journal file along with your commands, you must delete any of these messages that appear before saving or running the syntax file (see Fig. C.5).

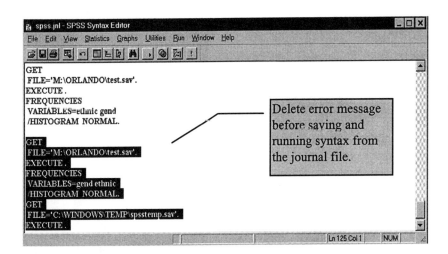

Fig. C.5. Editing the journal file.

To run or edit the journal file, see above.

Running Syntax Commands

You can run single commands, selected groups of commands, or all commands in a syntax window. The following options are available on the **Run** menu (see Fig. C.6):

- **All**. Runs all commands in the syntax window.
- **Selection**. Runs the currently selected commands. This includes any commands partially highlighted.
- **Current.** Runs the command where the cursor is currently located.

- **To End**. Runs all commands from the current cursor location to the end of the command syntax file.

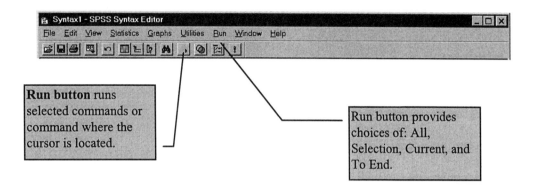

Fig. C.6. Syntax editor toolbar.

APPENDIX D

The HSB Codebook and How to Develop It

The purpose of a codebook is to identify clearly each variable so that both you and other investigators will know what the data represent. *Tables D.1 and D.2 are the HSB codebook that can be generated from the hsbdata file by clicking on **Utilities** and then **File Info**, while the data file is showing on your screen.* We have edited the codebook to make it more compact and typed in the transformation formulas (in middle column) of Table D.2 to make the codebook more complete.

The left column gives the *variable names* in 8 characters or less. Notice that these names are the same as those across the top of the data editor (see Table 2.1). The second column in Table D.1 provides several pieces of information for each variable. First, there is a longer name called the *variable label*. Second is the print and write formats, which indicate the number of columns and decimal places. Third, the variables have the *value labels* specified. Thus, for example, grades can take on values between 1 and 8; 1 indicates grades of less than a D, 8 is a grade average that is mostly A, and numbers 2 through 7 are grade averages in between. Likewise, the values for math grades are 0 for less than A-B and 1 for mostly A-B. These values are categories or levels of the variable (see chapter 1).

Certain variables are considered to be essentially continuous and thus do not have labels for each value. Visual mosaic and math achievement are such variables in this data set. We have, however, identified the highest and lowest value for each of these variables, indicating the range of possible scores for these continuous variables. For example, visualization scores could range from -4 to 16 and mosaic from -28 to 56. Math achievement, the variable in position 11, can range from -8.33 to 25. The minus scores are probably due to an adjustment for guessing so that a person who is just making wild guesses would get a score of less than zero.

The *print format* and *write format* are always the same and indicate the number of columns the variable can fill, for example, an identification number can be 3 columns, any number between 000 and 999. The visualization score format is 6.2, which means that it can be up to six columns with two places after the decimal point.

Table D.2 provides a codebook for the new or transformed variables that were computed, recoded or counted in Assignments C and D. It is important to keep track of such new variables and label them appropriately. The middle column shows how these variables were computed, recoded, etc.

Now let's think about the scale (or level) of measurement of each of these variables (see the data set in chapter 2 and also see chapter 3). If identification number were a variable in this study, which it is not, it would be considered a *nominal* or unordered categorical variable because the identification numbers for each participant are merely names and have no inherent order to them. Participant 2 is neither more nor less than participant 1 or 3. Visualization score, which varies from -4 to 16, is, like most test scores, considered to be approximately *interval* scale data because it is assumed that there are equal intervals between the scores; e.g., the distance from 1 to 2 is the same as from 2 to 3 and so on. *Ordinal* scale data are merely *rank* ordered, like 1st place, 2nd place, 3rd place and do not necessary have equal intervals between the ranks. As discussed in chapter 3, test scores and ratings, especially if composites, are considered approximately interval scale. Using the nominal, ordinal, and interval scale terms, how would you classify mosaic pattern test scores? How about grades in high school? Math grades? Gender? Ethnic group?

Table D.1. *File Information - Codebook*

List of variables on the working file

Name	Variable label, format, and Value label	Position
ID	IDENTIFICATION PRINT FORMAT: F3 WRITE FORMAT: F3	1
VISUAL	VISUALIZATION SCORE PRINT FORMAT: F6.2 WRITE FORMAT: F6.2 VALUE LABEL -4.00 LOW 16.00 HIGH	2
MOSAIC	MOSAIC, PATTERN TEST PRINT FORMAT: F6.1 WRITE FORMAT: F6.1 VALUE LABEL -4.0 LOW 56.0 HIGH	3
GRADES	GRADES IN H.S. PRINT FORMAT: F1 WRITE FORMAT: F1 VALUE LABEL 1 LESS THAN D 2 MOSTLY D 3 HALF CD 4 MOSTLY C 5 HALF BC 6 MOSTLY B 7 HALF AB 8 MOSTLY A	4
MATHGR	MATH GRADES PRINT FORMAT: F1 WRITE FORMAT: F1 VALUE LABEL 0 LESS A-B 1 MOST A-B	5

```
ALG1        ALGEBRA 1 IN H.S.                                      6
            PRINT FORMAT: F1
            WRITE FORMAT: F1
            VALUE    LABEL
              0        NOT TAKEN
              1        TAKEN


ALG2        ALGEBRA 2 IN H.S.
                                                                   7

            PRINT FORMAT: F1
            WRITE FORMAT: F1
            VALUE    LABEL
              0        NOT TAKEN
              1        TAKEN


GEO         GEOMETRY IN H.S.
        8
            PRINT FORMAT: F1
            WRITE FORMAT: F1
            VALUE    LABEL
              0        NOT TAKEN
              1        TAKEN


TRIG        TRIGONOMETRY IN H.S.                                   9
            PRINT FORMAT: F1
            WRITE FORMAT: F1
            VALUE    LABEL
              0        NOT TAKEN
              1        TAKEN


CALC        CALCULUS IN H.S.                                      10
            PRINT FORMAT: F1
            WRITE FORMAT: F1
            VALUE    LABEL
              0        NOT TAKEN
              1        TAKEN


MATHACH     MATH ACHIEVEMENT                                      11
            PRINT FORMAT: F7.2
            WRITE FORMAT: F7.2
            VALUE    LABEL
            -8.33      LOW
            25.00      HIGH


FAED        FATHER'S EDUCATION                                    12
            PRINT FORMAT: F2
            WRITE FORMAT: F2
            MISSING VALUES: -1
            VALUE    LABEL
              2        < H.S. GRAD
              3        H.S. GRAD
              4        < 2 YRS VOC
              5        2 YRS VOC
              6        < 2 YRS COLL
              7        > 2 YRS COLL
              8        COLL GRAD
              9        MASTER'S
             10        MD/PhD
```

```
MAED        MOTHER'S EDUCATION                                      13
            PRINT FORMAT: F2
            WRITE FORMAT: F2
            MISSING VALUES: -1
            VALUE    LABEL
               2     < H.S.
               3     H.S. GRAD
               4     < 2 YRS VOC
               5     2 YRS VOC
               6     < 2 YRS COLL
               7     > 2 YRS COLL
               8     COLL GRAD
               9     MASTER'S
              10     MD/PhD


GEND        GENDER                                                  14
            PRINT FORMAT: F1
            WRITE FORMAT: F1
            VALUE    LABEL
               1     MALE
               2     FEMALE


Q01         QUESTION 1                                              15
            PRINT FORMAT: F2
            WRITE FORMAT: F2
            VALUE    LABEL
               1     VERY ATYPICAL
               4     VERY TYPICAL


Q02         QUESTION 2                                              16
            PRINT FORMAT: F2
            WRITE FORMAT: F2
            VALUE    LABEL
               1     VERY ATYPICAL
               4     VERY TYPICAL


Q03         QUESTION 3
                                                                    17
            PRINT FORMAT: F2
            WRITE FORMAT: F2
            VALUE    LABEL
               1     VERY ATYPICAL
               4     VERY TYPICAL


Q04         QUESTION 4                                              18
            PRINT FORMAT: F2
            WRITE FORMAT: F2
            VALUE    LABEL
               1     VERY ATYPICAL
               4     VERY TYPICAL


Q05         QUESTION 5                                              19
            PRINT FORMAT: F2
            WRITE FORMAT: F2
            VALUE    LABEL
               1     VERY ATYPICAL
               4     VERY TYPICAL
```

```
Q06          QUESTION 6                                                      20
             PRINT FORMAT: F2
             WRITE FORMAT: F2
             VALUE    LABEL
                1        VERY ATYPICAL
                4        VERY TYPICAL


Q07          QUESTION 7                                                      21
             PRINT FORMAT: F2
             WRITE FORMAT: F2
             VALUE    LABEL
                1        VERY ATYPICAL
                4        VERY TYPICAL


Q08          QUESTION 8                                                      22
             PRINT FORMAT: F2
             WRITE FORMAT: F2
             VALUE    LABEL
                1        VERY ATYPICAL
                4        VERY TYPICAL


Q09          QUESTION 9                                                      23
             PRINT FORMAT: F2
             WRITE FORMAT: F2
             VALUE    LABEL
                1        VERY ATYPICAL
                4        VERY TYPICAL


Q10          QUESTION 10                                                     24
             PRINT FORMAT: F2
             WRITE FORMAT: F2
             VALUE    LABEL
                1        VERY ATYPICAL
                4        VERY TYPICAL


Q11          QUESTION 11                                                     25
             PRINT FORMAT: F2
             WRITE FORMAT: F2
             VALUE    LABEL
                1        VERY ATYPICAL
                4        VERY TYPICAL


Q12          QUESTION 12                                                     26
             PRINT FORMAT: F2
             WRITE FORMAT: F2
             VALUE    LABEL
                1        VERY ATYPICAL
                4        VERY TYPICAL


Q13          QUESTION 13                                                     27
             PRINT FORMAT: F2
             WRITE FORMAT: F2
             VALUE    LABEL
                1        VERY ATYPICAL
                4        VERY TYPICAL
```

```
ETHNIC      ETHNICITY                                                    28
            PRINT FORMAT: F1
            WRITE FORMAT: F1
            MISSING VALUES: 9
            VALUE    LABEL
                1      EURO-AMER
                2      AFRICAN-AMER
                3      HISPANIC-AMER
                4      ASIAN-AMER
```

Table D.2. *File Information for Transformed/New Variables*

Name	List of variables on the working file	Transformation	Position

```
VISUAL2    VISUALIZATION RETEST      NEW VARIABLE                    29
           PRINT FORMAT: F4
           WRITE FORMAT: F4
           VALUE    LABEL
               0      LOWEST
               9      HIGHEST

MATHCRS    MATH COURSE TAKEN         COUNT                           30
           PRINT FORMAT: F2          MATHCRS=ALG1+ALG2+GEO+TRIG+CALC
           WRITE FORMAT: F2
           VALUE    LABEL
               0      NONE TAKEN
               5      ALL MATH COURSES

FAEDR      FATHER'S ED REV           RECODE                          31
           PRINT FORMAT: F2          (2,3=1)(4-7=2)(8-10=3)
           WRITE FORMAT: F2
           VALUE    LABEL
               1      HS GRAD OR LESS
               2      SOME COLLEGE
               3      BS OR MORE

MAEDR      MOTHER'S ED REV           RECODE                          32
           PRINT FORMAT: F2          (2,3=1)(4-7=2)(8-10=3)
           WRITE FORMAT: F2
           VALUE    LABEL
               1      HS GRAD OR LESS
               2      SOME COLLEGE
               3      BS OR MORE

Q06R       Q06 REVERSED              RECODE                          33
           PRINT FORMAT: F2          (1=4)(2=3)(3=2)(4=1)
           WRITE FORMAT: F2
           VALUE    LABEL
               1      NOT TYPICAL
               4      TYPICAL

Q10R       Q10 REVERSED              RECODE                          34
           PRINT FORMAT: F2          (1=4)(2=3)(3=2)(4=1)
           WRITE FORMAT: F2
           VALUE    LABEL
               1      NOT TYPICAL
               4      TYPICAL
```

PLEASURE   PLEASURE SCALE   COMPUTE   35
           PRINT FORMAT: F4.2   PLEASURE=(Q02+Q06R+Q10R)/3
           WRITE FORMAT: F4.2
           VALUE   LABEL
           1.00   VERY LOW
           4.00   VERY HIGH

Q04R   Q04 REVERSED   RECODE   36
           PRINT FORMAT: F4   (1=4)(2=3)(3=2)(4=1)
           WRITE FORMAT: F4
           VALUE   LABEL
           1   NOT TYPICAL
           4   TYPICAL

Q05R   Q05 REVERSED   RECODE   37
           PRINT FORMAT: F4   (1=4)(2=3)(3=2)(4=1)
           WRITE FORMAT: F4
           VALUE   LABEL
           1   NOT TYPICAL
           4   TYPICAL

Q08R   Q08 REVERSED   RECODE   38
           PRINT FORMAT: F4   (1=4)(2=3)(3=2)(4=1)
           WRITE FORMAT: F4
           VALUE   LABEL
           1   NOT TYPICAL
           4   TYPICAL

Q11R   Q11 REVERSED   RECODE   39
           PRINT FORMAT: F4   (1=4)(2=3)(3=2)(4=1)
           WRITE FORMAT: F4
           VALUE   LABEL
           1   NOT TYPICAL
           4   TYPICAL

COMPETNC   COMPETENCE SCALE   COMPUTE   40
           PRINT FORMAT: F4.2   COMPETNC=(Q03+Q05R+Q09+Q11R)/4
           WRITE FORMAT: F4.2
           VALUE   LABEL
           1.00   LOWEST
           4.00   HIGHEST

MOTIVATN   MOTIVATION SCALE   COMPUTE   41
           PRINT FORMAT: F4.2   MOTIVATN=(Q01+Q04R+Q07+Q08R+Q12+Q13)/6
           WRITE FORMAT: F4.2
           VALUE   LABEL
           1.00   LOWEST
           4.00   HIGHEST

FAEDR2   FATHER'S ED BY STUDENT   NEW VARIABLE   42
           PRINT FORMAT: F8
           WRITE FORMAT: F8
           VALUE   LABEL
           1   HS GRAD OR LESS
           2   SOME COLLEGE
           3   BS OR MORE

MAEDR2   MOTHER'S ED BY STUDENT   NEW VARIABLE   43
          PRINT FORMAT: F8
          WRITE FORMAT: F8
          VALUE   LABEL
              1   HS GRAD OR LESS
              2   SOME COLLEGE
              3   BS OR MORE

PAEDR   PARENT'S ED REVISED   COMPUTE   44
          PRINT FORMAT: F8.2   PAEDR= MEAN(FAEDR, MAEDR)
          WRITE FORMAT: F8.2
          VALUE   LABEL
           1.00   HS OR LESS
           2.00   SOME COLLEGE
           3.00   BS OR MORE

APPENDIX E

Answers to Interpretation Questions

Assignment A (Chapter 4 - Checking Data and Descriptives)

1. We would look to see if any of the minimum or maximum scores in Output 4.1 were outside the ranges specified on page 19 and in the codebook in Appendix D. Note that the maximum scores for Questions 1 and 2 are too high; four should be the maximum.

2. Ethnicity and gender are the clearly nominal variables, but because gender is dichotomous, the mean and standard deviation can be interpreted meaningfully. The mean for ethnicity is not meaningful. There are six other dichotomous variables, math grades, algebra 1, etc., that some would consider nominal, but we think it is better just to think of them as dichotomous variables (see chapter 3).

3. Using Output 4.2:
    a) At least 75 because that is the biggest N for any variable.
    b) 67 (valid N listwise)
    c) 79%. The mean of a dichotomous variable indicates the percentage of those with the higher number, in this case .79 = 79% took algebra 1.
    d) 2 = minimum, 10 = maximum. Yes.

Assignment B (Chapter 5 - Descriptive Statistics)

1. Using Output 5.2:
    a) No
    b) 41.3%
    c) 44
    d) 78.7%. The percent and valid percent are the same because there are no missing data.

2. Using Output 5.3:
    a) No
    b) Yes, for mosaic pattern test.
    c) They tell us if the assumption of normality has been markedly violated.
    d) Visually none look very much like a normal curve. However, the skewness and kurtosis calculations say only the mosaic pattern test is not normal.
    e) 5.24
    f) 64.0%
    g) 12.0%

3. Using Output 5.4:
    a) Both distributions are approximately normal.
    b) The average male math achievement score is 14.765, and the average female score is 10.75.

c) 3

d) We learned that there were no outliers or extreme scores for either male or female math achievement scores. The highest scores for males and females were similar, but the minimum scores for females were lower.

e) The average male math achievement score is 14.761 and the average female score is 10.75.

Assignment C (Chapter 6 - Data Transformation)

1. Using your HSB data file or the data file in chapter 2:

   a) 5

   b) We recoded father's and mother's education because the education variables had a flaw; i.e., a parent with 1 week of college would get a higher score than a parent with 2 years of vocational school. *Faedr* for participants 2, 5, and 8 should be 1, missing data, and 2.

   c) The pleasure scale scores for ID 1 should be (4+3+3)/3=3.33.

   d) To be sure that the variables were transformed correctly.

2. We reversed Questions 6 and 10 because they were worded to measure low pleasure. We needed to get them in the same direction as Q2, which was positive, before adding them together.

3. The Motivation scores are not markedly different from a normal distribution because the skewness and kurtosis statistics each divided by their standard error are less than 2.5. However, the competence scores are significantly different from the normal distribution.

Assignment D (Chapter 8 - Cross-Tabulation)

1. The observed and expected counts in each cell are very similar (e.g., 23 vs. 22.4). When this is the case the results are likely due to chance and the appropriate statistic will not be statistically significant.

2. Assuming that both variables were nominal, we should use Cramer's V because the matrix is larger than 2x2. There is a very low positive association of .036, which is not significantly different from zero ($p = .95$). Thus, we cannot be confident that there is any relationship at all.

3. The appropriate measure of association for ordinal data would be Kendall's tau-b. In this example, Kendall's tau-b is .028, which is also a very low, nonsignificant association, suggesting no relationship between *faedr* and *mathgr*.

4. In Output 8.4, the appropriate eta value is .33 because math achievement is the interval scale dependent variable. This is probably a statistically significant association between math achievement and gender, but it is not strong.

Assignment E (Chapter 9 - Correlation)

1. In Output 9.1:
   a) The correlation coefficients tell us the strength with which the two variables are associated or related.
   b) r squared = .254 This signifies the percentage of variance in common between the two variables. In this case, it is the percentage of variance in math achievement that can be predicted from high school grades.
   c) The Pearson correlations have higher values than the Spearman and Kendall's tau-b correlations, but they have similar significance/p levels. Usually the Pearson r is somewhat more powerful.
   d) If one or both of the variables are clearly ordinal data, we would use the Kendall's tau-b or Spearman's rho.

2. In Output 9.2, there are 10 statistically significant correlations.

3. In Output 9.3:
   a) There are 21 correlation coefficients.
   b) 11 are statistically significant.

4. a) There was a statistically significant correlation, r (69) = .80, $p < .001$, between math courses taken and math achievement. Thus, we reject the null hypothesis of no/zero association. There is a strong positive association between number of math courses taken and math achievement. In general, those with a lot of math courses have high math achievement; those with few math courses have low math achievement, and those in the middle on one variable will probably have a middle score on the other variable.
   b) There was not a significant correlation, r (69) = .10, $p = .40$, between the pleasure scale score and math achievement. There is not evidence to reject the null hypothesis. In simple terms, there seems to be no association or relationship between the pleasure scale and math achievement. We do not know anything about math achievement based on a student's pleasure score.

5. With pairwise exclusion SPSS goes through the data and excludes only those instances where there are no data for one or both of the particular pair of variables. In the listwise exclusion, SPSS deletes an entire case/participant if they have even one score missing. In listwise deletion, the number of subjects (Ns) for each correlation in the matrix will be the same (71) and no more than the lowest N in pairwise deletion.

6. In Output 9.5 and 9.6:
   a) In Output 9.5, the points scatter widely with little pattern. The $r^2 = .05$ ($r = .21$), indicating a weak positive correlation, may well be due to chance. In Output 9.6, there is a very strong positive correlation $r^2 = .63$ ($r = .79$).
   b) In Output 9.5 the quadratic ($r^2 = .10$) appears to be better than the linear correlation ($r^2 = .05$) , suggesting that there may be a curvilinear correlation. In 9.6 the quadratic is no

better than the linear, suggesting that the Pearson linear correlation describes the data adequately.

c) Scatter plots are helpful because they give the researcher a view of where all the data points fall and how near they are to the regression line.

Assignment F (Chapter 10 - Factor Analysis)

1. Using Output 10.1:
   a) Highest correlations:
      Questions 5 & 1 = -.745 (low competence and motivation) different scales
      Questions 5 & 3 = -.743 (low competence and competence) same scales
      Questions 3 & 1 = .626 (competence and motivation) different scales
      Questions 12 & 13 = .607 (motivation and motivation) same scales
      Questions 8 & 7 = -.606 (low motivation and motivation) same scales
   Lowest correlations:
      Questions 13 & 6 = .001 (motivation and low pleasure) different scales
      Questions 13 & 11 = -.006 (motivation and low competence) different scales
      Questions 10 & 3 = .027 (low pleasure and competence) different scales
      Questions 2 & 13 = .028 (pleasure and motivation) different scales
      Questions 12 & 6 = -.044 (motivation and low pleasure) different scales
   Thus, the pairs of items/questions with the highest correlations tend to be the same conceptual scale and very likely will be in the same factor or component. Those with the lowest tend to be on different scales and will be in different factors.
   b) Component 1 = Questions -5, 3, 1 - 11, 2 = "competent and persistent at math"
      Component 2 = Questions 4, -7, 8 = "low math motivation"
      Component 3 = Questions 12, 13, 9 = "persistent and competent at math"
      Component 4 = Questions 10, 6, 11, -2 = "math pleasure"
   c) Questions 11 and 2 are loaded above .40 on two components so they did not factor cleanly. Questions 1 and 9 did not load most highly on the component for which they were intended. Perhaps the questions are ambiguous. These statistical components would seem to break motivation into two more specific components, one negative (#2) and one positive (#3).

2. Using Output 10.2:
      Component 1 = Questions -5, 1, 3, -11 = competence
      Component 2 = Questions 12, 13, -8, -4, 7, 9, = motivation
      Component 3 = Questions 10, 6, -2 = pleasure
   This is more like our conceptual clusters, but item 1 has moved from motivation to competence and 2, 9, and 11 might need to be dropped or rewritten because they are still problematic.

3. Using Output 10.3:
   a) The determinant is .562 which is satisfactory. KMO, which should be at least .50, is only .468, which is not adequate because mosaic is the only score to represent the second

261

component and you need several. The Bartlett test should be significant (<.05) and it is at $p = .000$.
b) Components 1 and 2 have eigenvalues > 1.0. and their total cumulative variance is 69%, or over 2/3 of the variance is accounted for by these two factors.
c) The correlation matrix shows that no correlations are high, but the lowest ones tend to be with mosaic. The rotated matrix shows two components: *mathach, grades*, and *visual* with loading of .864, .757, .629, and mosaic alone at .978. The plot also confirms that *mosaic* should be in a separate factor/component.

Assignment G (Chapter 11 - Reliability)

1.

Output	Scale	Mean interitem correlation	Alpha coefficient	Reliability
11.1	motivation	.385	.791	adequate
11.2	competence	.488	.796	adequate
11.3	pleasure	.278	.528	poor
11.4	modified motivation	.442	.798	adequate
11.5	modified competence	.592	.856	high

2. For the competence scale, the item with the lowest corrected item-total correlation is Q09 with .405. If item Q09 was deleted from the competence scale, the alpha would rise from .796 to .832.

3. In Output 11.6, the reliability coefficient for the visualization score is .886. Yes, it is acceptable, given that measures of reliability should be .70 or greater.

4. In Output 11.8, the kappa coefficient is .632. This is somewhat below .70 so even though it is statistically significant $(p < .001)$, it usually is considered to be low for reliability. Note that although 17 out of 20 ratings were in agreement, there was little agreement about mothers with some college.

Assignment H (Chapter 12 - Multiple Regression)

1. In Output 12.2:
   a) Four steps were done.
   b) Grades, gender, father's education, and motivation were identified as significant predictors of math achievement.
   c) The final multiple R is .654
   d) The adjusted R^2 is .392 which means that 39% of the variance in math achievement can be predicted by a combination of these independent variables.
   e) In Output 12.1, $R = .666$, $R^2 = .444$, and adjusted $R^2 = .379$. With the enter method, R and R^2 are slightly higher because there are more variables entered into the prediction equation and each adds a little. However, the adjusted R^2 is higher in Output 10.2 because less adjustment is necessary, given that there are fewer predictors.

2. Controlling for gender does not change the results *in this case*, except on the first step. The multiple R remains .654 and R^2 remains .392 because the same variables are in the equation although in a different order.

3. Output 12.4 uses the new composite variable of parent's education revised and omits competence and pleasure. R is now .688 and the adjusted R^2 is .443. Combining and/or eliminating predictor variables that are moderately or highly correlated (show collinearity) may lead to a more meaningful combination of predictors and improve the adjusted R^2.

Assignment I (Chapter 13 - Logistic Regression and Discriminant Analysis)

1. Using Output 13.2:
   a) The variables that combine to predict who took algebra 2 are competence and father's education revised.
   b) The overall predication is 71% accurate.
   c) The significant variables correctly predict 61% (22 out of 33) of those who would take algebra 2.
   d) The significant variables correctly predicted 81% of those who would NOT take algebra 2.
   e) The overall prediction is slightly lower in Output 13.2 (71%) than 13.1 (74%) because all six variables were used in 13.1 and each add a little, but not enough to be significant, to the prediction.

2. In Output 13.4:
   a) Father's education revised and competence combine to predict algebra 2.
   b) Overall, the prediction classification of who took algebra 2 is 71.8% accurate. Discriminant analysis predicted better who did *not* take algebra 2 (81%) than who did (62%).

3. A comparison of Outputs 13.3 and 13.4 reveals that both outputs agree that father's education and competence are the best combination of the of six predictors of who took algebra 2 and who did not. The two outputs are different in that the pooled within groups correlations in the structure matrix are higher in 13.4 than those in Output 13.3 for father's education (.819 versus .723) and competence (.492 versus .434) because the discriminant function for the stepwise method is based on only these two variables. As might be expected, the analysis in 13.3, which entered all six variables, correctly classified slightly, but not significantly, more participants (72.5%) than the stepwise method (71.8%).

Assignment J (Chapter 14 - t tests)

1 In Output 14.2:
   a) The variances for grades in h.s., math achievement, and math courses taken are roughly equal; however, the variances are significantly different for math grades ($p = .006$) which means that the assumption has been violated.

b) The appropriate *t*, *df*, and *p* for each *t* test are:

grades in h.s.	$t(73) = -.90, p = .369$
math achievement	$t(73) = 2.70, p = .009$
math courses taken	$t(73) = 2.97, p = .004$
math grades	$t(72.28) = -1.90, p = .055$

c) The *t* tests for math achievement ($p = .009$) and math courses taken ($p = .004$) are statistically significant.

d) Boys and girls do not differ significantly in average grades in high school (5.50 vs. 5.33). However, boys scored statistically significantly higher than girls on math achievement (14.76 vs. 10.75).

e) 95% of the time, the mean difference for grades in h.s. will fall within the range from -1.06 to .40. The difference is not significant because the signs are different; 95% of the time, the mean difference for math achievement will fall within the range from 1.05 to 6.97. Because zero is not included in the range (i.e., the signs are the same), the difference is significant.

2. In Output 14.3:
   a) The Mann-Whitney tests are statistically significant for math achievement ($p = .01$) and math courses taken ($p = .003$).
   b) Boys had statistically significantly higher mean *ranks* (46.01) than girls (31.35). On math grades, boys and girls do not differ significantly in mean ranks.
   c) When we compare Output 14.2 and 14.3, we find that with both parametric and nonparametric tests, boys and girls differ significantly on math achievement and math courses taken. The Sig. values are also similar, but the values for the *t* test are generally lower, indicating that it is the more powerful test.

	Output 14.2	Output 14.3
grades in h.s.	.369	.413
math achievement	.009	.010
math courses taken	.004	.003
math grades	.055	.058

3. In Output 14.4:
   a) The (Pearson) chi-square is not statistically significant ($p = .056$). This means that the relationship between two categorical variables (gender and math grades) is not statistically significant. Therefore, we cannot be confident that males and females are different on whether or not they get high math grades.
   b) Yes, according to footnote b in the chi-square tests table, the expected counts in all of the cells are > 5.
   c) Comparing Output 14.4 with the part of Output 14.3 that deals with math grades, we find that in both analyses boys and girls do not score statistically significantly different on math grades.

4. From Output 14.5:
   a) The paired samples correlation for mother's and father's education means that father's and mother's education are significantly correlated ($r = .681$). More highly educated fathers tend to marry more highly educated mothers and vice versa.
   b) Even though they are moderately correlated, the fathers of these students have statistically significantly more education than the mothers ($p = .019$). We can see in the Paired Samples Statistics table that the average level of fathers' education is 4.7 while the average of mothers' is 4.1. The two visualization scores are also statistically significantly different ($p = .001$). The visualization mean is 5.2, and the retest is 4.5.

5. In Output 14.6, which is a nonparametric test for two related samples:
   a) The Wilcoxon tests are statistically significant for parents' education ($p = .037$) and for visualization tests ($p < .001$).
   b) Both the parametric and nonparametric tests indicate statistically significant differences in parents' education and visualization scores and similar Sig. values..

Assignment K (Chapter 15 - One-Way ANOVA)

1. In Output 15.1:
   a) The assumption of homogeneity of variances was justified (not violated) for *grades* and *visual* ($p = .220$ and $p = .153$). However, a significance level of $p = .049$ for *mathach* tells us that the assumption of homogeneity of variances for *mathach* was violated--barely. Therefore, for *mathach,* we should use the equivalent nonparametric test (Kruskal-Wallis) or Dunnett's C for a post hoc test.
   b) The three fathers' education groups differ somewhere on their average grades in the high school, $F(2, 70) = 4.09$, $p = .021$. Math achievement scores are also significantly different, $F(2, 70) = 7.88$, $p = .001$. Average visualization scores did not differ significantly, $F(2, 70) = .76$, $p = .47$.
   c) For visualization scores, the mean for the low, medium, and high father's education groups were 4.67, 6.02, and 5.46, respectively. None are significantly different from each other. For grades, the group means were 5.34, 5.56, and 6.53, respectively. Because the overall F was significant, we know that there is a significant difference somewhere, but we don't know yet where.

2. In Output 15.2a, the pairs of means that were significantly different are the grades of students with low (h.s. grad or less) and high (B.S. or more) fathers' education ($p = .017$). In Output 15.2b, with the Dunnett's C multiple comparison test, students whose fathers had some college and those with B.S. or more were statistically significantly different on math achievement from those students whose fathers had only high school or less. We used Dunnett's C instead of the Tukey HSD post hoc test for math achievement because variances (Levene's test) were not equal.

3. In Output 15.3:
   a) The Kruskal-Wallis tests are statistically significant for math achievement ($p = .001$) but not for mosaic pattern test ($p = .899$).

b) The mean ranks (35.41, 38.03, and 38.32) for mosaic are not statistically different.

c) When we compare Output 15.1 and 15.3 for math achievement, we find that they both have the same Sig. value ($p = .001$).

4. In Output 15.4:
   a) No, there are not significant differences between the ethnic groups ($p = .104$).
   b) No, we do not need to do post hoc tests, because the ANOVA for ethnic groups was not statistically significant.

5. None of the more conservative (Scheffe) post hoc tests are statistically significant for ethnicity. One of the more liberal (LSD) post hoc tests is statistically significant when comparing African-American and Asian-American ($p = .016$).

Assignment L (Chapter 16 - Factorial ANOVA and ANCOVA)

1. In Output 16.2:
   a) Yes, the interaction between math grades and father's education is significant, $F(2,67) = 3.97, p = .024$.
   b) Examining the profile plot, we note that the lines are not parallel, indicating an interaction. This plot seems to indicate that for students with high math grades (mostly A&Bs) achievement increases as education of the father increases, but for those with lower grades (less than A&Bs) math achievement does not go up as education increases. Math achievement depends on both grades and father's education.

2. In Output 16.2:
   a) The main effect of father's education on math achievement is significant ($p < .001$). Eta squared is an index of effect size; .243 is a relatively small effect.
   b) Likewise, the effect of math grades on math achievement is significant ($p = .002$).
   c) The word "effect" can be misleading by inferring that math grades "caused" the differences. We can't know that for sure because this is not a good randomized experiment.
   d) Focusing on the main effect would be misleading because there was a significant interaction and the results depend on both variables.
   e) Because the main effect of father's education was significant we compared the three education groups with a Tukey HSD test in Output 16.3. However, because the interaction of math grades and father's education was significant, it would have been better to test the simple effects, by using Select Cases (see Appendix B) to do this Tukey test separately for those with high and low math grades.

3. In Output 16.3, high school grad or less versus some college, and hs grad or less versus B.S. or more, both are significantly different. Some college versus B.S. or more is *not* statistically different.

4. In Output 16.5:
   a) The adjusted main effects of gender remain significant, $p = .007$.

Appendix E - Answers to Questions

b) The adjusted math achievement means for males (14.77) and for females (10.73) do not differ much from the unadjusted means.

c) The above makes sense because the effect of the covariate, *mosaic*, is not significant at p =.056.

Assignment M (Chapter 17 - Repeated Measures and Mixed ANOVAs)

1. In Output 17.3:
   a) When we assume that the product scores are ordinal or that assumptions (e.g., sphericity) are markedly violated, then we use a nonparametric test for several related samples (i.e., Friedman). Based on the results, we did find an overall statistically significant difference between the mean ranks of the product ratings.
   b) For a complete interpretation to determine which pairs of products have significantly different mean ranks, we need to run an appropriate post hoc test. Unfortunately, SPSS does not have post hoc tests built into the Friedman test. We could also run six Wilcoxon tests, one pair at a time, but if so it would be prudent to divide the Sig. required for significance by 6 to adjust for the multiple comparisons.

2. In Output 17.4:
   a) The assumption related to sphericity is violated because the Mauchly statistic is significant (p = .01). What we do, therefore, is either use the multivariate approach or correct the univariate approach with the Greenhouse-Geisser or other similar correction.
   b) With this analysis too, the products are significantly different ($p < .001$). Although the multivariate Fs in Output 17.4 and 17.2 are both significant ($p<.001$ in both cases), the F is larger in Output 17.4:

   > In Output 17.2, $F(3, 9) = 19.07, p < .001$
   > In Output 17.4, $F(3, 8) = 23.15, p < .001$

   The F in the 2-factor (mixed) ANOVA is larger because it divides the error in a manner that lowers the error term by putting part of the error into the interaction.
   c) Yes, the interaction between product and gender is significant ($p < .007$, with the Multivariate Test). The product ratings are affected by both product and by gender. Males and females rate the products differently. If we plot the lines, they will not be parallel; they will cross somewhere. We could plot the interaction if we computed the mean rating for each gender separately, either with a calculator or by using Select Cases (see Appendix B).
   d) No, there was no significant difference between the genders ($p = .130$). No post hoc multiple comparison test is needed because the F is not significant. Even if it was significant, we would not run a post hoc because we only run post hoc tests with three or more groups.

Assignment N (Chapter 18 - Multivariate Analysis of Variance--MANOVA)

1. In Output 18.2:
   a) The multivariate tests are statistically significant, $F(3, 71) = 8.03, p < .001$ (cf. Wilks' lambda). This means that the genders differ on a linear combination of the dependent

267

variables (grades, math achievement, and math courses taken). Wilks' lambda is a commonly used multivariate statistic.

b) In the univariate "Tests of Between-Subjects Effects" table, we see that the dependent variables of math achievement and math courses taken are statistically significant for gender. Therefore, there are differences between male and female students on math achievement and math courses taken but not grades.

c) The results are similar to those in Output 14.2 in that the means, standard deviations, and univariate Sig. for grades in high school, math achievement, and math courses taken are exactly the same. Therefore, several independent samples t tests and the univariate tests from a one-way multivariate analysis of variance yield the same results. The results are different from those in Output 14.2 in chapter 14 in that $F = t^2$, and Output 18.2 provides the multivariate test.

2. In Output 18.3:
   a) The multivariate tests are not statistically significant for the interaction between math grades and gender ($p = .832$). Therefore, we can safely interpret the main effect for math grades and gender. The multivariate tests are statistically significant both for math grades, $F (3, 69) = 5.94, p = .001$ (cf. Wilks lambda) and for gender, $F (3, 69) = 6.05, p = .001$ (cf. Wilks' lambda). Therefore, math grades and gender each seem to have an effect on a linear combination of the three dependent variables (math achievement, mosaic, and visualization).

   b) The significant main effects of math grades for individual dependent variables are math achievement ($p < .001$) and visualization ($p = .019$). This means that students with low math grades differ from those with high grades on the dependent variables of math achievement and visualization. In addition, the males differ from females on the same dependent variables (math achievement, $p < .001$, and visualization, $p = .004$).

   c) The results are similar to Output 16.1 in that the descriptive statistics (means, standard deviations, and Ns) are exactly the same for math achievement. In addition, the univariate "Tests of Between Subjects Effects" are also exactly the same for math grades, gender, and math grades * gender on Type III Sum of Squares, df, Mean Squares, F, Sig., Eta Squared (Effect Size), and Observed Power in both Output 16.1 (GLM General Factorial, 2-Way ANOVA) and Output 18.3 (GLM 2-way Multivariate Analysis of Variance). Therefore, both analyses yield identical results for the univariate analysis. However, the MANOVA also provides a multivariate analysis and results for visualization and mosaic as part of this analysis.

Bibliography

Abelson, R. P. (1995). *Statistics as principled argument*. Hillsdale, NJ: Lawrence Erlbaum Associates.

American Psychological Association. (1994). *Publication manual of the American Psychological Association* (4th ed.). Washington, DC: Author.

Davidson, F. (1996). *Principles of statistical data handling.* Thousand Oaks, CA: Sage.

Davis, J. A. (1985). *The logic of causal order*. Newbury Park, CA: Sage.

Gibbons, J. D. (1993). *Nonparametric measures of association*. Newbury Park, CA: Sage.

Gibbons, J. D. (1993). *Nonparametric statistics: An introduction*. Newbury Park, CA: Sage.

Gliner, J. A., & Morgan, G. A. (in press). *Research design and analysis in applied settings: An integrated approach*. Mahwah, NJ: Lawrence Erlbaum Associates.

Grimm, L. G., & Yarnold, P. R. (1995). *Reading and understanding multivariate statistics*. Washington, DC: American Psychological Association.

Hinkle, D. E., Wiersma, W., & Jurs, S. G. (1994). *Applied statistics for the behavioral sciences* (3rd. ed.). Boston: Houghton Mifflin.

Huck, S. J., & Corimer, W. H. (1996). *Reading statistics and research* (2nd ed.). New York: Harper & Row.

Jaeger, R. M. (1990). *Statistics: A spectator sport* (2nd ed.). Newbury Park, CA: Sage.

Keppel, G. (1991). *Design and analysis: A researcher's handbook* (3rd ed.). New York: Prentice-Hall.

Keppel, G., & Zedeck, S. (1989). *Data analysis for research designs*. New York: W. H. Freeman.

Kerlinger, F. (1986). *Foundations of behavioral research* (3rd ed.). New York: Holt, Rinehart & Winston.

Kim, J., & Mueller, C. W. (1978). *Introduction to factor analysis: What it is now and how to do it*. Newbury Park, CA: Sage.

Lewis-Beck, M. S. (1980). *Applied regression: An introduction*. Newbury Park, CA: Sage.

National Opinion Research Center. (1980). *High school and beyond information for users: Base year data.* Chicago: National Research Center.

Newton, R. R., & Rudestam, K. E. (1992). *Surviving your dissertation.* Newbury Park, CA: Sage.

Shavelston, R. J. (1988). *Statistical reasoning for the behavioral sciences* (2nd ed.). Boston: Allyn Bacon.

Siegel, S., & Castellan, N. J. (1988). *Nonparametric statistics for the behavioral sciences (2nd ed.).* New York: McGraw-Hill.

Spector, P. E. (1992). *Summated rating scale construction: An introduction.* Newbury Park, CA: Sage.

SPSS. (1997). *Advanced statistics 7.5.* Chicago: Author.

SPSS. (1997). *SPSS base 7.5 users' guide.* Chicago: Author.

SPSS. (1997). *Professional statistics 7.5.* Chicago: Author.

Stevens, S. S. (1951). Mathematics, measurement, and psychophysics. In S. S. Stevens (ed.) *Handbook of experimental psychology (pp. 1-49).* New York: Wiley.

Tabachnick, B. G., & Fidell, L. S. (1989). *Using multivariate statistics* (2nd ed.). New York: HarperCollins.

Vogt, W. P. (1993). *Dictionary of statistics and methodology.* Newbury Park, CA: Sage.

INDEX

Index

Define variables, 20-21, 40, 216

df, see Degrees of freedom

Degrees of freedom, 86-87, 192-193, 221-223, 264, 268

Descriptive statistics, 22-23, 29-32, 35-39, 42, 45-64, 179, 240, 244, 258

Design classification, 80-81

Determinant, 113, 115-117, 122

Dichotomous variables, 26, 258

Discriminant analysis, 22, 85, 154-157, 163-171, 263

    enter independents together, 154-157, 163-167

    stepwise, 154, 157, 167-171

Dunnett's C, 189, 194-195, 202, 222, 265

Editing outputs, 38

Effect size, 86, 87, 207, 213, 228-229, 231, 266

Eigenvalues, 113, 116, 118, 120, 165, 170, 262

Entry of new data, 39-41, 215-216, 220-221

Epsilon, 221, 223, 226

Equivalent forms reliability, see Reliability

Eta, 84, 89, 91, 96, 207, 209, 213-214, 231-233, 235, 259, 266, 268

Exclude cases listwise, 99-100

Exclude cases pairwise, 98-99

Exit, 44

Explore, 22-23, 52-53

Factor analysis, 23-24, 111-124, 261

Factorial ANOVA, see General linear model

Filter, 44, 240-244

Frequencies, see Frequency distributions

Frequency distributions, 22-23, 29-31, 50-52, 54-61, 245-246

Frequency polygon, 29

Friedman test, 24, 84, 215, 218-219, 221, 224, 267

General linear model, 22-23, 199-210, 219, 221, 228-229

    general factorial ANOVA, 199-202, 204-205

    multivariate, see Multivariate analyses of variance

    repeated measures, see Repeated measures ANOVA

    simple factorial ANOVA, 203, 208

Get/Retrieve data, 33

GLM, see General linear model

Goodness of fit, 24, 159, 213-214

Graphs, 20-21, 51-52, 99-100

Greenhouse-Geisser, 221, 223, 226, 267

Help menu, 21-22